Whispers of the Unseen

Whispers of the Unseen

The Quest for Sixty-Four Yoginis

S.Beena Unnikrishnan

Title: Whispers of the Unseen: The Quest for Sixty-Four Yoginis
Author: S. Beena Unnikrishnan

ISBN: 978-93-92209-66-6

First published in India 2024
This edition published 2024

Published by:
BluOne Ink Pvt. Ltd
A-76, 2nd Floor, Sector 136, Noida
Uttar Pradesh 201301

Website: www.bluone.ink
Email: publisher@bluone.ink

Copyright © 2024 S. Beena Unnikrishnan

S. Beena Unnikrishnan has asserted her rights under the Indian Copyright Act to be identified as the author of this work.

All rights reserved under the copyright conventions. No part of this publication may be reproduced or transmitted in any form or by any means, electronic or mechanical, including photocopying, recording or any information storage or retrieval system, without the prior permission in writing from the publishers.

This book is solely the responsibility of the author(s) and the publisher has had no role in the creation of the content and does not have responsibility for anything defamatory or libellous or objectionable.

BluOne Ink Pvt. Ltd does not have any control over, or responsibility for, any third-party websites referred to in this book. All internet addresses given in this book were correct at the time of going to press. The author and publisher regret any inconvenience caused if addresses have changed or sites have ceased to exist, but can accept no responsibility for any such changes.

Printed and bound in India at Nutech Print Services

Kali, Occam and BluPrint are all trademarks of BluOne Ink Pvt. Ltd.

To my Sreebala

Contents

	Foreword by Bibek Debroy	xi
	Preface	xiii
1.	My Mentors	1
2.	Love for the Goddess	5
3.	Dr David	7
4.	The Srividya Conundrum	26
5.	In Search of My Femininity	29
6.	Ardhanareeswarar	33
7.	Ganesha	36
8.	Bhairavas	40
9.	The Sixty-Four	43
10.	The Sixty-Four Yoginis	45
11.	Yogini Chandi	51
12.	Yogini Tara	54
13.	Yogini Narmada	57
14.	Yogini Yamuna	59
15.	Yogini Manada	62
16.	Yogini Varuni	64
17.	Yogini Gowri	66
18.	Yogini Indrani	68
19.	Yogini Varahi	70
20.	Yogini Manasa	72
21.	Yogini Vanaramukhi (Anjana)	76
22.	Yogini Vaishnavi	79
23.	Yogini Vajra Varahi/Pancha Varahi	82
24.	Yogini Vadhyaroopa	84
25.	Yogini Charchika	87

26. Yogini Vetali	90
27. Yogini Chinnamasta	92
28. Yogini Vindyavasini	95
29. Yogini Jalakamini (Jayanthi)	98
30. Yogini Ghatavara (Jagadathri)	100
31. Yogini Kakarali	102
32. Yogini Matangi	105
33. Yogini Virupa (Apah)	109
34. Yogini Kauberi	111
35. Yogini Balluka (Jambavati)	113
36. Yogini Narasimhi	115
37. Yogini Viraja (Girija)	118
38. Yogini Vikatanana (Katyayani)	120
39. Yogini Mahalakshmi	122
40. Yogini Kaumari	124
41. My Visit to the Adi Shakti Peeths	126
42. Dream of a Girl	139
43. Yogini Vayu Veena (Swasti)	141
44. Yogini Surya Putri (Tapati)	143
45. Yogini Ajita	145
46. Yogini Sarvamangala	147
47. Yogini Gandhari	149
48. Yogini Dhumavati	151
49. Yogini Ganga	154
50. Yogini Murati (Rohini)	158
51. Yogini Chamunda	161
52. Yogini Vayuvega	164
53. Yogini Chandrakanti	166
54. Yogini Aditi	168
55. Yogini Agneyi (Svaha)	170
56. Yogini Jwalamukhi	173
57. Yogini Brahmani	176

58.	Yogini Bhudevi (Samudra)	178
59.	Yogini Narayani	181
60.	Yogini Uma	183
61.	Yogini Kali	187
62.	Yogini Stuti	191
63.	Yogini Ghatabhari (Bhavani)	193
64.	Yogini Kamayani (Trishna)	195
65.	Yogini Kamakshi	198
66.	Yogini Maheshwari	201
67.	Yogini Kumari (Bala Tripura Sundari)	204
68.	Yogini Vindyabalini (Kurukulla)	210
69.	Yogini Vinayaki	212
70.	Yogini Bhadrakali	214
71.	Yogini Bhairavi	218
72.	Yogini Yasha (Yakshini)	221
73.	Yogini Sarpasha (Surasa)	223
74.	Yogini Karkari	227
75.	Yogini Rathi	230
76.	Yogini Mahamaya (Lalitha Tripura Sundari)	234
77.	My Fiftieth Birthday Celebrations	240
78.	Sreebala	242
79.	Navigating New Horizons	244
80.	Sacred Sojourn: Traversing Temples in a Twelve-Day Documentary Odyssey	247
81.	Scripting	275
82.	Reflections	298
	Acknowledgements	301
	Bibliography	310
	About the Author	311

Foreword

The word *yogini* has several meanings. At one level, yogini is simply the feminine of yogi, and the word can be applied to humans too. At a more elevated level, yoginis are divine or semi-divine. They are Shaktis, manifestations of Devi. The names and number of yoginis vary from text to text. But, traditionally, in most texts, the number is given as sixty-four. There are sixty-four yogini temples in various states of disrepair and disuse. Typically, they are hypaethral, with no roof. Perhaps, the most famous of these, in better states of preservation, are the two in Odisha (Hirapur and Ranipur-Jharial). The one in Mitaoli, Morena, is also worth mentioning, although the statues of the sixty-four yoginis are missing there. In addition, there are Khajuraho and Bhedaghat. Down the years, several temples have been plundered and looted. It is obvious that the yogini cult spread across a vast geographical swathe of Bharatvarsha, especially the north and the west. Yet, beyond the somewhat superficial, there hasn't been much work on yoginis. The books by Vidya Dehejia and Stella Dupuis are exceptions. One can understand why. As with tantra, there is an aura of secrecy, and it is difficult to elicit information.

Beena Unnikrishnan's book on sixty-four yoginis is a book with a difference. It is not an academic treatise. It is written by someone to whom the sixty-four yoginis manifested themselves. It is a journey that is not just physical and geographical but one that is internal and spiritual. It is a book of self-discovery. Therefore, it is permeated with a sense of bhakti and immersion. She describes how she was dragged along this path involuntarily rather than consciously. She describes the sixty-four yoginis in Ranipur, Jabalpur-Narmada, Dudhai and Khajuraho. It is a remarkable story of personal journey. In the process, we have some documentation of the yoginis and the temples. But that, valuable though, is incidental. The primary thrust of the book is the journey of self-realisation. It is a personal and personalised account, and readers should thank her for having decided to go public with what has been a personal pilgrimage—a book remarkable in its conception and worth reading even if one is not interested in yoginis.

Bibek Debroy, chairman, EAC-PM
December 2023

Preface

I am neither a poet nor a writer. This book is the result of a metamorphosis of the colours that have spilt from my palette into words. When I say "I", I mean that I am just a brush or a pen of an infinite source of energy that I call Sreebala, the reflection of my love for Bala Tripura Sundari in me.

Writing this book was an artistic and spiritual journey that wove together my imagination, trust, clairvoyance, and blessings, all imbued with my love for Tripura Sundari, the universal Shakti. My love and trust in her have given me the strength to perceive this life with a new vision, to decipher mysterious patterns, to connect seemingly unrelated phenomena and thoughts, and to unleash the power of the feminine within.

My journey of painting the sixty-four yoginis is a testament to the supreme spiritual truth. I realised this when I contemplated my artistic endeavour and the sequence of my paintings. This journey maps spiritual experiences from my early years. I entrusted my life to the universe with an unquestioning mind, and the universe unveiled the mysterious pattern and made me experience the force of the unknown energy. This book is all about my mystic journey towards the goddess, and I realised that my journey was inwards, dispelling all my fears and insecurities while empowering the dormant female essence. It was a conscious awakening and reconnection to the harmonious feminine power.

My paintings are the visual representation of my journey to my inner goddess while harmonising with the cycles and rhythms of the universal Shakti through creativity, the most potent means to unite with your inner self. This journey may be seen as an illusion woven from thoughts shaped by my deep devotion to my goddess. The way you choose to interpret it is entirely up to you. I deeply respect every religious practitioner's discipline and practices while recognising that their path is not destined to be mine in reaching her. However, I have met many of them, and they have bestowed their blessings. That is the fuel for my journey.

I was never alone in this eventful time. I had many co-passengers who walked in and out, sharing their part of karma towards the goal of my life. I would like to express my deep-felt gratitude to all of them, and I will introduce them one by one in the coming chapters. I am indebted to all of them. Every person I encountered contributed value to my undertaking. Everyone in my past conveyed messages and connected me with experiences, people, and insights that guided me along the way. I have been fortunate to have several significant individuals who played pivotal roles: My parents, T. Rajendran Nair and Sobhana, bestowed upon me the gift of life. My husband, Col. Unnikrishnan, stands as my unwavering support. My sons, Arjun and Akash, have been pillars of strength. My core strength is my family. My brothers, Biju and Binu, and their families were always there for anything I wanted. Simba, my silent companion, remained by my side like a shadow. Thanks are due to Annamalai Subbiah for his moral support and to Jain Joseph, who guided me in unlearning and helped me to align my experiences to gain a broader perspective on this subject. Dr Harbeen Arora

Rai's trust in me is connected to the power of the feminine worldwide. My gratitude is due to Dr Bibek Debroy, who made this book a reality.

Mata (mother), Pita (father), Guru (teacher), Daivam (God)—I prostrate to all my gurus and guides seen and unseen. My Bala, the energy that placed trust in me and chose me from among millions, deserves my deepest gratitude.

1

My Mentors

A mentor is someone who dissipates the darkness inside you and moulds you. With his knowledge, he guides you to introspect and discover the source of light within you.

I was born in Kollam in Kerala, India, to a God-fearing family that consisted of my dutiful father who worked as a bank officer, my sincere mother who is a homemaker, and two younger brothers. When I was growing up, spiritualism in my household was nothing more than the lighting of a lamp in the evenings, going to temples occasionally, or having homams (a sacred fire ritual with prayers to God) at home on certain occasions and festivals. I did not know the essence or meaning of these rituals. I had a good childhood.

At the age of twenty, I married an army officer. As his postings changed every few years, I had the opportunity to travel across the country with my husband. I was constantly kept occupied with the duties of a "defence wife" and as the mother of two young boys who were quite a handful. Apart from all the socialising, I also tried to set time aside for my endeavours, which included my artistic projects. Art has always been a big part of my life and continues to be. Life was busy, to say the least.

The year was 1997. My husband was posted in Tiruchirappalli, a small town in Tamil Nadu, India. I have always valued my independence and tried to make the most of it. Hence, I started a spa in that quaint little town. Back in 1997, spas were not particularly common, especially in a conservative town such as Tiruchirappalli. I figured, however, that there would be a market for it. As always, I kept myself occupied.

One day, I started to feel a tad bogged down by all the work and had a particularly bad headache. My close colleague, Gayathri, offered to heal me with reiki. I was not familiar with the term but was open to the experience. Little did I know that it would change my life. The healing process left me overwhelmed with a feeling I cannot put into words. I grew curious about this healing technique. This experience consequently led me to search for a reiki teacher.

The following year (1998), my husband was transferred to the picturesque city of Shillong in Meghalaya, a state in Northeast India. There, I landed a job at Arena Multimedia as the head of the academic department and was quite busy. I was still in search of a reiki guru. People often say that when you put a thought out into the universe, it will manifest. I am a firm believer of this mantra, given the experiences I have had in life.

In Shillong, I came across Mrs Moorty, the wife of another army officer, who was a reiki expert. I trained under her for six months or so and completed all the levels, including the grandmaster level. I was very fascinated by the term *grandmaster*, but I eventually came to realise that it went deeper than what I had learnt. Despite completing all the levels, my thirst for knowledge on the subject had not been entirely quenched. I did not give adequate time to practising the art and just raced through the levels in an attempt to satisfy my curiosity on what the grandmaster level entailed. I felt the learning was inadequate. I was restless to do the process again and do it right, which set me off on yet another search for a guru. That is how I eventually met Mrs Saradha Jain.

When I hear the word *guru*, the first person that comes to my mind is the late Mrs Saradha Jain. She was the one who kindled the spiritual fire in me. She worked on healing an acquaintance of mine, and so I had seen her at my office a few times. Her presence felt very calming, and her energy zen-like. I was magnetically drawn towards her. I approached her one day and asked her to teach me her practice. To my surprise, she rejected my request. I avoided mentioning that I had already learnt it, but somehow, she knew. Her response at the time seemed odd to me. She told me, "The time hasn't yet come for you to learn." I was disheartened.

About six months later, she herself approached me at my workplace and asked me to join her the next day. I was thrilled. The time had finally arrived. She asked me to bring a flower while coming to our first class. The next day, after work, I bought an entire bouquet and made my way to her house.

"I had asked you to bring just one flower. Why did you buy an entire bouquet? Just pluck one from somewhere and bring it with you every day henceforth," she said. She then directed me towards a small room in the corner of her house. I entered this dark space and was immediately transported to another world. It was dimly lit and decorated with crystals of all shapes and sizes. There lay pictures of several deities and one of Mikao Usui's, the father of reiki. I laid the bouquet down in front of his picture and said a little prayer to begin my journey as a student on a good note.

Mrs Jain's teaching of reiki was quite different. Right at the start, she told me that the teaching process would not be academic or theoretical, but I would learn through practical experience. I began to visit her every day, and I would place a flower in front of the shrine in the healing room as directed. One day, however, she stopped me from entering the room to avoid disturbing a healing process that was taking place inside.

This happened for the next few days. My curiosity was piqued because I did not sense any presence inside that room. I tried my best to catch a glimpse but in vain. One day, a breeze blew the curtain out of the way, and just as I had guessed, the room was empty. I was upset as I did not quite understand why she had stopped me from entering the healing room. I questioned her, but her response made me feel uneasy.

"Just because you don't see something doesn't mean it isn't there. There are beings that exist outside your realm of reality," she told me curtly. She told me a soul was undergoing a healing process in that room. At that moment, she changed the way I perceived the world forever.

While practising reiki, I have had several experiences, but the one that really stands out is the vision of my great grandfather, Annapoornalayam Gopalanpillai, during my meditation session. He was a sage who has been given a space in our family temple as a Yogeeswaran (a respectful position given to a personality who has attained spiritual enlightenment). Now I realise that the vision was his blessing. Our ancestors are our unseen spirit guides. I prostrate in front of that great soul.

I connected deeply with people and felt gratitude for being able to heal them of any issues. Thanks to Mrs Saradha Jain, I was able to read energies and auras and do my little bit. I practised, meditated, healed, and really enjoyed every bit of the reiki-learning experience. Reiki is a tool that connected me to the infinite energy within and outside us.

2

Love for the Goddess

My family, like many other native Malayali families, firmly believes in astrology. My keen interest and involvement in reiki concerned my mother. Such practices were not common in Kerala, and my conservative mother assumed that it is some sort of supernatural ritual. So she visited our family astrologer, Krishnan Potti. After looking at my horoscope, he asked my mother if I am a Kali Upasaka (devotee of Goddess Kali). I was very curious to know the reason behind this strange question.

I paid him a visit on my next trip to my hometown, that same year, and we had an intense discussion on the matter. He remained adamant in his view, saying that if I was not a Kali Upasaka, then I would be some day. After this thought-provoking conversation with him, I was keen to find out more about the presence of the feminine power that was reflected in my horoscope, and I continued to regularly interact with him over phone to gain clarity.

Krishnan Potti's stories and narratives gave me a lot of insight into the spiritual world. I began to realise that I was magnetically drawn to a feminine power, a feminine power that I had had no inkling of so far in my life. Unbeknownst to me, I was gently entering the powerful orbit of *yantra*, *mantra*, and *tantra*. In a way, I could also say that Krishnan Potti slowly led me to it through my interactions with him.

He often discussed the subject of Sri Yantra or Sri Meru. Sri Yantra is a mystical diagram that is a symbol of the great Divine Mother principle, the source of all energy, power and creativity. I wanted to perform a Sri Meru pooja every day, but it is said that a guru is crucial to guide one, owing to its complexity and sacredness. When I confided in Krishnan Potti about my wish to do the pooja, he, being a devotee of Lord Shiva, said, "The *Skanda Purana* equates the guru to Lord Shiva himself; a guru is Shiva himself manifesting as a human."

He then wrote a mantra on my tongue with a sharp tool that is used to write on metals and said to me, "Lord Shiva himself is your guru, and you can recite any mantra after praying to him." Then he proceeded to gift me a silver figurine of the mugam (face) of the Adiyogi (a reference to Lord Shiva, who is considered as the first guru).

I have never been one to follow any discipline. Working within a framework or a set of rules has always made me uncomfortable, but what really drew me into this world of spiritual philosophy was the symbol of the Sri Yantra, a beautiful geometrical drawing, owing to my deep interest in art. Unconsciously to me, these small instances pushed me deeper and deeper into a realm of auspiciousness.

My love for the subject of goddesses and the sacred feminine divine started to reflect in my artistic expressions on the canvas. The deep desire to know the energies of "circles" and "squares" evolved into a keen interest in yantras and mantras and the fantasies behind them. Yantra is a geometric design drawn in the space of worship as a representation of the god. Mantras are sacred texts recited during worship that have immense power. This unseen but strong force took me to the doorsteps of Dr David, my mentor.

3

Dr David*

Painting has been a hobby of mine since childhood. I have always had an affinity towards painting gods and goddesses. I am not a "trained" artist. I have not attended art school or learnt from an expert. I am self-taught—art is in my blood, and I paint passionately.

I mainly enjoy painting portraits, but around 2011, I developed a deep love for yantras and geometrical patterns. Often, during religious ceremonies, mandalas or large geometrical patterns are drawn on the ground to invoke the gods and goddesses. That these patterns could open a portal into the heavenly world fascinated me, but unfortunately, these were not my forte. However, I do believe leaving one's comfort zone and stepping into an unknown area can be a wonderful experience. I believed that I had the blessing of God, and my strokes swayed along with the energies of every breath. I was mesmerised by the rhythms and patterns of this universe. All the art I painted had a deep mystic dimension that was beyond my immediate understanding. I eventually tried my hand at geometric patterns and found it to be a rather meditative process. I enjoyed breaking out of my comfort zone.

---

* In the interest of safeguarding the privacy of individuals associated with this person, I have chosen to employ a pseudonym instead of his real name. This decision has been made out of respect for his family.

Even though I enjoyed painting these geometric patterns and yantras, I felt that the hues I used to paint and the mystic geometries were not as vibrant as I had visualised them. The colours seemed lifeless, and they were communicating a different language. I wanted to breathe colours and life into my work, my art.

I discussed this with my family friend in Delhi. I spoke to him about my desire to meet someone who could guide me through this. He offered to introduce me to someone who, he believed, perceived tantra and yantra in an unconventional way. As much as I enjoyed painting these geometrical patterns, I was unable to put my heart and soul into my art without truly understanding it. I wanted to understand the real essence of tantra.

My geometric paintings were a result of the inspiration I received from yantras, which are the geometric patterns used to worship deities in the tantric religious system. As previously mentioned, these diagrams are often drawn to invoke deities during sacred rituals. Tantra is a technique of worship where the energies and powers of gods and goddesses are invoked using different rituals and practices. A person well versed in this technique is known as a tantric. I felt as though my geometric paintings lacked that energy and seemed lifeless, and I wanted to understand how to bring in the same energy.

My friend in Delhi spoke about Dr David. However, my friend was hesitant to share Dr David's contact details because Dr David did not approve of anyone sharing his contact details without his knowledge. I believed that the right time for me to meet had not yet arrived. For two years, I tirelessly enquired about Dr David in Chennai but to no avail. I never managed to find his contact details or a trace of his whereabouts. Spiritual people often say that the universe always responds to true seekers, which proved to be true in my quest for Dr David.

Dr David worked in a creative field and was also a scientist who studied the intricacies of human life and existence. He had a keen interest and understanding of various spiritual philosophies pertaining to different religions and practices.

I saw Dr David in New Delhi for the first time in 2012 at the home of my friend. I knew that I was standing at the edge of a bridge that would connect me with this unknown formless cosmic energy. I felt I was entering an aura of deep love, surrender, and faith. Dr David was very different from the spiritual teachers and gurus that I had previously encountered.

The first thing he told me was that he was not a "guru" but I could join him on his spiritual journey provided I refrained from questioning him. But I was free to ask questions. He said that if I did have questions, he may have answers. I felt an instant gravitational pull and irresistible energy that drew me to him. Overnight, I quit the project I was working on and joined him on his spiritual journey without too much thought. A deep faith engulfed me, and I knew I was making the right decision. At this point, I must write about some of the experiences I had with him and the goddesses who guide me every day in my life. This book would be incomplete without those experiences.

Our first spiritual trip together that year (2012) was to Kerala. Now when I think about it, it seems to be part of a master plan. On that trip, he met all my close friends and my parents and told them not to worry about me. I was intrigued by this. He also met my bedridden grandmother, who passed away two weeks after meeting him, almost as though he helped her clear her karmic debt and go in peace.

On that trip, I also took time to introduce him to the priest Krishnan Potti. Dr David thanked him for keeping my interest in spirituality alive and for not misleading me. His statements were quite thought-provoking, and I wondered why he said that. In hindsight, I realise that Krishnan Potti's guidance was what had led me to meeting Dr David. If I had been taught differently, breaking out of the wrong thought process and entering the right one would have been difficult. Fortunately, I was a blank slate with minimal awareness on the subject, and Dr David was glad that he could show me the right light. After this, we also visited my family temple and offered prayers to the family deity.

Once, during an intense spiritual discussion with him, Dr David mentioned that I must learn to practise detachment for my spiritual growth. He believed that detachment from the material world was important for spiritual growth. This thought lingered in my mind always, and I wondered how I would reach that state of detachment.

We proceeded with the trip. No meetings had been planned when we started out on the trip, but as I said, it seemed like a master plan later. The end of that journey took us to Thirunelli Temple in Wayanad, Kerala, to perform rituals for Dr David's departed family members.

The Pithru Shradh is a sixteen-day sacred ritual in which Hindus revere the souls of their departed ancestors, and the Thirunelli Temple is famous as a place where people perform the last rites for family members. This ritual often includes taking a "holy dip" in any water body near the pilgrimage site to rid oneself of any ancestral karmic baggage and to ensure the peace and well-being of the departed souls.

Dr David suggested that I accompany him and perform the ritual. I had my apprehensions, since it is uncommon for someone whose parents are alive to perform the Pithru Shradh. He reasoned that I could pay my respects to my forefathers, which somewhat convinced me.

When we reached the Thirunelli Temple, the sky was overcast, adding an air of eeriness to the experience of being at that holy site. The place was crowded with over twenty people waiting for their turn to take the dip in the pond, which added to my anxiety. However, as I entered, the crowd started to make way and clear a path in front of me. It seemed like a grand welcome gesture. The only ones who remained were a mother and her child, sitting by the stairs leading down to the pond, almost as though offering me moral and mental support at the time.

My mentor used to say that when one is performing the holy dip, having the sun above is a great omen, as if the sun is acknowledging the act. This exposure, if followed by gentle rain, is a sign of divine blessings being showered upon you. I looked up at the dark sky almost cynically. Not even a speck of sun was visible. The water was cold, and it took me a few seconds to adjust to its temperature. Then, I took my first dip. I collected a handful of water, as one does when performing this ritual, and held it in front of my heart.

What happened next still gives me goosebumps. The clouds right above me parted, just enough to offer a small clearing for a stream of light to pass through and fall straight into my hands, the water glistening in its illumination. I stared in awe. My actions were being watched. Some sudden chanting in the background floated into my ears and ushered me back to the present.

I completed the rest of the ritual and paid my respects to the generations of my forefathers. Right as I was about to finish, I felt a drop of water trickle down my face, and then came the blessings, a gentle shower of rain. The rain came down diagonally to, in a way, coexist with the sun shining right above me. At that euphoric moment, I felt the existence and presence of divinity.

Dr David and I took 108 dips that day, a number with deep spiritual and sacred significance in Hinduism. I was filled with utmost satisfaction, peace, and serenity. Just as we exited the pond, the crowd started to form again. It felt as though that short period was reserved for me to pay my respects and it was witnessed by the Almighty who thought me worthy enough to be exposed to the sun's brilliance for a few brief moments. The experience taught me that I am never truly alone as long as I choose to see it that way.

Spiritual seekers often claim that the supreme divine power manifests time and again for the benefit of humankind, and if you are lucky enough to experience this in your lifetime, you should consider yourself blessed. There have been several instances during my extensive travels when I have sensed a certain divine presence watching over me. Sceptics may call these coincidences or mere hallucinations, but to me, they were reassurances from a higher realm of reality.

My First Visit to Kodungallur, Kerala

My next trip to Kerala with Dr David was in 2013. We visited numerous temples, including Padmanabha Temple, Mannarasala, Guruvayur, Kodungallur, Chottanikkara, Triprayar, Ernakulathappan, and Ettumanoor. All these temples are very sacred and believed to be touched by God.

After a wonderful darshan (auspicious sight of the deity's statue) of the Kodungallur Bhagavathy Temple in Thrissur district, I kept feeling uneasy when I took a round of the temple premises. I felt as though someone was talking to me. Was it real? Was it my imagination or just tiredness? Later as I got into the car to leave the temple, two fingers on my right hand became frozen, and I felt someone whispering in my ears. I immediately turned to Dr David, and as I was telling him this, my two frozen fingers distanced themselves from the other fingers. He laughed and, in a mischievous tone, said, "Who knows? It must be Kodungallur Amma!" I felt a sense of eeriness when I heard him say this.

When we proceeded by road to Chottanikkara in Kochi from Kodungallur, we got delayed because of some traffic due to a political rally. During this two-hour journey, I still was not at ease, and my only source of strength was Dr David. We reached Chottanikkara Temple past its closing time, but fortunately, it was kept open on that day for a special ritual happening in the temple premises. When I stood in front of the goddess, I felt as though I was not present at that moment in time. I did not understand what was happening to me, but I journeyed on.

Next, we went to the Ernakulathappan Temple (dedicated to Lord Shiva) in Ernakulam. During the car journey, Dr David kept narrating stories about gods, but my mind was busy conversing with someone else. We then went to a hotel for an overnight stay, but as we walked there, I felt as though I was being followed. Oddly, I also consumed a lot of food on that day, more than I normally would. What was happening to me? I had no answers, nor did I think of questioning my feelings.

The next morning, I spoke to Dr David about the uneasy feeling. My body felt warm and feverish almost. He asked me to apply some coconut oil on my head, palms, and feet and take a bath. I followed his instructions and, after a shower, made my way back to his room. He had a guest over, who was a very close friend of his. I noticed that he was having his breakfast quite early and asked him why.

"I'm feeling really hungry," he said.

"Didn't you get enough dinner last night?" I asked him.

"Beena, you never gave me my dinner. You ate it," he joked.

I was surprised and started to get defensive because I did not remember it.

"See, there is someone with you who is doing this," he said.

"What do you mean? How could you say that?" I responded fearfully.

He slowly started to narrate instances from the previous evening and mentioned my various antics. His words came as a shock to me because I was unaware of what had happened.

The next day, we flew back to Chennai from Kochi, and as we made our way to my house, I felt as though I was going crazy. I felt the same presence with me. I could not explain it, but a strong feeling possessed and overwhelmed me. As soon as I got home, I pulled out a blank canvas and some charcoal pencils and decided to sketch to divert my mind from what I was experiencing. Intuitively, I started sketching this dark goddess, but that did not lift the heavy load I felt off my shoulders.

I went to meet Dr David the next day and said to him, "I can feel her in my hands, and I feel like moulding her with my hands." Unhesitatingly, his immediate response was, "Then you should do just that."

I really did not know anything about sculptures, or the materials needed to mould them. On my way back home, I picked up some putty, plaster of Paris, and glue. I started sculpting that very same night. Art, for me, always means impulsivity and living in the moment without any planning. I took up the challenge of working with clay, a material I had not worked with before, and it seemed to have a mind of its own as soon as my hands touched the clay.

I was transfixed and in deep meditation, transferring all the energy I was experiencing into the mixture in my hands. It was a mystical experience; my head and hands moved around like an expert as I moulded a beautiful goddess. I could feel her—the smoothness of every curve on her face, the divinity—as she took shape before my very eyes. She was beautiful.

She stayed with me for a day. I had told Dr David that I would hand her over to him once she was done, but her beauty made me think otherwise. The sculpture had turned out beautifully, and I also added some gold foil to make her resemble a Tanjore painting. I wondered if I could keep her rather than give her away. Later that evening, when I entered my room, I noticed that her face seemed a bit out of shape. I smoothed it out and corrected it, but then again, there seemed to be something else that seemed off about her face structure. The energy emanating from her was extremely strong and dynamic, and I felt as though I was not able to handle her. I also took this as a hint that she was not meant to be with me. The next day, I handed over the goddess's sculpture to Dr David, and it occupied a place of pride in his study. I came back and slept like a log, peacefully, without any of the strange whispering in my ears. Again, many may believe this to be my imagination or hallucination, but to me, her presence was real. She emerged before me through my art. She had shown me her presence, and I felt truly blessed.

Kali Temple, New Delhi

Prior to meeting Dr David in 2012, I worked at a multinational company in New Delhi. A colleague, on finding out about my interest in the feminine divine, mentioned a Kali temple situated in Nigambodh Ghat, one of the biggest cremation grounds in the city. Nigambodh Ghat is on the banks of the river Yamuna and is the oldest crematorium in Delhi. It is believed that Lord Brahma, the lord of creation, bathed in the river and recovered his lost memory. Hence, the ghat is known as Nigambodh (realisation of knowledge), an apt name for this cremation ground as this is the only place that can remind us of the power of our breath and life. However, I knew about the temple but never visited it because I did not have the courage to step into a cremation ground. A couple of years later, during one of my many spiritual discussions with Dr David, I mentioned this temple to him.

In the blazing summer of 2013, we took a trip to New Delhi. While stepping out of the aircraft, Dr David mentioned that he was planning on visiting the Nigambodh Ghat Kali Temple that afternoon. I was not in the habit of asking him if I could accompany him to any temples, and neither did he ask me to join him in this instance.

In Delhi, we were staying at different locations. We reached my hotel, and just as I was getting out of the car, he said, "If you are interested, you can come with me to the Kali temple." He also told me to bring an extra pair of clothes. I did not quite understand why, but I also never asked him to explain. Such was my relationship with him. I refrained from asking too many questions, afraid that he would ask me not to join him. I just followed his cues.

It had been my dream to visit this Kali temple. I was quite excited, but, at the same time, I was not too comfortable around *death*. Given that a body was brought to the ghat for cremation every three minutes, I was quite apprehensive. Moreover, in Hindu culture, women generally do not visit cremation grounds, but my urge to see the goddess and the compelling presence of Dr David made me let go of some apprehensions and fears.

We left around 4 p.m. for the temple. Just as I entered Nigambodh Ghat, my legs froze. I was unable to move. There were more than ten bodies awaiting their turn at the pyre at the crematorium. There was not a single woman in sight. Summer was at its peak in Delhi, and the heat emanating from the burning pyres made me dizzy.

Dr David asked me if I was afraid as there were no women around, and I replied, "Why fear when you are here?" We went towards the temple.

The Kali temple is located at the far-left corner of the cremation ground, and one had to walk between burning pyres to see the goddess. Suddenly, the body of a youngster was brought in before me. I bottled up the fear and emotions I felt as I saw the young man's body and just followed Dr David to the temple. Just as we reached, a woman with a strong piercing gaze came out of the little shrine with prasad (a devotional offering made to God, typically food which is later distributed amongst devotees). Dr David turned around to me immediately and said, "Now you can be at peace, since you have seen a woman here and know you are not the only one."

The Kali temple was a small one, and you need to bend down a little to see the goddess. Dr David sat in front of the idol. Between the sanctum sanctorum and him, there was a homakund (a fireplace used in a holy ritual in Hinduism where offerings are made to God) that had seen many homams and was filled with some pieces of old burnt wood. Dr David told me he was unhappy that he had come empty-handed to see the goddess. An offering, like flowers or fruits, is always given to a deity, and he had brought nothing with him. He then asked me to sit down. We noticed that there was a Sardarji praying nearby. Since he had no offering with him, Dr David decided to perform the Manasa pooja (a ritual where offerings are made from the mind, symbolic of material ones such as flowers and water) and started to chant the mantras.

After about ten minutes, a blaze of fire suddenly erupted from the homakund. A small piece of burning wood flew and fell in front of the goddess at her feet. I was speechless! The Sardarji, who had watched the whole scene, got up in a frenzy and prostrated in front of Dr David. Dr David calmly asked him to bring the burning piece of wood from near the goddess and put it back in the homakund. The piece of wood immediately started burning again in the homakund.

I turned to look at Dr David, who seemed oddly different. He asked me, "Beena, what do you want?"

I did not know what to ask for after what I had witnessed at the temple. So I simply replied, "It is extremely hot today. All I can ask for is that Delhi needs a good rain." He smiled, raised his hand to the sky, and snapped his fingers three times. He then lowered his hand and continued the pooja.

Several moments later, I felt a drop of water roll down my cheek, and to my shock and surprise, it started pouring heavily. What I had just witnessed was nothing short of a miracle.

As per the *Rigveda*, if yagnas (a ritual of offerings in front of a sacred fire) are performed well, there would be blessings in the form of rain—Agni Deva, the god of fire, invokes Varuna, the god of rain. If one knows how to control the Pancha Bhutas or the five elements, then also one can call upon the rains. Words cannot possibly describe the feelings I experienced that day.

My mind was blank. Half my body was warm, and the other half was frozen cold. I shut my eyes and entered a deep meditative state with the subtle pitter-patter of rain in the background. It continued to rain for another forty-five minutes or so. I was on cloud nine. It was a state of bliss, a state I had never experienced before.

Suddenly, Dr David's voice broke through my meditative trance, and he asked me, "Beena, shall we leave?"

I slowly opened my eyes and got up.

"Not so soon. You are not a young girl anymore who can go about running around in the rain. It has to stop, doesn't it?" he said, in a cheeky tone. I used to tell him that on schooldays, I never took umbrellas deliberately during the rainy season to get wet.

Again, he raised his hand to the sky and snapped his fingers three times. Slowly, like clockwork, the rain started to calm down and stop.

The pyres had stopped burning because of the rain. I turned to look at the pyres. Dr David mentioned how bad he felt that the rain had disrupted the young boy's cremation process. The boy's pyre was in an elevated position, about 50 metres away from where we stood. Dr David turned to look at the boy's pyre, and just as he pointed his fingers towards it, the pyre was ablaze once again! The puddles of water at my feet were so hot, and I just could not fathom what was happening around me. I seemed to be on some metaphysical plane that I had no cognisance of.

From Nigambodh Ghat, we returned to Dr David's guest house, where he asked me to take a bath since we had visited a cremation ground. As I was leaving the guest house, I asked for his permission to touch his feet. When I lowered my head towards his feet, I felt something wet on my hands. I assumed it was water after my bath, but when I opened my eyes, I was shocked to see blood oozing out of my nostrils like a river. However, I was not worried. I was in a different frame of mind. Dr David asked me to sit down and relax for a while before I headed back to my hotel. It was one of those nights in life where I slept extremely peacefully.

This incident is just one of the mystical and inexplicable experiences I had with Dr David in my years of travelling with him on this spiritual journey. I have been fortunate to have had these experiences. I would need to write another book to talk about them, but even that would not be enough because every second I spent with him was an experience. He was my source of strength, a strong pillar and foundation in my journey that continues today.

The Nakshatra Paintings

Yet another year of travelling and exploring the world of spiritualism with Dr David passed by. I frequently visited his home. On a fine day in 2014, on one such visit, he said to me, "You came to me to learn tantra, but you are not doing anything about it."

As I said earlier, I always found it best to never ask him for anything. From this statement of his, I presumed he would start teaching me something about the subject. Instead, he said, "Start painting—the subject is twenty-seven nakshatras, the twenty-seven constellations."

I just could not stop laughing when he said this to me. "I don't know anything about them. What will I paint?" I asked him.

Dr David responded, "Tantra is nothing but distilling information from the universe. *Yat Pinde Tat Brahmande*. All that exists outside of you (macrocosmic universe) also exists within you (microcosm). It is just a matter of connecting cables and distilling the information. We all are just coexisting energies. That distilling is called tantra. Tantra is the technique of distillation."

Let me be frank here. Everything he said went over my head. I had no idea what he was talking about. He, however, did not seem perturbed at all and proceeded to recite the mantra of the first nakshatra or constellation while meditating. Once he was done, he asked me to go ahead and paint. He refused to divulge anything more.

"In the world, there exist many systems to classify the world population, such as country, creed, colour, and caste, but nothing is accurate. If you must be accurate, divide the people of the world into twenty-seven as per the nakshatras they are born under," he said, sending me off on a new journey to discover the twenty-seven constellations.

The next day, I began working on my first painting of the Nakshatra series. I did some basic research on the attributes of each nakshatra so that the paintings may look different from each other. My first piece was the nakshatra Ashwathi, and from then onwards, everything about the nakshatras just seemed to unveil themselves onto the canvas in fluid strokes.

It took me nine months to complete the entire collection of twenty-seven nakshatras. During this period, the only time I ever stepped out of the house was to visit the temple one day. I did nothing but paint for nine months, devoting myself to the constellations. During this period, I learned the real meaning of tantra. I also understood that every experience with Dr David was a teaching process. Practising detachment, selflessly thinking beyond what you see, connecting the energies, killing the fear within you—he taught me all these, and I absorbed everything like a sponge soaking up the wisdom and knowledge without questions.

Dr David seemed to appreciate my art, and together we started planning an exhibition of the nakshatra paintings.

As an artist and as any other normal human being, I started building castles in the air with dreams of how the exhibition would turn out. I came back to the ground with a thud when Dr David asked me not to sign the paintings. "No one can take the rights away from you. They are yours and yours only," he reiterated. But I could not accept it.

I was upset. He did not speak to me for two days. I guess it was his method of punishment. When he spoke to me later, he said, "If you want to know these energies, you need to be a *nishkami*, a person without desires. Great artists sign behind their paintings and practise detachment."

Nothing seemed to convince me. I was no less adamant than my guru. I took a few days to think about it and decided to leave the paintings at his house even though he asked me not to.

"We will go to the twenty-seven nakshatra temples. I want you to sign each of them in the presence of that energy," he told me. Still, I was not ready to listen to him.

"They don't belong to me. I'd like you to accept them as my guru dakshina (an offering made to the teacher to give thanks). The day you finalise the exhibition, I will complete the paintings," I responded in defiance.

Later that week, I went to his house with the paintings, handed them over, and sought his blessings. I do not know if it was my arrogance or ego, but it was then that I really learned the meaning of the word *submission*. I trusted that he would never exhibit the nakshatra paintings without my signature on them and gifted them to him in good faith.

Today, when I look back at this incident, I realise that the paintings were a rough sketchbook where he taught me to envision the energies I had encountered and to understand the meaning of tantra. It was through learning the method of distillation that I understood my inner strength. I learned to be detached, to be a *nishkami*; it was merely an exercise that my mentor made me go through. He taught me how to receive energy from the universe and convert it to vivid colours on the canvas through my palette.

A Day of Great Loss

"It is time for me to vanish."

A year prior to the fateful day, Dr David would constantly make such remarks.

He would often come and tell me, "Today is a bonus day for me." I grew a bit concerned but brushed it off. He often spoke in such a stoic tone. At one point, he used to visit my office several times a week, but the visits eventually reduced to just once a week.

Dr David was unwell, but he had always refused to go to doctors. Even if he did on the rare occasion, he would not follow their advice. One morning, he called me and asked me to come over to his house. I spent close to six hours with him that day.

At that point, I was working on a film script with a good friend of his, Mr Anil Kumar. The script had been completed, and so I asked him to attend the script reading. "Why do you need my physical presence? I am always there with you. You are a strong woman, and you can take it forward, Beena Anandamayi," he responded.

Beena Anandamayi—that is what he called me when he was very happy. Little did I know that those would be his last words to me.

He spoke quite a bit to me that day. He had attended an event a day earlier without me. I normally accompanied him, but this time, he specifically called me and asked me not to. "You take rest. You must be fed up listening to me talk," he said.

That day he was so happy about the event and kept talking about it. He told me that people were calling him to get back into movies. I jokingly asked him to make his comeback in the film Anil and I were working on.

He said to me, "There is a surprise for you tomorrow, but I don't want to tell you anything about it now." I said okay because I never asked him for a reason.

While leaving, I did a sashtanga namaskaram (prostrated) in front of him as I was about to leave his house. Normally, he would stop me, saying a woman must not do a sashtanga namaskaram. On that fateful day, however, he did not.

We stepped out of the house, and he walked me to the gate.

"I am not feeling well. My leg is very painful. Let's go to Kerala tomorrow evening. In the morning, I am going to another place." I told him that he should rest, and he replied, "In Kerala, I will rest."

"Okay, we'll go tomorrow," I told him. *No* was a word I never uttered to him. I always only nodded in affirmation to any request or thought he had.

Eight years have passed by, yet the surprise I got the next day is one that I will never get over. Early the next morning, we got a call from his family, informing us that he had been admitted to the hospital. My husband and I rushed to the hospital. My mind was numb the entire time. I knew he had left us. I do not want to write about that day. I cannot get over the scene that I saw when I reached the hospital. Just as he had wished, we travelled to Kerala the next day with his lifeless body to perform the last rites.

My life has changed drastically since then. It feels vacant without his presence. A couple of days after his passing, I dreamt of him consoling me. I asked him not to appear to me that way again as I did not wish to see him in that form. It only hurt me further. He left a huge impact on all those he held close, and to this day, his absence is felt. It took me a long time to mourn his loss, but he will always be by my side in spirit, if not physically.

My travels with Dr David helped me understand the bridging of science and the Sastras (religious treaties). I understood the power of the five elements of earth, water, fire, wind, and space, the power of thoughts, and the real meaning of tantra. He always looked for scientific explanations or reasoning behind religious or spiritual matters. He claimed that in the current times, one could only wholeheartedly follow spiritual rules if one understood the scientific reasoning behind them.

Dr David always said, "A real guru grooms the disciple to be independent of the guru." I know he is with me. Otherwise, I could not have done what I am doing now.

Before I move on, I would like to do my sashtanga namaskaram to my guru, friend, and mentor, to the divine soul. I pray that Dr David will always be there to guide me and bless me in this project. Without him, it is impossible.

A few years earlier, on one of our trips to Thiruvananthapuram, Kerala, Dr David took me to meet his guru, a popular astrologer. We had a wonderful time, conversing on various subjects around spiritualism. When we were about to leave, he said something about the doctor.

"Just like the sky, Dr David is incomparable. He is not one in a million; he is the only one," he said to me in a sombre tone.

These words perfectly describe the incredible human being that I have been blessed to call my friend, philosopher, and guide—Dr David.

4

The Srividya Conundrum

Like a child standing in front of an ocean without understanding its enormity and depth, I stood in front of my inner calling. The perpetual cadence of the ocean stirred my restless mind, its gentle waves beckoning me into the deep waters of the mystery of Srividya or knowledge. The vast ocean, seemingly conspiring with the flow and ebb of the water swelling and cascading at my feet, urged me to wade further and deeper into the infinite sea of knowledge.

An interesting discussion took place between me and Dr David prior to his demise in 2015.

"Paint and write on the subject of Srividya," urged Dr David with a smile one evening.

Returning the same demure smile, since I had no clue what he was referring to, I jokingly enquired, "Which Srividya?"

There is a south Indian actor named Srividya with whom I was more familiar. I know he was referring to Srividya, the divine tantric feminine.

He looked at me with his piercing eyes and asked, "Can't you?"

"If the goddess blesses me, I can paint without any knowledge of the subject. But writing is impossible. I don't have the confidence to write a single page on this subject. I have not studied it; moreover, I don't have the talent to write also," I replied nervously.

He opened his desk drawer, took out an ancient book wrapped in a yellowing old plastic cover, and handed it to me.

"Time will reveal when you should, and this book will guide you," he told me.

I took it from him and kept it in my bag without uttering a word. I knew there was a reason for everything and that all will be revealed when the time is right. Such was my unwavering faith in the goddess and in him.

Several times after that, I asked him to teach me the Srividya Upasana as it is the primary prayer of Sri Yantra, which, as previously mentioned, was a subject that interested me. He would just smile.

Srividya is a tantric Hindu religious system devoted to Goddess Lalitha Tripura Sundari, one of the highest forms of Shakti, the divine feminine. The following of this practice and devotion to the goddess is said to bring material prosperity as well as enlightenment. In this form of worship, the divinity within oneself is worshipped. The traditions followed by this sect of Hinduism vary in different literatures but have similarities to Kashmiri Shaivism, a non-dualistic Shiva–Shakti worship tradition that originated in Kashmir, India.

Whenever Dr David recited the Shodashi Mantra (a sixteen-syllable mantra recited in worship of Goddess Lalitha Tripura Sundari), he would do so loudly and gesture to me to listen. Shodashi is another name for Goddess Sri Lalitha Tripura Sundari. This mantra consists of a series of syllables and sounds that are considered seed mantras or Beej Mantras, and it possesses its own power. The mantra is chanted to grant both material and spiritual benefits and is said to increase one's magnetism.

"Just love her, and when she realises your selflessness, she will appear before you. Keep your mind clean to receive her, and at that time, I will be by your side to guide you," he told me.

Everything he said to comfort me wiped away my worries. If I was destined to receive this divinity, it would happen.

The year following his death, I did not realise the days and months passing by as my mind grieved his loss. The reminders to fulfil his expectations passed through my mind like a breeze caressing my thoughts. His words crept through my brain whenever I was silent. "Paint and write on Srividya."

I waited.

5

In Search of My Femininity

All my life, I have always been surrounded by masculine energy, and naturally, I have imbibed some of it as well. Professionally, I have worked in male-dominated fields. Moreover, I am always surrounded by men: I grew up with two brothers, and my family consists of two sons and my husband. I have always thought of myself as having more masculine qualities than feminine. How could I paint and write on Srividya if I had completely lost touch with my femininity?

In the rush of life, women tend to get carried away with responsibilities and lose touch with their feminine nurturing sides. I missed the little girl in me. Back in school, I was known to have a reputation for fluttering around like a butterfly. I missed my womanly side.

Even though Goddess Lalitha Tripura Sundari (the presiding deity of Srividya) was one of my all-time favourite subjects, I did not know much about Srividya. I felt an inner calling towards it, but I could not identify it. I also did not know where and how to start painting and writing on the subject. If I was not able to connect with my inner femininity, how could I connect with and paint the divine feminine?

Nothing was inspiring me, and unfortunately, I had forgotten where I had placed the book Dr David had given me. I had made sure to keep it in such a safe place that even I could not find it!

The season of Navaratri, an annual Hindu festival observed for nine days in reverence of the Adi Parashakti or the divine feminine, was approaching. It is a celebration of Goddess Durga, the feminine power, and the victory of good over evil. As a penance, I decided to fast for the nine days of Navaratri and have nothing but water, hoping to gain some clarity on where to begin. I was hoping to connect with my inner femininity during this penance.

Surprisingly, during this time, whenever I meditated, I could see the shadows of two men, one of them reciting the *Lalitha Sahasranamam* with me. The *Lalitha Sahasranamam* is a text of ancient religious chants of 1,000 verses in praise of Goddess Lalitha Tripura Sundari. Their faces were unclear. It is always said that you should look beyond what you see to see the goddess's mystic plans for you.

I also felt the presence of divine male energies during my meditations. Therefore, to show reverence to that masculine spirit, along with the feminine spirit that I had originally set out to paint, I started on my first painting—the Ardhanareeswarar (the composite male–female figure of the Hindu god Shiva together with his consort Parvati).

Around the penultimate day of Navaratri, I caught glimpses of the shadows again, but this time, their faces were revealed to me. One person was my business partner Manjula's friend, Mr Annamalai, whom I had met only once. I grew curious about why I kept seeing him and asked Manjula about his whereabouts.

The second person I saw resembled a good friend of mine Mr Madhav. I assumed that he would be the person to help me write about my spiritual journey with the goddesses as instructed by Dr David.

I was not confident about my writing skills as I did not have much experience. I was born and raised in a small town where English was not commonly spoken. I knew I needed someone I could depend on. I decided to meet my friend and discuss it with him. My plans seemed very unclear to myself, and convincing such a dynamic personality was going to be a tough task.

My prior interactions with my friend Mr Madhav had never revealed his interest in spiritualism. He was a very simple and honest human being whom I only knew on a professional level. What I had was a checkpoint, the *Lalitha Sahasranamam*, as I had seen him reciting it. I enquired further about his interest in the subject, and to my surprise, he had vast knowledge. That was my green signal.

At this point, I still was not sure of what to paint or write. I had not decided what I was going to paint exactly, but I knew that I was going to paint something related to Srividya. The exact topic was only revealed to me later as I progressed on the journey. I knew that I had to write on the divine feminine as instructed by Dr David, and I believed that the first step towards knowing the goddess was to understand the meaning and significance of the *Lalitha Sahasranamam*.

As a start, I requested Mr Madhav to recite the *Lalitha Sahasranamam* and explain its meaning. He agreed, and being a disciplined man, he said we would discuss a few verses every day.

I thought his disciplined approach would help me to create a road map for my work, which would hopefully give me more clarity. Sometimes, though, things do not happen as planned. Every passenger we meet on our journey has a place to disembark. My friend recited 90 per cent of the 1,000 verses to me. Then he said that once he was done with the entire mantra, we would have to discontinue our regular conversations about the subject. Due to his work schedule, the circumstances had changed.

For some reason, I decided to put an end to the sessions at that point where 10 per cent of the mantra was yet to be recited and explained. I am not sure why I felt the need to, even though he magnanimously offered to complete reading it. Call it a gut instinct. Sometimes I wonder if I expected too much, but everything has a reason. We all are a part of the master plan.

I decided to explore the last ten verses on my own as I felt that this was my solo journey and it required only me and no one else to go beyond what I was merely exposed to. From the bottom of my heart, I thanked my dear friend for reciting the *Lalitha Sahasranamam* to me.

Later, while researching the mantra, I came across a story that parallels mine. According to a tale from the *Lalita Mahatmya* (an ancient Puranic text about Goddess Lalitha Parameshwari), the 1,000 names of Lalitha were first recited to the ancient sage Agastya by Hayagreeva, an incarnation of Vishnu. I wondered whether Mr Madhav would have embodied the role of Hayagreeva in my life if he had completed explaining the meaning and significance of the remaining 10 per cent of the mantra. However, maybe that was not part of the master plan.

This incident was an indication for me to go on this journey alone. I came to realise that, in this path, I may have different co-passengers who will do a bit of their karma and leave. My journey and destination should be independent of all that. My journey was internal, and I could not have a companion tag along. I realised that I needed to gather energy from within and move forward.

6

Ardhanareeswarar

Despite being asked to paint and write about Srividya or the divine tantric feminine, during my meditations, I strangely felt drawn to a masculine force. A vision of a male deity kept appearing before me. Therefore, to honour the masculine in me, I decided to start my project with a painting of the Ardhanareeswarar or the form of Lord Shiva combined with his consort, Goddess Parvati.

Red, green, blue—there was a riot of colours around me. I kept my mind clear as a blank canvas. In that silence, the shades of yellow and red drifted onto my canvas, the colour of the glowing sun, my spectator.

Even though I felt a stronger masculine force around me, I started with the feminine half, or Parvati, of the Ardhanareeswarar, and she came out beautifully. I am not one to praise my own work, but when the feminine divine expresses herself well, you feel peace within. This journey was not just for me to show off my artistic skills but for me to connect with higher realms and the divine feminine energy.

I encountered the traces of the colours of the male half, Shiva: dark blue or the true blue. I realised that the colour of the male in me was enhancing my wisdom, empowering me with the power of the union of male and female (the centre point of the Sri Yantra).

It felt as though blue was the colour of my breath. Every brush stroke on the canvas induced calmness and peace in me. He emerged on my canvas as a charming young man, amalgamating with my feminine power. The painting held my conscious and subconscious existence very empathetically and dramatically.

The image of Ardhanareeswarar was forming in my mind. The painting was signifying the presence of both the forces in me, without which I could not have taken the next step. I started to celebrate my life.

The Ardhanareeswarar form explains how inseparable the masculine and the feminine in us are. It represents the presence of masculine and feminine power in us. The realisation of the power of this duality in us can take us to a perpetual state of ecstasy. The union of Prakriti and Purusha is the source of power of all creation. I realised why I wanted to start with Ardhanareeswarar.

As per Indian philosophy, Prakriti is often described as the fundamental cosmic essence from which all existence emanates. In contrast, Purusha embodies the very spirit that orchestrates our lives and defines our perception of reality. The presence of these cosmic forces is not confined to the cosmos alone; rather, they find their dwelling within us, shaping our very essence. Just as our bodies comprise the elemental building blocks known as the Pancha Bhutas or the five elements, so do they contain traces of Prakriti and Purusha, rendering us microcosmic universes in our own right.

The whole world came into existence through this form. A human being is not a purely unisexual organism. An embryonic genital has two parts—the inner part has the potential to develop into testes and the outer cortex has the potential to develop into ovaries. The presence of one Y chromosome causes the cortex to retreat and the testes to form. The testes secrete a small amount of oestrogen along with androgen, the male hormone, and the ovaries secrete a small amount of androgen along with oestrogen. Each energy nurtures the other.

The concept of Ardhanareeswarar aspires to resolve the paradox of opposite in unity. This concept transcends the distinction between the genders and the limitations of being male or female and takes us beyond genders, resulting in liberation.

7

Ganesha

Ganesha is another of my all-time favourite subjects. According to Hinduism, every project begins by taking his blessings. He is one of the most popular deities in Hinduism. In this case, I sought his blessings to start my project by painting the Ardhanareeswarar form first instead of him, because this occupied my thoughts. I have always felt a connection with Lord Ganesha, who is known to be the remover of obstacles. Therefore, I was in the habit of collecting his idols. I have also been blessed with a son who was born on Ganesh Chaturthi (festival celebrating Lord Ganesha).

The one thing that confused me, however, is what form of his I should paint. I confided in my husband about the confusion I had, and he pointed at a Tanjore painting of mine that I had done a few years before and asked me to copy the same form.

The Tanjore painting was of a sitting elephant, the Lord himself, with five faces. I meditated on that form for an answer, but for some reason, the image of a lion kept popping up in my mind. I had never seen an image of Lord Ganesha on a lion, but I realised this journey was to paint what is unseen. So I decided to paint Ganesha with five heads sitting on a lion.

Four heads of the Ganesha faced the four cardinal directions, and one faced the centre, which is the axis controlling the five elements—water (north), fire (south), wood (east), metal (west), and the earth in the centre of the spirit, that is, the five vital forces that move through the body. On further research, I discovered that this form does exist as one of the thirty-two forms of Lord Ganesha; it is called Herambha and has strong roots in tantrism.

Ganesha is the representation of universal intelligence. After painting Ardhanareeswarar and understanding the existence of male and female forces in a body, I realise that knowledge can be manifested only by such a body.

The most beautiful part of painting such energy is when you look and feel it beyond what you paint. Then you merge with that energy. I always look for an answer from the universe repeatedly to confirm if I have taken the right path.

It was Akshaya Tritiya, the day Maharishi (Sage) Vyasa is said to have begun to narrate the great Indian epic of the Mahabharata to Lord Ganesha. Before going to work, I had to deliver something to a friend who lived nearby. When I reached her place, she was getting ready to go to a jewellery store, and I tagged along with her. I asked my office driver to pick me up from the jewellers', but he came late.

As I waited for my driver at the jewellery store, the salesperson took out a silver Ganesha pendant and said to me, "This is a beautiful piece. Why don't you buy it?"

I wondered why he showed me that specific piece, but I took it as a sign from the gods and bought it happily. It may seem like a mere coincidence to others, but I believe when you are immersed deep into a subject, nothing is a mere coincidence. I wore that pendant every single day until I completed my artistic endeavour.

After I finished the Ganesha painting, I received a call from Senthil, a priest at the Adi Kamakshi Temple adjacent to the Kanchi Kamakshi Temple (one of the Shaktistalas, holy places of worship dedicated to Goddess Sati, where the navel of Sati had fallen) in Kanchipuram that Dr David and I used to frequently visit, asking me to drop by, since it had been a while. I decided to make the short trip from Chennai to Kanchipuram, and as we were heading there, I decided to visit both the Adi Kamakshi as well as the Kanchi Kamakshi temples.

The Adi Kamakshi and Kanchi Kamakshi temples of Kanchipuram are both dedicated to Goddess Kamakshi. My first stop was the latter. While doing the *pradakshina* (the rite of circumambulating in a clockwise direction around an image, relic, shrine, or other sacred object), I spotted an altar of Lord Ganesha. There were some words in Tamil that I could not read. Just as I crossed the altar, I suddenly heard someone calling me from behind. I turned back to find an older gentleman.

"Do you know who this is?" he asked me.

"This is Ganesha," I responded, assuming he asked me out of curiosity.

"He is Herambha, the tantric version of Ganesha, seated on a lion, and closely associated with Srividya," he replied.

I was stunned. I was trying to suppress my surprise, but it was evident on my face and he noticed it. He smiled again and moved on. It was a confirmation of my connection with the Lord and a confirmation that I was on the right path. I had been to Kanchipuram several times, but not once had I noticed this. I was overwhelmed by emotions and started to cry.

Beyond the eyes lie all the mysteries of life.

My next stop was the Adi Kamakshi Temple. The place brought a wave of memories of the times I would accompany Dr David when he performed rituals to worship the goddesses.

He would buy sixty-four lotus flowers and perform a pooja, sitting in the mandapa (a pavilion where rituals are performed). He would ask me to create mandalas or geometrical figures on the ground using the flowers to invoke the gods and goddesses. I never bothered to ask why sixty-four flowers. After this, he would also perform the Kalabhairava pooja (a ritual to invoke the fierce manifestation of the Shaivite deity Lord Bhairava).

When I entered the temple premises, the flower seller spotted me and hurriedly came towards me, saying he had fresh lotuses. He remembered me from the times I used to accompany Dr David. He counted the number of lotus flowers, and there were exactly sixty-four in number. I still did not quite understand the significance of the number and its relation to the pooja Dr David performed for the goddesses and Kalabhairava. Therefore, I asked Senthil, the priest.

"It could be because there are sixty-four Bhairavas," he replied.

This reply sent me on a voyage, with fresh eyes, in search of the mystery behind the number sixty-four. I knew the journey would take me deep into my soul, and I felt I was ready.

8

Bhairavas

Lord Bhairava and I go way back. In 2009, I worked as the director of corporate affairs for a company in New Delhi. My job required me to handle legal affairs; hence, I had to visit the court regularly. For some reason, courts made me uncomfortable. I am not sure why, but I never liked being in that space. Seeing my plight, a colleague suggested that I visit a Kalabhairava temple nearby, which was famous for protecting people from legal entanglements.

So, thereafter, visiting the court meant visiting Kalabhairava at the famous Prachin Bhairav Mandir near Delhi's Old Fort where liquor is given as a religious offering. It is said that the temple was constructed by the Pandavas, the mythological brothers from the Mahabharata. I became a regular visitor at the temple.

Later, when I met Dr David, I learnt that he was a great devotee of Kalabhairava. I became aware of the deity's power only after meeting him. Every Ashtami, the eighth day of the waxing or waning of the moon, Dr David would perform a pooja for Kalabhairava, since the day is dedicated to him.

Kalabhairava is the lord of time. He is the wrathful manifestation of Shiva. Hindu mythology has several stories on gods and goddesses. Even though Hinduism believes in the ultimate God "Brahman" (the creative principle by which the whole world functions), each god has manifested as different forms and each story of that manifestation has deep value, solutions for life, and lessons on how to exist in society.

We have the freedom to perceive God based on our experiences. The origin of Bhairava is attributed to a story from the *Shiva Purana* (the ancient text on Lord Shiva). Once, Lord Brahma started a heated argument with Lord Vishnu and Lord Shiva, claiming him to be the lord of the universe, since he was the creator. Brahma's attitude angered Lord Shiva, which led him to incarnate as Kalabhairava and behead one of Lord Brahma's five heads. Kalabhairava, in doing so, had committed the great sin of Brahmahatya (killing a Brahmin). To rid himself of the sin, he was advised by Lord Shiva to take a dip in the Ganga, after which he was relieved of the karma.

Another beautiful fact is that, usually, in temples of Shiva and Shakti, the key to the temple is placed in front of an idol of Lord Bhairava, since he is considered the protector or guard of sorts. Siddhas (enlightened souls) are known to worship him before embarking on a journey. Are any more reasons needed to answer my inner calling and paint a form of this great deity?

The more knowledge I gained about him, the closer I got to understanding the essence of the number sixty-four. Kalabhairava has eight manifestations that guard eight directions of the universe. Each Bhairava has seven Bhairavas under him. Therefore, there are sixty-four Bhairavas in total.

Every stroke I did on the canvas struck a familiar chord. I could feel a presence and an energy that I knew and understood very well. He came as a tinge of dark blue and captured my canvas with the mightiest power. Swirls of indigo represented clearer perception, and splashes of royal blue indicated both lust and peace. He emerged as a powerful, handsome man with piercing eyes, almost as though he came down to burn the fear in me, destroy the ego and doubts in me, and inculcate trust and faith about my further travel. According to the ancient sages, praying to Kalabhairava before you start a journey ensures your protection until you reach the destination.

Moreover, he is said to be the presiding deity of Rahu (one of the nine celestial bodies in Hindu astrology, said to bring an inauspicious time in the lives of those impacted by its presence during a specific period). Being a strong believer in astrology, this connected me with him deeply as I was going through the period of Rahu in my life at that point.

I was starting to decode the blueprint. I had torched the mystic number sixty-four. To know more, however, he was the energy I needed to hold on to, as he would lead me to the consorts—the sixty-four yoginis, the sixty-four forms of the divine feminine or Goddess Lalitha Tripura Sundari.

As an ice-cold glacier in the sun, I melted into the ocean that was my purpose. Everything up until that point had led me to the yoginis. I came to realise that this was my ultimate project: to paint and write about the sixty-four yoginis.

I felt the presence of Rahu as Sarpa (snake) and Bhairava in the form of Chandrakala (moon). Therefore, I decided to have the symbolic representation of the two in every painting of mine, as silent spectators witnessing and guiding me through my journey to Lalitha Tripura Sundari.

9

The Sixty-Four

You are not a drop in the ocean. You are the entire ocean in a drop.

—Rumi

Sixty-four is not only a sacred number in Hinduism but also part of science and technology and other religious and spiritual philosophies such as Buddhism and Christianity. The number sixty-four fascinates in both the scientific and the spiritual realms. It is the smallest number with seven divisors and is both a perfect square and a perfect cube, revealing its mathematical significance. In spirituality, sixty-four is revered in Hinduism through the sixty-four Tantras, texts in Tantrism, a mystical and ritualistic approach to life. In culture, the number is represented in the sixty-four squares of a chessboard, symbolising strategy and intellect. Intriguingly, some theories propose the existence of sixty-four dimensions in the universe, with the sixty-fourth being the highest. Historically, in ancient India, mastering the sixty-four traditional arts or Chausath Kalas was crucial for cultural sophistication. This blend of science and spirituality makes sixty-four a uniquely powerful number.

Human DNA has sixty-four codons. A codon is a sequence of three DNA or RNA nucleotides, and each set of codons is called a genetic code. A genetic code includes sixty-four possible permutations and combinations of three-lettered nucleotide sequences.

The points where the *mamsa* (muscles), *shera* (veins), *snayu* (ligaments), and *asti* (bones) unite are called the marma points. These are the vital parts of the body, which are considered the seats of life. In our body, out of 107 marma points, sixty-four are called Kulamarma points, which are deadly and said to hold life itself.

Sage Agastya is considered the founder of the science of marmas, the Marmashastra. Marma points are located along with the *nadis* (the energy channels) through which *prana* (life force) flows. According to ancient texts, *Purusha* (pure consciousness or ojas) and *Prakriti* (principle of manifestation of time and space or *tejas*) interface with prana at marma points.

There are eight major marma points that are essential to life:
1. Sahasrara (crown)
2. Sivaanandha (posterior of crown)
3. Brahmanandha (anterior to crown)
4. Yaju (third eye)
5. Shanka (left and right temple)
6. Hridayam (heart)
7. Naabhi (umbilical)
8. Nadha (anus)

Eight goddesses are said to govern these energy centres. There was so much to explore in this realm. These numbers had a deeper meaning, and everything seemed connected. Science and spirituality work hand in hand. I came across all this information while doing further research on the numbers sixty-four and eight, which I found to be very relevant. I was happy that I was on the right path.

10

The Sixty-Four Yoginis

Gaining knowledge of the yoginis is the true awakening of the feminine power and the creative life force deep within us. She, the divine feminine, is the luminous wisdom weaving all the sixty-four cosmic powers within us.

As mentioned, after painting Lord Bhairava, I knew and had decided that my next undertaking would be to paint the sixty-four yoginis. I had never heard of yoginis prior to this, other than as part of certain slokas, nor had I visited any yogini temples. I cannot say for sure when exactly the word entered the realm of my thought and became the purpose of my life.

My mind was full of questions, and I did not know where to start. The easiest and most accessible source of information was the internet, or I could go the old-fashioned way and read books. Whatever information I could gather only managed to confuse me further.

There are several references to the feminine divinity of yoginis in ancient sacred Puranic texts and scriptures such as *Brahmanda Purana, Skanda Purana, Agni Purana, Kalika Purana, Nandikeshwara Purana,* and *Chandi Purana.* The numbers and names differ.

A compelling legend sheds light on the emergence of these sixty-four yoginis. The demon Mahishasura left the gods, goddesses, and celestial beings in despair. They turned to Goddess Lalitha Tripura Sundari in prayer. Their plea was simple: protection from Mahishasura.

In response to their supplications, Goddess Lalitha Tripura Sundari, the ultimate divine force, reassured them by manifesting Goddess Durga from her divine essence. From the very body of Goddess Durga emerged eight demi-divine beings known as the Ashta Matrikas. From each of these Matrikas, an additional eight yoginis sprung forth, culminating in the manifestation of a total of sixty-four yoginis.

United with the divine might of Goddess Mahishasuramardini, these sixty-four yoginis joined forces to vanquish the demon brothers Sumbha and Nisumbha, along with their entire asura army. This heroic act established an unbreakable bond between these yoginis and Goddess Lalitha Parameshwari, the embodiment of divine grace and power.

Adi Shankara was an 8th-century Indian Vedic scholar and teacher known for his philosophy of Advaita, which talks about the existence of a single reality. According to him, Lalitha Parameshwari is not just guarded by sixty-four yoginis but 640 million yoginis. Bhaskara Raya, a great scholar who wrote a commentary on the *Lalitha Sahasranamam*, was tested on his knowledge about yoginis by a group of learned scholars who asked him to list the names of the 640 million yoginis who are said to surround Goddess Lalitha Parameshwari. When he started listing the names without a thought, another sage saw an apparition of the goddess herself seated on Bhaskara Raya's shoulders and warned the scholars. Bhaskara Raya's recitation confirmed that Adi Shankara was right about there being not just sixty-four yoginis but 640 million.

In the ocean of unknown and unheard information on the 640 million yoginis, my brain was ready to take a step back. I was constantly finding other reasons to not take this journey forward. Financially, at that point, I was not in the best situation. Hence, I thought of taking a step back from this artistic journey. One day, I received a call from Mr Annamalai, a friend of my business partner, Manjula. During my Navaratri fast, I had seen glimpses of him during my meditations and, therefore, kept enquiring about him to Manjula. She informed him about my queries, which made him call me.

Annamalai, being a very pious person, met me to discuss reiki healing for him. I told him that reiki would be a commitment and that I was not in a position to commit to timings. The best I could do was pray for him. He noticed all my paintings, and I told him about my undertaking. Without much thought, he immediately asked me how he could get involved. I confided in him that I may need financial support so I would not have to halt the project midway. Much to my surprise, Mr Annamalai readily agreed to support me financially. He has selflessly been a part of my journey; he, too, played his karmic role in this entire process.

I worked on my paintings, trusting my instinct as I recalled Dr David's words, "If you worry too much about money, no work can take place. Keep moving and the money will fall in place." I just focused on a few things: trust the path that unfolds in front of you; have blind faith in her energy; and love her as you would love yourself.

Every day I tried learning more about the subject, but the more I read, the more confused I was. I did not think it best to discuss it with anyone else either because then I would follow their path rather than forge my own way. I knew if I found someone, I would need to go through the process of initiation and the procedure of worship (*sadhana*). I wanted my mind to delve deep without any restrictions.

I could feel an energy around me that wanted to take shape on my canvas, one that was forcing me to paint and asking me to create my own path. It was a very compelling force.

Apart from this, there were also the practical issues like my lack of knowledge of Sanskrit and having to hire someone else to translate the texts for me.

Each list of yogini names I came across differed from the previous one. I deeply meditated on all these lists and felt drawn to the one from the Chausath Yogini Temple in Hirapur, Odisha, also known as the Mahamaya Temple.

I immediately got started on the paintings, one by one. I find the painting process to be quite meditative; my art was based on how the divine feminine appeared to me during this mediation. The Hirapur list was just a reference.

After completing four of the sixty-four paintings, I decided to visit Hirapur. Mr Annamalai also accompanied me. Situated a little distance away from the hustle and bustle of Bhubaneswar (Odisha), Hirapur is a small town surrounded by paddy fields. Built in the 9th century, the temple is non-functional and under the protection of the Archaeological Survey of India (ASI) today. It is a small circular shrine made of sandstone. I had never been to a temple with such a structure before. The place had a lot of stories to tell, and I felt a deep connection to it.

All the structures looked beautiful. The black stone had a sheen to it. Each goddess's sculpture had a beautiful smile and well-combed hair and was adorned with gorgeous jewellery. The four paintings I had finished looked quite different from the sculptures. I felt the presence of the rest of the goddesses and that they wished to be painted as well and expressed on my canvas.

I sat in front of Mahamaya, the presiding goddess. I had only one question in my mind: "Am I on the right path?"

To my utter surprise, I heard someone replying, "What you are doing is the right decision. Yoginis that you can handle will come to your canvas."

I turned to see a well-built man seated near me, answering the question I had in mind. I looked at him, perplexed. How could he have possibly known?

He smiled and said to me, "She has her own method of answering your question."

He was Jasyindar Singh Sihdu from Malaysia, a true devotee of the goddess. Thereafter, whenever he visited India, he would visit me, and whenever I had any doubts, I would call him. It felt as though he was the answer to what I was seeking.

I bought a book, *Sixty-Four Yogini Temple* by Suresh Balababtaray, from Hirapur, and that was a reference which I followed, but as the painting process continues, I just painted where my subconscious mind led me. Almost every goddess was unknown to me. During that time, I had a lot of interesting experiences and met a lot of interesting people, which all led to very intense incidents and experiences. I realised the changes that were happening in and around me. Every painting was a unique experience for me.

The next challenge I faced was with the texts about the yoginis. I tried to research about the yoginis. Every source of information differed from the next. The goddesses were known by different names in different sources. I was required to do a tremendous amount of research if I had to document my journey. Then I came across a book titled *Yogini Cult and Temples* by Vidya Dehejia. This book seemed to offer a lot of insight on the subject but somehow confused me further. Therefore, I thought it would be better to not use any references and just trust my intuition. I read her book after completing my paintings, and following my heart and mind was the right decision.

Apart from this, yoginis can be commonly divided into two groups, one including the Matrikas or "group of mother goddesses" and one excluding the same. The Hirapur list I used as a reference did not seem to include the Matrikas, but, surprisingly, I had painted them as well.

What I came to realise was that I never followed any list. It was purely as per the Divine's directions. The Hirapur yogini list was just an anchor. I was allowed to move around, and I painted yoginis who were ready to express themselves. As I have said, we did not decide anything. It was her master plan and her actions. I was just a tool in her hands. I tried to connect the initial few paintings with body, chakra, and positions. I realised that it was not right to give directions to my journey and I should wait for the divine interventions.

When I turn back and look at 30 per cent of the master plan that has been revealed, I really feel blessed for being a part of this divine planning.

11

Yogini Chandi

When I sat in front of my blank canvas, murmuring riddles and unspoken words, my heart and toes tapped to an unheard voice. My hand, which was holding the brush, was trembling. I was afraid to express the first yogini as colours on my canvas.

I really missed Dr David's presence. My thoughts had no direction. I surrendered myself to the sixty-four yoginis. I knew that this entire experience would mould me and change my life. I had to breathe out the "me" in me and learn to adapt myself to become the receiver of energy. I had to be free of doubt and transform her energies into my painting.

Chandika or Chandi in Hirapur, Odisha, was the first yogini on my list. In Hirapur, she stands on a corpse in the Tribhanga pose (a standing pose where the body bends in one direction at the knees, the opposite direction at the hips, and then again bends at the shoulders and neck). Her iconography made me more fearful. Her energy was beyond my imagination. However, every stroke I laid on the canvas erased my fear. I prayed to her, hoping she would come to me in a peaceful form.

Chandika is a powerful form of the divine feminine that was manifested to destroy evil. She is the main deity of the famous *Devi Mahatmya*, a poem of 700 verses on the goddesses. She is the fierce manifestation of Shakti, the symbol of feminine power. She is revered more in the southern and eastern parts of India where the Shakta tradition of tantrism is followed. Goddess Chandi is said to have a dark complexion, which signifies her fierceness. She wears a garland of human skulls called Mundamala and is said to have twelve arms, each holding a damaru (a small two-headed drum), trishula (trident), sword, snake, khatvanga (skull mace), thunderbolt, severed head, kapala (skull cup), and a panapatra (goblet).

I made sure not to get influenced by the information that was available to me on the goddess. I wished to explore her essence on my own. My Chandika just bloomed on my canvas, blazing a luminescence as bright as a thousand suns, with three piercing eyes and adorned with a crescent moon. She reflected love in her strong eyes, just as I expected her too. I have always felt the eyes, hair, and breasts of a woman are her energy centres, and my Chandika reverberated with energy.

After I had completed the painting, I decided to visit the temples in Kanchipuram again. I wanted to buy sixty-four lotuses, just like Dr David would, and offer them to the resident deity. There are flower shops on the pathway leading up to the temple, but I could not find sixty-four lotuses anywhere, which was a little upsetting. The temple was not too crowded. I made my way into the shrine and sat down in front of the deity. I told the goddess about my painting of Chandika and how I was hoping to get a sign of acknowledgment from her. Once I finished praying and got up to leave the shrine, I heard someone call out to me. I turned back to find the priest, who said, "Avaluka Podunga" (Put this for her), and he handed me a garland of sixty-four lotuses. I could not believe my eyes. My tears flowed like a river. My heart was overwhelmed when I took the garland from him.

My tears flowed the entire journey back to Chennai from Kanchipuram. I got home and placed the garland on the painting of Chandika. Later that evening, I received a call from Mr Annamalai, who mentioned that he had visited a spiritually inclined friend of his for some business discussions. His friend abruptly and very randomly asked him, "How was the Chandi Homam (sacred ritual in worship of Goddess Chandi)?" Mr Annamalai, surprised, asked which Chandi Homam his friend was asking about.

The friend responded, "I don't know why, but I felt you had performed a Chandi Homam."

The conversation seemed out of the blue, and neither of them was aware that I had been painting Goddess Chandi. When Mr Annamalai said this to me, I felt as though the very process of painting the goddess was like performing a Chandi Homam because homams involve invocation of the goddess. These are not coincidences. They are signals from the universe reconfirming that I was on the right path. Goddess Chandika was the remover of my fear. I believe all the demons in the mythological stories in Hinduism are a representation of a negative force. Killing a demon signifies the killing of the negativity in you. Fear is the biggest enemy to humankind.

12

Yogini Tara

Tara was a familiar name to me thanks to my practice of reiki and basic knowledge of Buddhism. She is one of the Mahavidyas. The ten Mahavidyas are forms of Goddess Mahakali, the ruler and goddess of time and death.

In Hirapur, Tara is a two-armed figure mounted on a corpse. I was ready to paint the corpse, but my mind refused to accept that form. When I sat in front of the canvas, my soul pulled me towards the colour blue. I wanted to paint a form of hers that I had previously been exposed to, but I took my time with it. The shades of blue somehow infused compassion in me.

Tara and Kali are very similar in appearance. Kali wears a girdle of severed heads on her arm, while Tara wears tiger skin. Both have a ferocious look, but to me, Tara is the goddess of compassion and healing, maybe due to her connection to reiki.

There are several interesting mythological stories about Goddess Tara. She is the wife of Brihaspathi (Hindu deity associated with fire and the ruler of the planet Jupiter) and mother of Budha (Hindu deity associated with the planet Mercury). She is considered the reason the sun came into existence during the creation of the earth, but the most popular story about her is one that talks about her compassion.

During the churning of the ocean of milk, a powerful poison, Halahala, emerged from it. To protect the universe, Lord Shiva consumed the poison, which made him unconscious. Goddess Tara placed Shiva on her lap in the form of a baby and nursed him. The healing power of the mother's milk and her compassion helped Shiva regain consciousness. Thus came alive the form that was reflected in my mind. It took me time to imagine Tara and a lot more time to paint the image. My slow progress concerned me a little, but I saw her in the form of a mother to Shiva. I could see a mother's compassion in her piercing eyes. Her expressions were very different as her mystical energies were revealed to me. I came to realise that if one concentrates on one's actions and thoughts, the Divine starts to trust and comes towards one more profoundly, which gives a lot of clarity. To me, as already mentioned, she appeared as the goddess of compassion, but at the same time, she exhibited a strong and ferocious nature that could go to any extent to protect her disciples and her children. In certain sects of Buddhism, especially Mahayana Buddhism, Tara is considered a female Bodhisattva, a person on the path of enlightenment. She is seen as someone with healing powers who embodies compassion and mercy.

Interestingly, she is known as Neela Saraswati (blue Saraswati), and Lord Shiva is known as Neel Kant as his throat turned blue after consuming the poison that emerged during the churning of the ocean of milk. She is also called Shabda Shakti (power of sound). She is the goddess of speaking power and perception, which could be because she is the feminine form of Om, the primordial sound of life.

The marma point associated with speech is called Neela Manya, which is in the throat region. Tara Devi's location on the human body is the Manipura Chakra (third chakra), which is the navel centre. I am convinced that the sixty-four energy points in the human body, called the Kulamarma points, are governed by the sixty-four yoginis. The mastery of locking and unlocking these energy centres is an esoteric science in itself and is often taught in the advanced stage of certain spiritual and martial art disciplines.

I took a lot of time to paint Yogini Tara. I kept feeling that there is something more to do about her. She was so much more communicative. I was getting used to the intense communication process with the Divine. Hence, I still feel the same. There is so much to discuss whenever I sit in front of her.

13

Yogini Narmada

Unlike Tara, who took her time to express herself, Goddess Narmada was ready to flow, peacefully, onto my canvas. I never felt as though I was painting. Rather, it felt as though I was moulding her with clay as I always felt the presence of clay in my hands.

> Like clay,
> In a sculptor's hand
> Eager to be moulded
> In the fold of her curves
> I could feel the moisture of her body
> I saw her—so earthy and mystic
> She flowed so smoothly
> I didn't realise
> When I slipped into her depths.

I painted her without any hindrances, but several times, I noticed something. When someone would ask me which goddess I was painting during that time, I would never remember her name and would reply, "I don't know who I'm painting."

The story of Narmada's origin surprised me. She is said to have been born from the sweat of Lord Shiva, which accumulated while he meditated and then started flowing as a river. Narmada was very beautiful. All the gods and rakshasas (demons) wished to marry her. She had the habit of running away and hiding to avoid them. I perceived this as her playing hide-and-seek, exactly like how she slipped in and out of my mind and I forget her name. Narmada surrendered herself to Lord Shiva, who blessed her to become a holy river. Even a mere glance at her is said to rid one of all sins. Narmada embodies the playful aspect of the feminine. She radiates an innocent positivity that one may experience at the mere sight of her.

Legend has it that Lord Shiva named her Narmada, which stems from the word *narma,* meaning tenderness, owing to her virtuous and kind nature. She is free-flowing and devoid of the burdens of negativity. Blessed with lifelong liberation by Lord Shiva, she slipped through the fingers of all the gods that tried to capture her.

Narmada is also known as Maa Rewa. True to the nature of a river, she welcomes everyone to take a dip of purification and sees no distinction in class, creed, or lineage. Somewhere, I felt a deep connection with her, reminiscent of my childhood days. It was as if I had known her since my youth or as if I were gazing upon my own reflection. The clarity of this connection was elusive, but it brought me closer to my soul and heart. She has evolved into more than just a goddess. She has become a dear friend of mine, an integral part of my life.

14

Yogini Yamuna

Once I have completed a painting, I keep the canvas ready for the next. I put a tilak (bindi) on the canvas, welcoming the energy of the goddess. I give myself the required time, sitting in front of the blank canvas and meditating on the unknown energies until I start feeling her presence. Interestingly, there is a story attached to this painting. My brothers—Biju and Binu—stay in Dubai, and we meet once or twice a year. For some reason, while I was waiting to paint Yamuna, I started to miss them, and my heart was filled with love for them. I started to reminisce about our younger days, going through old photographs. I then wondered what Goddess Yamuna had to do with my relationship with them.

> While painting her,
> I was mesmerised by notes of love
> That had bound me at birth
> Branching out into different directions
> To see the desires and dreams
> Truly the priceless nostalgia of life.

Throughout the time I was painting her, my mind was on my brothers. I enriched every moment I painted her with the love and protection my brothers showered on me. Yamuna is one of the holiest rivers in Hinduism. Its confluence with the Ganges and the mystic Saraswati, called the Triveni Sangam, is a holy pilgrimage site located in Prayag in India. When I delved further into her story, I came to realise why my brothers occupied my thoughts so much.

Yamuna or Yami is considered the twin sister of Yama, the god of death. She is the daughter of Surya and Sanjana. Her other siblings are the Ashvins, the twin sons of Surya and physicians of the gods, and the planet Saturn. With such mighty siblings, she is the powerful sister of the universe and known as the "Lady of Life". Yamuna's relationship with her brother Yama is documented in several ancient scriptures. They are said to be the first ever mortals born.

Yamuna, previously known as Yami, urged her brother to consummate their relationship so that humanity could proliferate. However, Yama, being righteous and religious, was against this incestuous proposition. Yami and Yama continued to foster their sibling relationship with love and affection. When Yama was killed in battle by Karthikeya, the son of Shiva, Yamuna grieved the loss of her brother deeply. Her undying love for her brother, despite him denying her advances, tells us that she is a symbol of unconditional affection.

At times, I ponder whether these are mere coincidences. However, when I heard Yamuna's story, I realised that I needed to let go of the idea of attributing everything to chance. Otherwise, I knew I would not fully grasp the energy of the yoginis. Just imagine how your perception of Yama, the god of death, as someone who takes you away from the earth shifts to Yama as a protective brother. I have truly started to relish these feelings.

According to the yogis, there are two nerve currents in the human spinal column called Pingala and Ida, and a hollow canal called Sushamna runs through the spinal cord. This is the underlying concept of Triveni Sangam. The nerve currents are represented by three rivers or three goddesses—Ida by Ganga, Pingala by Yamuna, and Sushamna by Saraswati. Therefore, these nerve currents reflect the flow of these three rivers and merge at the Triveni Sangam of the body. The confluence in the body is similar to that we see in nature.

15

Yogini Manada

In the abode of blissfulness
I swayed in peace and tranquillity
While I painted her

On my canvas, Goddess Manada emerged from a lotus with a peaceful smile, almost as though she was in a meditative state. I painted her in the same meditative state. Goddess Manada, as her name suggests, is the goddess of peace, seated on a fully bloomed lotus. She is a form of Goddess Lakshmi, the giver of wealth, life, and peace. The goddess's energy miraculously rubs off on all those who interact with her.

During this period, I seemed to experience great bliss. I believe the word *Manada* is derived from the word *ananda*, which means joy. *Man* also means mind; therefore, Manada's very essence is that of absolute blissfulness and elation.

The brain secretes several endorphins and hormones that keep us in a happy state of mind. Anandamide is an endogenous cannabinoid produced in our system that acts as a mood enhancer. The name *Anandamide* originated from the word *ananda*, which, as previously mentioned, means joy. The hormone Oxytocin stimulates the production of Anandamide. As per the *Chandi Purana*, Prana is protected by Kalyanashoba, who is Goddess Lakshmi herself spreading ananda through life.

Manada, being a form of Goddess Lakshmi, is the personification of true inner delight, a joy that develops within and is not dependent on happenings or belongings in the material realm. Being a form of Goddess Lakshmi, she is radiant, instilling peace in the minds of her devotees.

I had the habit of sending my work to my cousin Sreekumar for an opinion. The first thing he said when he saw her was "Wow! She looks peaceful. Who is she?" His reaction confirmed that I had indeed manifested her energies since the painting reflected what she stood for: peace.

Despite Lakshmi being the goddess of wealth, detachment from material possessions is encouraged in Hinduism to ensure long-lasting happiness. Manada captures the essence of true inner joy, which is devoid of any conditions. She represents the real wealth of life—true inner bliss or shanthi (peace).

16

Yogini Varuni

During the period in which I painted Goddess Varuni, I was going through quite a bit of turmoil in my personal life. My life was being churned between family duties and work commitments. My business was struggling to stay afloat and required quite a bit of restructuring and planning on my part. My husband had recently retired from army life, and we were adjusting to our new normal. We were also trying to chart the way forward for my children's higher education. I felt as though I was being pulled in all directions. I do believe churning to be an essential part of life. One can regurgitate all the negativity and create space for the grace of God to flow in. What troubled me was that everything came all at once. I took it in my stride as a part of the process of painting Goddess Varuni and hoped her blessings would relieve me of these pressures.

Durvasa, a great sage who was infamous for his temper, offered Indra a garland. When Indra ignored his offering, the sage felt disrespected. He cursed Lord Indra and all the other gods to lose their powers. Lord Vishnu came to help and suggested churning the ocean of milk to bring out a magical nectar, amrita, which would help the gods and Lord Indra regain their powers on consumption of this nectar. The gods needed the help of the demons to churn the ocean, which was a laborious task. During the churning, many things emerged from the depths of the ocean—treasures and wealth, a fragrant tree, poison, and so on. Goddess Varuni, too, emerged from the ocean, along with wine.

Spreading the flavours of the various floral
tones and spices of life
Penetrating my senses
She emerged so gracefully
draping the waves around
Intoxicating the world around

Every single person who saw Varuni's painting, without even knowing the context of her story, used the word *intoxicating* to describe her beauty. She is also known as Sura as she emerged with a wine that was first offered to the demons. They refused to consume it, assuming that they would not be offered the amrita if they did have it. Hence, they came to be known as asura or the deniers of Goddess Varuni's Sura.

Varuni is also another name for a medicinal herb called Indiravaruni. Lord Balrama, the brother of Lord Krishna, is said to have gone into a deep ecstasy on consuming Indiravaruni. Certain sects in Hinduism encourage the use of hallucinogenic herbs or plants to ascend to a higher spiritual realm. These intoxicants are believed by some to form a gateway into the world beyond.

I believe Varuni to be a transporter. The worship of this goddess takes one's mind to places beyond one's imagination. She represents the activation of parts of the mind that are said to be dormant. One may activate these dormant parts of the mind by indulging in meditative practices and penance. I believe that spiritual enlightenment is real intoxication. The physical intoxicants we are exposed to only take us so far. What ultimately raises us to a higher realm of spiritual existence is sincere devotion and unshakable faith, which provides one with the ultimate ecstasy.

17

Yogini Gowri

Goddess Gowri is the epitome of beauty. She seemed somewhat familiar to me. When I started painting, it felt as though I knew her, maybe because of the numerous Gowri poojas I had attended.

Everyone secretly wishes to be perceived as the most beautiful or magnetic in the room, especially in the eyes of those they love. All the goddesses I had painted so far seemed beautiful to me once I had completed them, but Goddess Gowri's beauty was something I had not witnessed before. I noticed it as the painting was taking life. Throughout the entire process, I felt my femininity come to the forefront. I embraced that gentle, motherly, and loving aspect of myself during the process of painting Goddess Gowri.

Gowri or Maha Gowri is one of the manifestations of Goddess Parvati. She is associated with the qualities of purity and sincerity. There are multiple stories attributed to her origin. One version is that after defeating the demon king Raktabeeja, Goddess Kali is said to have performed a penance to rid herself of her dark complexion, which, to me, symbolises her fierceness. She then became Goddess Gowri.

The story that resonates the most with me talks about Shiva's mockery of Parvati's dark complexion, which consequently led her to retreat into the forests and raise her own spiritual vibrations. Lord Brahma took notice of this and offered to grant her a boon. She wished for her dark complexion to be taken away so Shiva would find her attractive. Lord Brahma is said to have taken the darkness or the dark quality of ferociousness and created Goddess Kali out of this ferociousness. The nature that was left behind was the gentle and peaceful Goddess Gowri or Parvati with golden skin.

A powerful message this story gives us is to not brood over one's shortcomings but to instead build over it and evolve into our ideal selves. I believe colours to be perceptions of the mind. Her story spoke about skin colours, but metaphorically speaking, I believe her transformation stands for self-cleansing or the rejuvenation of oneself. It is the removal of older, worn-out layers of the self to become young and new, just like a snake sheds its skin or an eagle sheds its feathers as it grows and evolves. Gowri took pride in her evolution and rid herself of what needed to be left behind.

18

Yogini Indrani

As a young girl, I would often get envious when my mother spoke highly of my peers, and we would get into arguments. My mother warned me that this insecurity of mine would get in my way. As I grew up, however, I realised that everyone is on their own path, and there is enough space for everyone to thrive. I became far more secure with myself. I am also not one to blow my own trumpet. I know and understand the importance of humility, as it is important when receiving the Almighty's grace. For some reason, however, when I painted Goddess Indrani, I was overcome with a feeling of pride and overconfidence. I grew increasingly arrogant and haughty, which was reflected in my interactions with others. I was self-aware but could not help it. I realised that I needed to keep a check on myself and my attitude.

I knew Goddess Indrani as one of the Ashta Matrikas (group of eight mother goddesses) and the wife of Lord Indra but nothing more. Based on what I knew, I thought of painting her as a queen, owing to the various stories I had heard about her husband and king of the heavens—Lord Indra. However, she emerged on the canvas as a powerful woman with intensely fierce eyes and the strong features of a tribal woman. Her features seemed rawer and fiercer than the royal and delicate queen I had envisioned her to be. Quite often, the painting turns out different from my initial plan. I always make sure to go with the flow and trust the inspiration

I receive from a higher realm. Disconnecting from the "me" in me was necessary to paint her unconditionally. It is a truly overwhelming feeling when the goddesses reveal their characters as energies that we need to conquer.

Goddess Indrani is the consort of Lord Indra and the daughter of Puloman, an asura or demon king. She is the queen of heaven. She was a woman of incomparable beauty, and all the deities longed for her company. She was chosen by Indra, owing to her attractiveness, from amongst the several other women that competed for his attention. Legend has it that Lord Indra forcibly took Indrani away and killed Puloman, her father, the tribal demon king, before the latter could curse him for exploiting his daughter. She is said to have Kanakavarnah (golden skin) and is depicted as seated on an elephant.

Goddess Indrani's reputation is far from pure and godly. She is associated with negative attributes such as evil and jealousy due to her background, but I believe her to be a victim of circumstances. Lord Indra was a powerful man who got everything he wanted, including his wife. She was a woman who was snatched away from her family and suddenly put in the mould of a wife and on the pedestal of the queen of heaven. Additionally, Lord Indra had a reputation for chasing and desiring women. Therefore, to me, her arrogance and temper seem understandable. It is but natural for the frustrations of an unjustly treated woman to manifest as conceit and boldness. She is a powerful tribal queen, not cold-hearted but strong and unfazed.

19

Yogini Varahi

When I stood in front of my canvas, I suddenly felt a rush of heat waves inside me, exactly how you would feel when you have a high fever. The difference, however, was that I felt very energetic. Even the tinge of blue on my brush did not cool me down. Every person that entered the room felt unusually warm. I generally keep my windows shut to avoid too much dust from entering, but I noticed that my domestic help kept leaving them slightly open. I asked her why she kept doing that, and her response seemed so innocent.

"The room is getting very warm. I thought I'd leave it open for air circulation," she replied.

I believe the heat hinted at the presence of Goddess Varahi. This association between heat and the goddess could be because she led the other goddesses in the battle against the demon king Raktabeeja. I felt as though Varahi animated every atom in that room and every cell in my body, and that friction and vibration generated heat.

She played the role of a teacher, and I was a good student. I painted Goddess Varahi without any hindrance. I felt truly cleansed as her energies burned away the negativities inside me.

With the head of a boar, the body of a woman, and a fierce and aggressive demeanour, Goddess Varahi is yet another yogini who has her origins rooted in tribal culture. She is one of the Ashta Matrikas and the commander of the army of Goddess Lalitha Tripura Sundari, rightfully so. The goddess is revered as the protector of the land and a fearless warrior. She is said to have originated from Goddess Chandika's back during the battle against Raktabeeja.

Legend has it that Hiranyaksha, a demon king, was granted a boon by Lord Brahma to not be killed by any man or animal. While asking for the boon, he named every animal but, unfortunately, missed out the boar. Hiranyaksha wreaked havoc in hell, in heaven, and on earth. The gods begged Lord Vishnu for deliverance. So Vishnu incarnated as Varaha, a boar, both to lift the earth, which was submerged in the cosmic ocean, and to kill Hiranyaksha.

Varahi is the feminine energy of Varaha, from whom she derived her energy. Varahi symbolises courage, the ability to face challenges head on, and the ability to dive headfirst into a problem and tackle it fearlessly. She stands for resistance against force and is shaded with a tinge of rebelliousness. She is aptly a warrior goddess.

The lifting of the earth from the depths of the ocean by the boar also subtly implies that, sometimes, our steadfast and patient nature (symbolised by Mother Earth) may get submerged in the depths of emotional turbulence (represented by the ocean). Introspection and delving deep like a boar into the depths of our mind is needed to rediscover our true nature and lift it back to where it truly belongs.

20

Yogini Manasa

Goddess Manasa is the first female divine energy I personally experienced. She is an energy I hold close to my heart. Goddess Manasa and I go back almost thirty years. I was extremely fond of and close to my aunt Hema, who married into the family when I was a teenager. Aunt Hema had a particularly complicated pregnancy, which scarred me. I had decided then that I would not have any children of my own and would choose to adopt.

A couple of years later, in 1990, I got married and moved to the city of Chandigarh in northern India, where my husband had been posted. There I would frequent a temple dedicated to Devi Manasa, mainly because I enjoyed the prasad (religious offering, usually food, given to the deities as well as devotees) there, which was kadi chawal (a dish of cooked rice served with a yogurt-based gravy).

Like a typical mother, my mother's regular question, whenever she called me, was, "Is there any good news?", indirectly asking if I am pregnant. I started worrying because I used to think I did not want to have children due to the fear of delivery. My prayer was that I should become pregnant now.

Sometime later, we were to move from Chandigarh to the city of Pune in Maharashtra. A day prior to the final move, my husband and I decided to visit the temple yet again to seek the goddess's blessings. That day, as I walked down the stairs of the temple towards the exit, an older woman, her face wrinkled with age and experience, suddenly caught hold of me and said in her weak and quivering voice, "The next time you visit this temple, you'll be pregnant."

I was taken by surprise. I wondered if she had some sort of prescience. What surprised me even more was that I was going to Pune the next day, and I would not be coming to this temple for another six months. That meant there was a real chance for the goddess's blessing.

"If that's the case, then I shall offer the first morsel of rice to my child at this temple," I responded mentally to the deity at the temple.

In Kerala, we have a custom where a child is first fed solid food at a temple. It is celebrated as a ceremony. The universe truly has a strange way of communicating with you! As fate would have it, I was back in Chandigarh six months later, pregnant. I visited the temple once again. I was terribly afraid of the pregnancy and all the pain and complications that could arise from it as I had witnessed my aunt's struggles. I stood in front of the goddess's idol and surrendered to her, trusting that she would protect me.

"You have given me this child, so you take the pain," I thought. I repeated this phrase over and over again until it somehow entered my subconscious mind. My entire pregnancy was so smooth that I did not even feel pregnant! I continued to move as I would when I was not pregnant. In the eighth month, I moved back to Kerala temporarily so that I could have my parents around during the birth of the child. My mother constantly complained about how I was not careful enough. However, I did not feel any discomfort whatsoever and so did not feel the need to be overly careful with my movements.

Even during the ninth month, I felt so light that I would toss and turn abruptly in my sleep, instead of first rising and then turning to my side slowly. I kept hearing a woman's voice say, "Careful! Don't be so quick." I thought it was my mother and did not bother too much. One morning, I asked her why she kept checking on me in the middle of the night, but to my surprise, she said she had not checked on me even once. Every night, I slept with a picture of Goddess Manasa under my pillow. It was her hand that was holding mine throughout the pregnancy.

The day I visited the hospital to book my room, I was unexpectedly admitted to deliver. Unbeknownst to me, my cervix had dilated quite a bit. I was shocked, and so was the doctor. I felt no pain whatsoever. It is rare for a woman to not feel any pain during a delivery. The doctors even tried inducing labour, but I felt nothing. I asked the attender for a cup of coffee. When she stepped out to bring it for me, she ran into my mother, who asked when I would deliver. The attender seemed doubtful that I would deliver any time soon since I felt absolutely no pain. About five minutes later, while I casually sipped on my coffee, for a brief second, I felt a muscle cramp in my back. I looked at the doctor impatiently and asked how long it would take for me to deliver. "Maybe again after a couple of years," she said, with a chuckle. That is when I realised that I had already delivered. It was truly miraculous. Goddess Manasa protected me as fiercely as she does all her devotees. As I promised her, I offered the first morsel of rice to the baby at the Manasa Devi temple.

Years later, when I did a more detailed study on Manasa, I came to realise that she is the deity of snakes and is worshipped for deliverance from fertility-related issues. She is the mother of the sage Astika who was responsible for stopping the mass sacrifice of snakes conducted by King Janamejaya, the great grandson of the Pandava hero Arjuna. He conducted the sacrifice to avenge the death of his father, Parikshit, due to snake bite. On the advice of Astika, Janamejaya realised his folly and stopped the sacrifice in which thousands of serpents were about to be killed. Thus, Manasa Devi earned the gratitude and reverence of the celestial serpents for being the mother of the great sage who delivered them from the sacrifice.

In Kerala, serpent worship has deep roots in tradition. Most temples and palatial ancestral houses have a space reserved specifically for a serpent shrine, called a sarpa kaavu (abode of snakes) in Malayalam. Serpents are seen as guardians of ancestral treasures in Kerala. They are seen as the protecting deities of a clan called the Nagavamshi as well as the Nair clan that I belong to. It is believed that during times of poverty, the family prays to the serpents, and the treasure somehow surfaces. I have always felt drawn to that space, and I am at peace in the sarpa kaavu in the local temples in my hometown.

Goddess Manasa is worshipped as a formless entity. She is warm-hearted to her devotees yet brave in her mannerisms. She is the "mind-born" daughter of Sage Kashyapa and is also known as Manasa Krida Shakti or "mind play energy". I overwhelmingly felt her energy protecting me through my entire pregnancy. Painting her was a beautiful experience, almost as though I was revisiting an old friend. The creativity flowed out of me and onto the canvas.

21

Yogini Vanaramukhi (Anjana)

When one comes across a name that invokes a sense of familiarity, there is a certain sense of comfort in knowing that the energy is one you have interacted with in the past. Vanaramukhi means the one with the face of a monkey. This name naturally took me to one of the most beloved deities in Hinduism, Hanuman.

When I started on my painting of Goddess Vanaramukhi, I felt that the colours reflected my creative powers, and even during that period, I required a great deal of courage and strength. This period involved decision making. I had to evaluate my risk appetite to take certain personal leaps. When one connects with the goddesses, a transfer of energy takes place. The beauty of encountering such energies is how vivid they are. I imbibed the qualities possessed by Goddess Vanaramukhi and took chances.

The colours of my Manipura Chakra oozed onto the canvas continuously, strengthening my core energy. She emerged looking like a beautiful warrior. That is when I slightly distinguished her from the energy that I had previously known.

One may associate Hanuman with the qualities of bhakti (devotion) and dedication owing to his interactions with Lord Rama, whereas Vanaramukhi's eyes reflected a strong femininity that stood apart from Hanuman's energy. I have realised that outer appearances do not connect one with a person; their inner being is what matters.

Punjikastala was a beautiful apsara or heavenly nymph who was roaming around in a garden in the heavens. She noticed a monkey sage in deep meditation. Instead of not disturbing him, she started to laugh at and make fun of him. He was furious with her for disrupting his meditation and cursed her to take the form of a monkey. She genuinely apologised and begged for pardon.

"The curse can only be lifted if you give birth to an incarnation of Lord Shiva," he said to her.

She prayed to Shiva and once visited an ashram. There, she realised that people did not laugh at her. She was hesitant to tell them the story behind her monkey face. She introduced herself as Anjana, an alias. She left behind her past and decided to live there. She learnt that a huge demon called Sambasadan had been terrorising people in the forest in which the ashram was located. She made a small Shiva linga and started to pray to Shiva and Parvati to aid the people in the area. She heard a loud voice from the heavens say that the demon could only be defeated by his own blood. She was prepared to go fight him, but from somewhere, a warrior came to her aid. To her surprise, he, too, had the face of a monkey. He was Kesari, the king of monkeys. Together, the two of them went into battle with Sambasadan.

Kesari deeply wounded the demon. Anjana dipped her arrows in the demon's blood and fired them at him. With each hit, the demon began to melt and was finally defeated. She was approached by Kesari with the offer of marriage, and she happily agreed. Together, they worshipped Shiva and Parvati.

At the same time, King Dasaradha was performing a ritual to have children, and the prasad was meant to be shared between his three wives. The third portion was snatched away by a bird. When the bird dropped the prasad, it was taken by

Vayu to Anjana and Kesari as per the instructions of Shiva. Anjana heard a voice from the heavens asking her to consume it since it had the power of Vayu and the essence of Shiva. Thus was born Hanuman, whose birth eventually freed her from the curse. Hanuman came to be known as Anjaneya.

She reflected the energies I witnessed in Vanaramukhi. We have spoken about the interplay of male and female energies. Anjana had both energies within her. In Hirapur, the goddess is depicted as standing on a camel, and I realised that this could be due to the presence of Hanuman's energies as his vahana (mount) is a camel.

Goddess Vanaramukhi emphasises strength of character and inner being, rather than external appearance. One's inner being is what defines one's existence.

22

Yogini Vaishnavi

When the time came to paint Goddess Vaishnavi, I was confident of how I desired to see her on the canvas. Being a Keralite belonging to a family of staunch devotees of Lord Vishnu, or Guruvayurappan, as he is commonly called in Kerala, I thought I knew Goddess Vaishnavi well. After all, she is the feminine manifestation of the Lord himself.

I would sit in front of the canvas every day, but I was unable to form a single stroke. It felt as though all the creativity had been drained out of me. I grew tense. Why would she not come to me?

I decided to make a short trip to Guruvayur, a sacred town in Kerala, home to the famous and holy Guruvayurappan temple, to ignite the creative spark in me. The Guruvayur temple is quite crowded on any regular day as pilgrims from across India visit to seek the blessings of the Lord. Surprisingly, on that day, the temple was relatively empty. I stood in front of the Lord and apologised to him for my overconfidence. I asked him to bless me with the energies of the goddess.

The Almighty often has his ways of humbling you. To truly show devotion, one must rid oneself of pride and ego. We are all God's creations; therefore, our creations, too, belong to God.

While I prayed with my eyes shut, I heard a woman chanting a mantra where she said the name of Goddess Vaishnavi. I opened my eyes to see a stunning woman in deep prayer. She had long, lustrous hair, and her piercing gaze was directed upwards to the heavens. I stared in awe. She looked at me and smiled faintly. I slowly walked forward and went on to worship the other idols in the temple, but everywhere I went, I saw her, almost as though I was being followed.

When I finally reached the idol of Bhagavathy or the mother goddess, I said to the deity in my mind, "If Goddess Vaishnavi's presence is around me, I should see this woman when I open my eyes."

As soon as I opened my eyes and turned back, I saw the woman seated on the ground, in a dark corridor opposite to the shrine of the goddess, smiling at me in all her glory. Her face stayed with me the entire journey back to Chennai. She, to me, was the manifestation of Goddess Vaishnavi, and I decided to paint her as Goddess Vaishnavi.

Contrary to popular belief, Goddess Vaishnavi is not the consort of Lord Vishnu but his female manifestation. She is armed with the same weapons as Lord Vishnu, wears the same ornaments, rides the same vahana, and carries the same banner. As per the Devi Mahatmyam, the Ashta Matrikas emerged from various parts of the goddess's body, and Vaishnavi came out from both hands of the goddess. She is a ferocious warrior deity in the Puranas who accompanied Lord Shiva in his battle with Andhakasura. She is the ruling deity of the northern direction. In some stories, she was born from Lord Vishnu's energies into a Vaishnava family to destroy a demon king. In that story, she is a staunch devotee of Lord Rama from birth and desires to marry him. However, since Lord Rama is already married to Sita, he asks her to wait until his next incarnation. Goddess Vaishnavi is believed to be performing penance to this day, waiting for him on the Trikuta (three-peaked) mountains (one of the twenty mountains surrounding Maha Meru, the home of Lord Brahma) with deep devotion. I saw that same devotion and serenity in the eyes of the woman I came across at the temple. I knew it was a divine presence that was here to guide me through my journey.

The resemblance of the goddess in my painting to the woman I saw in the temple was uncanny. I am grateful to have had the chance to visit the temple and gain inspiration. I truly feel blessed to have been visited by the energies of the Divine, the evidence of which is present in my art.

23

Yogini Vajra Varahi/Pancha Varahi

My mind was completely blank yet very peaceful. It went completely beyond the name Pancha Varahi, which was included in the Hirapur list of yoginis that I used as my reference point. I found it difficult to connect with the way she had been portrayed. Vajra Varahi emerged very differently from the energy I had been exposed to. When you do not know what you are painting, it is a mysterious feeling. The relationship I had with painting was one of trust and faith. I could sense my cognitive abilities transforming into spiritual enlightenment. I was in the habit of regularly listening to spiritual music or sacred chanting of texts such as the *Lalitha Sahasranamam* while I painted. During this period, however, I found myself especially drawn to Tibetan or Buddhist meditative music as the chants would distract me. When I started to meditate on the music, I started to get a clearer picture on what to paint. I came to realise that I was working on a deity closely associated with Buddhism.

While painting, I also often found myself distracted by the sound of bells. The sound was not of anklets, which are generally worn as a traditional ornament in India. This sound was louder—it rang through my ears. Bells are often tied to cows and calves in India to keep track of where they are. So I would open my window to see if there were any cows passing by. For some reason, I felt the urge to draw this bell ornament around the waist of the goddess. I also felt like painting her with the face of a boar, as per her depiction at Hirapur. My further research led me to Vajra Varahi.

As I had expected, Vajra Varahi is an important deity in Buddhism and is predominantly worshiped in the Himalayas. She is a tantric goddess and a fierce manifestation of the Vajra yogini. Being an incredibly powerful force, she is worshipped for strength to achieve anything one sets one's mind to. Her iconography is similar to that of the Hindu goddess Varahi. With red skin, skull garlands, and the head of a sow, she represents ridding oneself of ego and ignorance (according to Tibetan legends) and the elimination of illusions.

24

Yogini Vadhyaroopa

When it comes to matters such as music and education, the only goddess that comes to mind is Saraswati. In Kerala, we celebrate Saraswati Pooja over a span of three days. As a child, it was a great three days for us as, according to tradition, one must not read books until the pooja had ended. This meant that no one would ask us to study!

I assumed that Goddess Vadhyaroopa had to be a form of Saraswati. Despite feeling as though I knew her well, I just could not paint her. I would sit in front of the canvas and recite prayers to Saraswati, but my efforts were in vain. By this point, I had come to realise that if there was a delay, that meant I needed to delve deeper into the subject matter. Moreover, I was heavily influenced by the idols at Hirapur, and the sculpture of Vadhyaroopa looked nothing like Goddess Saraswati. A notable fact is that she had protruding teeth. Her iconography in Hirapur impacted my thought process, and for some reason, I was drawn to her instrument, the mridangam (two-headed drum).

I felt as though the mridangam played some important role in Hindu mythology. Almost two weeks passed by, and this thought stayed with me. I started to read further about the mridangam, which is also known as Deva Vaadyam (the instrument of the gods). Nandi, the sacred bull of Lord Shiva, is said to have played it during Shiva's Tandava, or dance of rage, when Sati, his first wife, died by jumping into her father

Daksha's sacrificial fire. He carried her charred remains on his shoulders and performed this dance of rage to express his grief. The rhythm resonated across the heavens.

The word *mridangam* is derived from two words in Sanskrit—mrid (clay) and ang (body). Lord Brahma is said to be the creator of the mridangam, which was made from the blood-soaked cloth he pulled out of the demon Tripura.

I delved deeper and deeper into the subject when my friend Mr Resul Pookutty, Oscar-winning sound designer, called me to let me know that he would be visiting Chennai for some professional work. I went to meet him at one of the most spiritually divine musical places, the studio of A.R. Rahman, the maestro himself, an incredible composer and artist. I received very welcoming and positive vibrations from the studio and absorbed all the energy that I would use to paint. Vadhyaroopa emerged beautifully.

The day I was done, I received a message from a friend that included pictures of her performing a pooja. The pooja was done in celebration and worship of the sun god and to give thanks for supporting life on earth. Since I finished the painting that day, the bindi I painted on the goddess was inspired by the Chath festival. I felt, on deeper contemplation, that Vadhyaroopa perhaps represented that aspect of the Divine Mother that maintains the cosmic rhythm of the universe, the power that regulated everything in time and space to sustain the equilibrium in the cosmos.

There is a pattern and order in life, however random it may appear to the ignorant and naive. The purpose of any rhythm is fulfilled only when it supports a melody, and here, the divine melody is called life. This concept is exquisitely captured in the narrative of Devi Mridanga Saileshwari, who is revered as Goddess Saraswati, the deity ruling over knowledge and fine arts. Mridangam is an ethnic percussion instrument representing the rhythmic discipline that forms a skeletal support within which all wisdom, truth, knowledge, talent, and skill of the world is to be regulated and expressed.

25

Yogini Charchika

The day I started on my painting of Goddess Charchika, I was furious. I was unaware of where the anger stemmed from; it was unusual for me. My brush, too, seemed to echo my mood as it moved at a faster pace. I painted furiously, leaving behind every other thought. For some reason, I could sense that something major was ahead. I stepped away from the painting for a while and took a short nap.

I dreamt of a friend. He stood in the centre of an empty field, and the figure of a ferocious goddess appeared, running around the circumference of the land—howling—as she was unable to enter it. I woke up with a feeling of immense discomfort and immediately called up the friend to ask if he was alright. I told him that she was trying to convey to him that he was in a place where her energies and protection could not reach him. He assured me he was fine but did get a bit worried after I explained my dream to him.

I continued to feel restless. The same day, I found out that another dear friend had met with a serious accident, but by the grace of the goddess's protection, she narrowly escaped. The next day, I continued painting, but I kept getting visions of the same goddess, fighting someone with the weapons in her multiple hands as I clung to her for dear life.

Suddenly, loud beats started ringing in my ears, followed by powerful chanting. In walked my husband with his phone.

"I just heard this on YouTube and thought you'd like it. It is called the Chandi Kavacham," he said. "It talks about how every part of the body is protected by a goddess."

It was the first time I was hearing this sacred chant. I cooled down and held on to the goddess like a baby holds on to its mother. She held me closely and delicately as I painted my mind and soul on the canvas. I completed the painting, and my family loved it. They loved her even though she looked very ferocious.

I sent a picture of the painting to my cousin Sreekumar. He said that he could only look at her once as her energies were overwhelmingly strong. I slept like a log that night.

Charchika communicated well with me and, as usual, held me close. It felt as though more was to be unveiled.

The next morning, I sent some messages to the friend about my dream. They were delivered but not read by him. I felt restless, just as the goddess was running around the empty field, unable to enter it. I found out that he was trapped in some legal entanglements and had to face some enquiries, due to which he was unable to communicate. This was yet another shock to me, and I was unaware of how long it would take him to be relieved of these legal issues.

Charchika was a turning point in the series of paintings. I decided to continue and just prayed to her throughout the process for strength and guidance. Painting was my form of penance, as it continues to be even today. Goddess Charchika is a fierce form of Goddess Parvati and one of the chief yoginis. She is portrayed as deeply frightening as she adorns a garland of human skulls and stands atop a prostate human body. She is the feminine manifestation of Yama, the god of death, and, therefore, symbolises death, destruction, and decay. As per the *Matsya Purana*, Charchika was created by Lord Yama to protect Goddess Parvati. Therefore, for me, she represents the fiercely protective aspect of a woman's nature. As she is comforting to those who seek her support and security and unforgiving to those who threaten the safety of her dear ones, she is often associated with the slaying of demons and sinners. Her existence is owed to the need for providing safety and assurance, which, therefore, is her ultimate purpose.

Her presence in my dreams was a warning, so I could prepare myself for the worst that was yet to come. However, I knew that she held me close, and no major trouble would harm me or the ones I hold dear. I believe my friends narrowly escaped worse circumstances because she, the goddess herself, shielded us with all her might. Goddess Charchika always makes her presence known. Right before I started writing this, I was in a temperamental mood. I yelled at my son and my colleague and then realised whom I was about to write on—Charchika, my fuming goddess.

26

Yogini Vetali

It took me a while to start my next painting. I sensed an energy pushing me to a distance, almost as though I were being warned to keep a distance from her. I paid heed to the warning and settled my mind. At times, such stillness allows you to introspect. It makes you go deeper within yourself. Only once you acknowledge and face your demons and emotions can you connect with the infinite forces beyond our realm of being. I felt as though the goddess herself asked me to pause and pray. It is often said that we should visualise Vetali as she is an energy that could pacify any turmoil. In village folklore, Vetal and Vetali are often considered the guardians of the villages. This belief could have come about because Vetal is a soldier of Lord Shiva.

Even while painting Vetali, I sensed a detachment from her end. I realised that was her energy. In many temples, she is treated as the guardian of the deities inside. I felt as though she was safeguarding me from a distance, keeping a watchful eye on the devotees and protecting them with all her might. On several occasions, even after the completion of her painting, I have sensed her energy. She was an important part of my journey.

Vetali is another manifestation of Mahakali, the consort of Mahakala, a fierce aspect of Lord Shiva, whose references can be found predominantly in Shaktism. Puranic legend has it that Vetali escaped from the abode of the gods as she, being naughty and restless, could not put up with the restrictions imposed on her there. The story is an analogy for the release of hidden potential energy in us to explore beyond our comfort zone. The vehicle she used for her escape was the donkey, which is also again a representation of our hard work that can carry us through. Her donkey suffered a wound on its hind leg while being pursued, which miraculously transformed into an eye. This is nothing but a subtle depiction of the importance of alertness under all circumstances.

This devi (goddess) is depicted as holding a human skull, a sword, a mirror, and a three-pronged dagger in her four arms. The skull symbolically serves as a cup that holds the blood of ego that is slashed by the sword of knowledge. The mirror depicts the tool for introspection and realisation of the self within, and the three-pronged dagger denotes the killing of the three principal enemies within us: lust, anger, and greed.

The worshippers of Vetali Devi can perceive her as a mother, a friend, or even as a servant of her devotees according to their level of spiritual evolution and connection with her. She responds and guides her devotees accordingly. Vetali is also believed to be the guardian of certain traditional lineage practices in some Buddhist sects where she is considered the deification of the fierce feminine force that is invoked to ensure the regulation of peace and harmony.

27

Yogini Chinnamasta

After painting Goddess Charchika, my journey was quite different. On one side, my life was filled with legal entanglements and issues in my business and relationships. I managed to hold on to hope without fear because, on the other side of life, I encountered supremely divine energies at high frequencies. It was not easy to balance the two, but never once did I feel the fear taking over me, despite it being quite a traumatic period, emotionally and financially. However, I did seem to gain quite a bit of clarity on several issues. Truths were unveiled right in front of my eyes, which was clearing clusters of problems. I needed to believe that things would be fine. Strength was of utmost importance.

I had heard Dr David mention the Chinnamasta Sadhana on several occasions. It is the discipline followed by the sadhakas or disciples and the powers they possess. I only worshipped the goddess with all my heart. I considered myself illiterate and lacking discipline. I was not aware of any sacred literature on these goddesses. I knew that following structures and schools on these goddesses was not something I was capable of doing. I confided in the goddess and said that all I could do was love her every form unconditionally with intensity and purity sans any personal objectives. I understood that that is all that was expected of me. By trusting in the strength of my faith, I could raise my frequency to receive the goddesses and then have them express themselves through me on my canvas.

When I started painting, I felt peace within myself. Chinnamasta was very different from all the other goddesses I had painted. I realised that her wisdom was beyond my normal level of understanding and perception. As I painted her, I felt close to her and began to realise that half the issues we face are due to our ego. The process of painting her ignited an energy in me, and I felt as though I was able to channel it well. I was able to look at people beyond what was visible to me. I knew that the process of taking "I" out of my system would not happen in a few days, but she sowed the seeds of detachment in me.

"I" or ego always blocks the power of creativity. I reached a higher state of awareness as her colours were reflected on my canvas. I connected more deeply with her, and the bliss I experienced helped me face the challenges in my life head on.

Tantrism has several negative connotations. To any regular "non-expert", the practice is shrouded in mystery and taboo, mainly owing to the portrayal of goddesses such as Chinnamasta. With bright red, and at times black, skin, streams of blood spurting out of her neck, her decapitated head in hand, and standing atop a copulating couple, Goddess Chinnamasta is not one for the fainthearts. Her frightening persona tends to intimidate even devotees, let alone non-devotees, who do not quite understand her essence and what she stands for. To me, however, Chinnamasta is the ultimate symbol of earnestness and self-sacrifice for the sake of those who believe in and depend on her. She is a reliable force to reckon with.

There are a couple of stories about her origin. The one that stuck with me, however, is the one that gives us insight into who the goddess is deep down. Goddess Parvati was once bathing in the Mandakini river when her complexion turned a bright red shade, apparently owing to her sudden sexual desire. At that moment, Dakini and Varnini, her two ladies in waiting, approached her in desperate hunger, begging to be fed.

Goddess Parvati immediately decapitated herself and fed them her own decapitated head with the blood spurting out of her neck. When you understand the reasoning or the tale behind what is shown, you understand the innately humane and giving nature of the goddess. Her willingness to serve those in need proves to show her approachability, contrary to popular belief.

To me, the decapitation of the head also signifies ridding oneself of ego and, thereby, ascending to a higher realm of spirituality and connecting with the Divine above and within. Chinnamasta is also the personification of sexual desire, a naturally occurring human feeling. However, despite the esoteric portrayal of the goddess and her sexual liberation, she also symbolises the control of one's urges by standing atop the copulating couple Kama and Rathi (the god and the goddess of love).

Sexual desires can often be very strong, and exercising control over them can ensure that one does not get derailed from one's purpose. Goddess Chinnamasta is quite misunderstood, but she is a powerful symbol of selflessness and self-mastery. She represents detaching the "I" from oneself to gain a broader, more detached outlook on life.

28

Yogini Vindyavasini

After painting Chinnamasta, my soul went into a meditative state. I had no thoughts running through my mind. I just focused on my daily chores and household duties, which also was an important part of my journey.

I found it difficult to connect with Vindyavasini, but I could sense her energy and presence. I felt as though she was around me, almost as though she was saying "catch me if you can". The subtle energies she emanated seemed very content. It took me roughly a month and a half to start on her painting.

During this period, I visited Bengaluru with my friend Sakina, and we spent the night at the house of another friend, Lakshmi. The next day, right before we were about to leave, Lakshmi handed me a small box of prasad. The box had the image of a goddess imprinted on it. I asked her which goddess it was, and to my surprise, it was Vindyavasini. I had not discussed my paintings with Lakshmi. So this was unplanned. It felt as though I had visited her house just to seek the blessings of the goddess so I could paint her.

I was overjoyed. I wanted nothing but to come home and start painting her immediately. When you are open to the universal flow of energy, you seamlessly connect with the infinite Divine. I felt very content before I started on her painting. During this phase, I came to realise that the overcoming of negative qualities is a powerful strength.

Vindyavasini is another name by which Goddess Durga is known. She got this name as she chose to reside in Vindhyachal mountains after her battle with Mahishasura. As per Puranic lore, Goddess Durga delivered the world from the terror of Mahishasura, a demon in the form of a buffalo who terrorised the good and virtuous. He had a boon that he could not be defeated by any male. The gods appealed to the divine universal mother Durga for her help, and she obliged by eliminating Mahishasura after nine days of battle in the Vindhya mountains. After that, she chose to stay there and bless her devotees who came to worship there. The story is about how, with the help of Devi, one can conquer one's baser animal instincts and tendencies and rise to a higher level of consciousness. The nine days of battle are observed every year as Navaratri through vows and austerities, and the tenth day is celebrated as Vijayadashmi, the day of victory of good over evil through Devi's grace, the good and evil being within one's own self.

In my painting, I have depicted the demon Mahishasura as a godly figure because I believe that by slaying the demon, the goddess helped relieve him of his sins and attain salvation, which turned him into a supremely divine soul. His slaying symbolises the killing of one's inner demons to evolve to a higher state of being.

Today there stands a temple in Vindhyachal (in present-day Uttar Pradesh) dedicated to Vindyavasini, where devotees from all over visit throughout the year to seek blessings. Vindyavasini is addressed as Padmanabha Sahodari, the sister of Padmanabha or Lord Vishnu, in the *Lalitha Sahasranamam*. This form of address alludes to the tale associated with the birth of Lord Krishna. The goddess incarnated as a daughter to Yashoda, the wife of Nanda, at the same time Krishna was born to Devaki and Vasudeva in King Kansa's prison. The babies were exchanged at birth. When Kansa tried to kill the baby girl, fearing she might be the cause of his death, she is supposed to have disappeared from his hands. This baby is Goddess Vindyavasini.

The devotees of Vindyavasini who approach her with all humility and attitude of surrender are always protected and blessed with peace, progress, and prosperity in their lives.

29

Yogini Jalakamini (Jayanthi)

Venus, beauty of the universe
She stood tall and majestic
Her femininity is set to the sensuous curves
Hiding under the fullness of her breast.
She places her utmost virtue of self-esteem.
Amazed by her grace, gorgeous in every way
But the vital elements unseen.
She is not just flesh and bones of triviality.
In her quiet murmurs, she roars like a lioness.
With strength as her unbreakable demeanour
She is an altruistic lady with opinions
With layers of deep thoughts and feelings.

This poem expresses the exact feeling I experienced on seeing Goddess Jalakamini. Beautiful, confident, and delicate, she flowed without hesitation onto my canvas. She reflected a lot of love and positivity. The 640 million yoginis are responsible for running the entire universe, and it is interesting when you can connect them with a planet that exists and is a tangible and known element that exists within science. In Hirapur, she is seated on a frog, which directed me to the energies of the planet Venus. Venus is ruled by the element of water.

Venus, or Lord Sukra, is seated on a frog in most depictions. The frog is called Manduka, a Sanskrit word that means "someone who dwells in satisfaction". I have always personally felt that the Venus in my birth chart was strong. I now understand why. I have always been blessed with the material comforts and pleasures of life, and my deep connection with the arts is a representation of Goddess Jalakamini's energy present in my life.

Jalam represents water, which, on a spiritual level, is the elixir of life. Sukra represents a similar elixir that brings materialistic riches and comfort. Interestingly, in Hinduism, water is a representation of wealth. As water is ever-flowing, wealth too must be.

The feminine aspect of Lord Sukra can be found in Jalakamini, who is the deified aspect of his wife, Jayanthi, whose name means victory. Jayanthi is the daughter of Indra and Shachi. She is one of the goddesses in the *Kubjikamatatantra*.

Jayanthi was sent by Indra to disrupt Sukra's deep penance as he was afraid that Sukra would receive immense power as a boon on appreciation of his prayers. Jayanthi was not on board with the idea but chose not to disobey her father. Throughout Sukra's penance, she served him and stayed by his side. At the end, Sukra was blessed with a boon, and Jayanthi requested him to make her his wife for ten years. During this phase, they are hidden from the rest of the world, embracing each other in a secret union.

If one requires a balanced life, both materialism and spirituality must be embraced. Generally, people tend to pick extremes, but both aspects are equally necessary to truly enjoy the gift of life.

30

Yogini Ghatavara (Jagadathri)

I started working on my painting of Goddess Ghatavara during the monsoon season. I thoroughly enjoyed the cooling showers of rain. It felt refreshing. To capture unknown divine energies, raising my energy levels was important for me. There was so much fluctuation of energy levels in me that it was often hard to get back to a normal state.

Ghatavara was a name I had not encountered before, but the iconography of the goddess at the Hirapur temple reminded me of the tale of Lord Shiva and Gajasura Samhara. According to an ancient scripture called the *Kurma Purana*, a demon called Gajasura, who had previously performed penance and been gifted with several powers, assumed the form of an elephant and started to terrorise, rob, and torment the Brahmins and Shiva devotees that resided in the holy town of Varanasi in northern India. On one such occasion, he disrupted a prayer session of some Brahmins who were performing a sacred ritual in front of a Shiva linga (a structure that is the abstract representation of Lord Shiva). Lord Shiva was enraged. Emerging from the linga, he killed the demon, ripping apart his elephant skin. The demon's soul, thereafter, requested Shiva to wear the elephant skin on his upper body so he could be blessed by forever touching the Lord's body.

Additionally, the pose struck by the sculpture of Ghatavara at Hirapur resembled a popular dance form in Kerala called Thaiyam. I am not exactly sure why, but I could sense strong drumbeats pounding through my ears. The immense rhythm put me in a trance. I felt her presence intensely dancing around me. She was ferocious yet very grounded, and I felt the essence of victory in her steps.

Goddess Ghatavara, also known as Goddess Jagadathri, is said to be the combined form of Sri Lalitha Tripura Sundari and Goddess Durga. Her origin story can be traced back to the *Kena Upanishad*. The gods of Svarga or the esoteric planes in Hindu cosmology—namely Agni (fire), Vayu (wind), Varuna (sky), and Chandra (moon)—were blinded by pride and so were tested by Ma Shakti or the divine feminine. She asked them to pull out a blade of grass. They all failed the test. They became aware of their faults and sought the forgiveness of Shakti. She appeared before them as Goddess Uma on a lion and destroyed their ego and pride, which manifested itself as an elephant. Thus, Goddess Uma seated on a lion and holding an elephant came to be known as Ghatavara.

Legend has it that the entire universe is held in Ghatavara's hands. The second she places the universe down, everything will end. Therefore, Ghatavara is an important deity in Hindu mythology. Ghatavara symbolises the multiple responsibilities and burdens a woman carries on her shoulders. We have all encountered these women—our mothers, siblings, wives, daughters, and even ourselves. When she ceases to perform as she always does, her absence is felt tremendously. The slashing of pride is also an important moral that the goddess demonstrates. Her ability to stay humble despite her great importance is exemplary.

31

Yogini Kakarali

A lone woman, in an outwardly sad and pathetic state, wandered the streets aimlessly. A group of dogs followed her, but she was unbothered by what was happening around her. She shared the little food she had with the dogs. Her clothes were worn and torn, and her appearance was unpleasant. However, there was strength in each step she took, and her eyes reflected peace.

I awoke suddenly from deep sleep. It was a strange dream. I did not know this woman, but her image was fresh in my mind when I started on my painting of Goddess Kakarali. My heart was overwhelmed with karuna or compassion. I started to pray for the crippled, unloved, diseased, unsafe, and unhappy. I prayed all the time I painted. I started to think about all the magnanimous people out there who served the needy, the ones who generously give. I introspected deeply, and for some reason, Florence Nightingale came to my mind. I started to find out more about her life and work. It is an absolute wonder when you are led by the universe to the character of the goddess. It seems dramatic, but you would be magnetically drawn to energies that resemble those of the goddess. Almost a year after painting Kakarali, my friend Lakshmi Menon visited my home. The second she saw the painting, she said it reminded her of Mayamma and went on to speak about her in detail. I was shocked to find out that this was whom I had dreamt of before I started painting.

Mayamma was a self-realised soul who roamed about the streets of Kanyakumari in rags with a few stray dogs for company. Though she never begged for alms, she accepted whatever food she received from kind people in the neighbourhood and never ate without first sharing it with her dogs. She saw the essence of divinity in all creatures. Although she knew many languages, she seldom spoke. But her silence was so eloquent that it led spiritual seekers to the path of light.

Many miracles are said to have manifested in her presence. She once completely healed a dog that was run over by a vehicle with a mere touch. This miracle grabbed the attention of the people, and soon, she became a much sought-after guide for spiritual aspirants. Many believe that she is an incarnation of the goddess of Kanyakumari herself.

In my painting of Kakarali, the depiction of a dog could not be avoided as that would be like depicting Lord Shiva without the snake. So I included my pet in the painting to complete it. That brings us to the pertinent question of whether a less evolved life form like a dog can be taken inside a temple. As much as we need to see divinity in all creation, the temple is a place where we worship within a certain ritualistic order and code of discipline. There are certain parameters of cleanliness and decorum that need to be maintained. Although God does not distinguish between his creations, it should be remembered that temples are not made for God but for humans to worship God. Hence, certain restrictions are required to maintain the sanctity of the temple or any place of worship. Therefore, we must be sensitive to these sentiments. There can be exceptions, but these exceptions would be a deviation that already exists in the tradition of the temple.

In certain parts of northern and western interiors of India, Kakarali or Hadkai Mata is a goddess associated with rabies and measles. She rose to prominence in the latter part of the 20th century and is worshipped for protection and cure from rabies.

Worshipping at the temple of Hadkai Mata, who is depicted as standing on a large chariot pulled by four dogs, is supposed to offer relief from rabies. She is also called Hadkamai, Hadaksha, Hadkabai, and Hulan. Hadkai Mata is popularly worshipped in many parts of Gujarat where one can find many stray dogs. Some of the hospitals and clinics that offer treatment for rabies also house mini shrines or statues of Kakarali.

32

Yogini Matangi

I had kept my canvas ready to get started on the next painting, and in came my husband with an unexpected gift: a beautiful baby parrot. We decided to name her Meetu. I wondered if this was Goddess Matangi before my eyes.

Meetu's favourite place to perch on was my palette. Her piercing eyes transferred wisdom to mine. It seemed as though she had much to say. I found a true companion in Meetu. She would often observe me while I painted and would land on my hands as I swept my brush across the canvas.

The iconography of Goddess Matangi, or Saraswati as she is more commonly known in Hirapur, was very interesting. She is said to be grabbing her cheek or a thick moustache on her upper lip. The idea of her having a moustache drew me in. Unlike any of the other paintings, I sensed the presence of Shiva. Even when I went through many of her stories, she was always present along with Shiva and Shakti. I will address this later in this chapter.

> In the cooling showers of morning glory
> I swayed with my twin flame
> Adding the fiery red waves
> Mesmerised with rhythms of his heartbeats he twisted me around and down to ground deeper and beyond his breath
> I moved with him wild in ecstasy
> Inhaling my spirits within.

While painting Matangi, I felt the spread of her essence around me. With every stroke, I felt her presence grow stronger. Her creative fire just flowed through me with colours so vibrant that I could not even paint some of them. I felt truly and deeply blessed to know her soulfully.

Matangi, the tantric form of Goddess Saraswati, is also known as Ucchista Matangi and is one of the ten Mahavidyas. The literal meaning of her name is "limbs that are intoxicated with passion", which is in complete sync with her many vivid forms in different stories. She is also known by other names such as Rajamatangi and Sumukhi-Matangi.

She is depicted differently in different contexts, but she is a goddess who holds exceptional powers. She originated from the leftover food of Shiva and Parvati from a feast that was arranged for Vishnu. This story is of great significance as it shows Matangi's unique and unconventional quality. Leftover food symbolises pollution and is not considered sacred. A notable observation I made is that Saraswati is commonly associated with higher castes and Matangi with lower castes. This differentiation between the goddesses could also be due to the segregation of castes based on professions in ancient Hinduism. Lower castes included people that worked menial jobs where they often found themselves surrounded by uncleanliness.

Caste and creed are all segregations imposed by humankind. God sees no difference between devotees. I believe that Matangi's unconventional associations are the inclusivity of the less privileged.

Saraswati may be the goddess of academic knowledge, but Matangi represents holistic knowledge of the arts, literature, and creativity. In ancient times, a lot of creative professions in the field of arts, music, dance, and artisanship were taken up by people belonging to "lower castes". She also imparts the wisdom required for one to see beyond manufactured social structures and not just follow hollow advice passed down by previous generations on what is right and what is wrong. She makes one think beyond what they are exposed to and pushes one to implement change to improve society at large.

As mentioned earlier, I noticed later that her iconography showed her holding her cheek or twirling her moustache, which drew me in. I sensed the equal presence of Shiva in her energies.

An interesting tale around Matangi that reaffirmed this feeling of mine takes us to the marriage of Shiva and Parvati. Parvati had gone to visit her father, and during the time of her absence, Shiva grew impatient and jealous. He took the form of a jewellery vendor and visited her. Parvati bought a bangle from the vendor and asked him for the price. The vendor asked her to pay with sexual favours. Parvati immediately recognised that this was Shiva and decided to play his game. She agreed to perform the sexual favours but only when the time was right.

Sometime later, when Shiva was in a deep penance, Parvati took the form of a Chandalini (tribal) girl and sensually danced in front of Shiva to seduce him. Shiva agreed to make love to her, and while performing the act, she turned him into a Chandala man. That was when Shiva realised that it was Parvati all along. From then on, Parvati swore to make the Chandala form of hers a permanent one, and she came to be known as Ucchista Chandalini.

I noticed that parrots were shown in the images of several goddesses, including Madurai Meenakshi. One may think it a mere coincidence that Meetu entered my life around this same time, but by now I knew that it was a sign of the presence of her energies around me. They are usually perched by the ears of the goddesses, and I assumed that maybe they were imparting the wisdom of the sixty-four arts.

I, too, have spoken wisely in this chapter. Could Matangi be speaking through me? I wonder.

33

Yogini Virupa (Apah)

After my painting of Goddess Matangi, I was drenched in creative juices, and my mind was full of wisdom. I had been exposed to society's blemishes, and all the negativity within me and the heat and dust of the summer outside me was being washed away as the first few droplets of rain trickled down my face. Monsoon was officially here.

At this point, there was a change in my speed of painting. The next goddess was ready to be painted. I finally felt a sense of control.

I checked the calendar. It was the last full moon of summer in all its glory. Honey is harvested at this time when the moon is said to be the sweetest. Since I had already done a series of paintings on the nakshatras, I knew that this moon was the Purva Ashada.

The day of Purva Ashada has the power to take one to the next realm of life. Like the gushing water of the universe, it clears any blockages by cleansing and purifying its path as it makes its way to the eternal cosmic ocean.

I went through the Hirapur list to see which goddess I was to paint next. Goddess Virupa presented herself to me, standing atop what seemed to be the carving of a wave. She had some connection with the element of water. I started to recognise her.

I personally believe her to be a form of Apah, the ancient presiding goddess of all water bodies who is often invoked in the *Rigveda* for relief against drought. This made sense to me because I started seeing signs of water bodies everywhere. Apah is also the presiding goddess of the constellation Purva Ashada. She rejuvenates, purifies, and nourishes our relationships by enhancing our intuitive wisdom.

Water is often considered the elixir of life for it not only purifies anything that comes its way but also rejuvenates and induces life and vigour. Indra may be the god of rain and Varuna the lord of the seas, but the essence of both rain and the sea is water. The character of water that flows and purifies is identified as Goddess Apah.

The waters in the *Rigveda* were both terrestrial and celestial. Before the creation of the universe, there was said to be nothing but the bottomless, uninterrupted, limitless water without light. Water is the mother of Agni and is, therefore, the producer of fire. The world moves with the pure and simple movement of the water. It washes away impurities and cleans the inconsistencies of human behaviour.

At a deeper level, this goddess also represents the spirit of unity of purpose. She symbolises the union of various streams, rivers, lakes, and backwaters that flow into the ocean. On a spiritual level, she is the deity of the cosmic consciousness, which is the collective consciousness.

Water is also the most adaptable of the elements. It takes the shape of whatever it flows into: a cup, a pot, a tank, or a riverbed. The worship of Apah basically calls for adapting and regulating our energies for constructive purposes. Unchecked water can cause immeasurable damage and destruction. Yogini Apah serves the higher purpose of establishing a balanced sense of achievement in our lives.

34

Yogini Kauberi

I often visited temples in between paintings. I found it a powerful way to recharge. My visit to the popular temple town of Tirupati to worship Lord Balaji was long overdue.

There are stories surrounding Lord Balaji. A popular one is that Lord Balaji had borrowed wealth from Kubera for his wedding with Goddess Padmavati. Kubera is said to be the guardian of the wealth of the universe. Stories such as these highlight the human aspect of these gods, which make them more relatable figures to worship. They also prove to show that divinity and the human experience can coexist.

When I visited the temple at Tirupati, it was not to invoke Lord Kubera or Goddess Kauberi. It was just a regular temple visit like any other, nor did I think there existed any connection to these gods at this temple.

After a wonderful prayer session, I started to visit the smaller sub-shrines to pray to the Upadevatas. A short, old lady approached and asked me if I had prayed to Lord Kubera. I looked at her in surprise. I had never heard of a Kubera idol in this temple. I grew curious and interested since the next goddess I had to paint was Kauberi. She led me to a smaller area, which was shrouded in darkness. A small flicker of light came from a lit lamp. Suddenly, I was approached by the security officials who asked me what I was doing there. I told them that I was brought there by the old woman, but she was suddenly missing. The security officials angrily led me out of the area. I asked several people about the presence of Kubera in that temple, but not many knew about it. Very few answered in the affirmative.

Goddess Kauberi, also known as Bhadra, is the queen of Kubera. She is the daughter of Surya, the sun god, and Goddess Chayya, the sister of Shani or Saturn. Bhadra, as the name suggests, stands for auspiciousness.

She is considered one of the Matrikas, and along with Lord Shiva, she is supposed to have partaken a portion of the deadly Halahala poison that emerged from the great churning of the ocean of milk. This act of hers symbolises the spirit of selfless sacrifice for the greater good. The worship of Kauberi is known to mitigate the effects of our previously bad karma.

Wealth and riches tend to bring the poison of greed. Kauberi is the remover of that poison associated with money. Consuming the poison is also an analogy for the goddess absorbing all the poison of negativity existing in her devotees, thereby, leaving them with positive energy to perform their karmas. On a physical level, she is said to be the goddess protecting the pores of our body, through which we excrete toxins. Therefore, she plays an important role in ridding the body and mind of metaphorical poisons and keeping them pure.

35

Yogini Balluka (Jambavati)

Goddess Balluka was incredibly feminine and beautiful, despite having the face of a bear. I felt as though I was in a garden surrounded by lovely flora and fauna, all of which reflected her love and dedication. I felt the presence of a sweet and pious energy around me.

From the time I had painted Matangi, a friend of mine, Ranjith, would often call. Every time, we would find ourselves discussing the expression of the energies I was painting. It is quite rare to find people who take a deep interest in subjects such as these. These discussions really broadened my horizon. I had clarity on Goddess Balluka's energies but somehow found it hard to find information about her. Then Ranjith's colleague put the thought in my head that Balluka may be Jambavati since the word *Balluka* means bear.

Jambavan is one of the Chiranjeevis (immortals). References to him can also be found in the great Indian epic Ramayana. He was a bear known for his wisdom, believed to have emerged from the mouth of Brahma. He served in the army of the monkey king Sugriva and assisted Ram in the rescue of Sita from the demon king Ravana. Jambavan is said to be the reincarnation of the king of the Himalayas, Himavat, who also happens to be the father of Goddess Parvati.

In the *Brahma Vaivarta Purana*, Lord Krishna claims to Brahma that in the Dwapara Yuga, Parvati would also reincarnate on the earth as the daughter of Jambavan, Jambavati.

An interesting tale is associated with the two. In the Dwapara Yuga, Lord Krishna was wrongfully accused by his friend Satrajit of stealing a precious gem. Krishna's search for the gem led him to the cave occupied by Jambavan, where he found it. A fight ensued between the two. On realising that Krishna was the reincarnation of Ram, Jambavan respectfully backed down and offered his daughter's hand in marriage to Krishna as a token of apology. The two eventually married.

Unfortunately, Jambavati was unable to have any children. Lord Krishna had to do a severe penance to please Lord Shiva to bless them with a son. Out of their union was born Samba, who was named thus because he was born out of Lord Shiva's grace. The story, however, takes an unfortunate turn. Samba, in his later years, was responsible for antagonising a group of holy sages who then cursed the entire Yadava clan (Krishna's familial clan) to perish due to infighting. Jambavati was grief-stricken and heartbroken. She left her body, took the ashes of Krishna, and became a river that eventually merged with the ocean.

People often take a dip in the Jambavati River in Gujarat, seeking protection from misfortunes and from the plight of widows. This ritual may have come about because Jambavati had known the pain of losing her family due to the actions of the child she was blessed with. She was a resolute woman who represents many others who are a victim of their circumstances. Remarkably, she radiated both grace and beauty, embodying a poise that inspired profound admiration within me.

36

Yogini Narasimhi

I found it extremely hard to start painting. Goddess Narasimhi was as clear as day in my mind, but I was unable to make a single stroke on the canvas. There was a riot of energy in me, which was very distracting. She was very much present in my heart and soul, but transferring that energy seemed impossible. It was very stressful.

The same evening that I started to work on this painting, I received a message from Ranjith asking about the painting. I confided in him about the fix I was in. I went on to explain in detail what I had visualised, especially her hair, and he listened very patiently.

In that same flow, I started to paint her hair. Something came over me, and I was not stuck anymore. The entire painting flowed out of me, and I discussed details with Ranjith every step of the way. Her strong energy flowed from me to him and then back to me. In this process of energy transferring, her energy seemed to become diluted, which made it easier for me to take in her energies and express them on my canvas. Within the time frame of that small conversation, I finished the basic sketch.

She was incredibly, unimaginably strong. Speaking to someone like Ranjith, who had the potential to take in her energy without any fear or doubts, helped soften her impact. Every cell in my body vibrated, generating tremendous heat. I believe that if a person is in direct contact with the highly powerful energies of the goddesses, they should know how to cool themselves. Such energy must not be taken for granted or used for any purpose in this material realm. It is meant to be used for greater, universal purposes and never personal ones. I learned to become selfless and channel her energy onto the canvas.

I feel a deep sense of gratitude to Ranjith for helping me without even understanding what I was attempting to do. Yogini Narasimhi had full control of the Pancha Bhutas or the five elements to bring down the energies of Lord Narasimha to a normal state. She used all the powers of the trinity and tri-shakti (the combined powers of Saraswati, Lakshmi, and Parvati) to do so.

Female representation in ancient Hinduism majorly contradicts the way women have been conventionally portrayed over the last few centuries, which was as meek and submissive. In mythological tales, feminine energies are unabashedly aggressive yet also exhibit qualities of sensitivity, empathy, and compassion. All these goddesses are part of the army under the supreme mother deity, Goddess Lalitha Tripura Sundari, who fought off several demon kings and brought justice to their victims.

Goddess Narasimhi is one such deity, one of the chief warriors of the army. She has the head of a lioness and the body of a human. Her thunderous roars could make even the bravest of the brave tremble in unimaginable fear. Her origin story differs in the Vaishnavite (a sect that worships Lord Vishnu as the supreme deity), Shaivite (a sect that worships Lord Shiva as the supreme deity), and Devi worship philosophies.

The tale of her origin involves Prahlad, a devotee of Vishnu, and his father, the demon king Hiranyakashyap.

Hiranyakashyap had attained a boon that he could not be killed by anything that was born from a womb, neither in the day nor at night, by man or animal, neither indoors nor outdoors, neither on land nor in water, and by no man-made weapon.

Angered by Prahlad's devotion towards Lord Vishnu, Hiranyakashyap tried to kill him, but Vishnu took the form of Narasimha, a half-man half-lion creature that emerged from a stone pillar. Narasimha placed Hiranyakashyap on his lap on the threshold of the entrance of his house at dusk and killed him using his long and sharp nails, thereby, finding a way around the boon.

Legend has it that Narasimha was in an uncontrollable rage. He went on a rampage, and no one could calm him down. Lord Shiva took the form of Sharabha, a large bird-like creature with two wings of Shakti, one Shoolini and the other Pratyangira. However, Narasimha, in turn, assumed the form of Gandabherunda and engulfed Sharabha. In answer to Lord Shiva's prayers, Pratyangira emerged from the wing, took her place as Narasimha's consort Narasimhi, and pacified him. Yet another tale states that Narasimha could be pacified by no one. Therefore, as a last measure, Goddess Lakshmi Devi took her secret tantric form of Narasimhi to calm him down.

Goddess Narasimhi, to me, represents balance. On one hand, she is a fierce and terrifying warrior who has the power to defeat demonic energies, but on the other hand, she represents the essence of peace and composure. In some texts, she is considered the protector of the universe. She douses the fire that was Narasimha's rage and represents how emotionally complex and multifaceted a human can be. Despite her unconventional appearance, she is as fascinatingly human as any of us.

37

Yogini Viraja (Girija)

Painting Narasimhi made me a powerhouse of creativity if I may say so myself. I was fully charged. Goddess Viraja emerged in a single thought, and I found her energy to be incredibly soothing.

In the vermillion of the setting sun, she blossomed like a moon. She was very poised and connected to universal energy. The dust and dirt that were remnants in my system because of the electrifying charge I experienced while painting Narasimhi were cleansed by Viraja and disposed of from my system. Painting her refreshed my mind and soothed my soul. The emotions and energies each goddess carries are truly mind-blowing.

As per Puranic texts, she is Girija, the daughter of Giri, the king of the mountains. The tale surrounding her birth talks about King Giri's unwavering devotion as he engaged in a rigorous penance, hoping for the goddess to be born as his daughter. One fine day, he ventured to bathe in the Padmatheertha Lake in the Himalayas and was met with a beautiful sight—a colossal lotus with thousands of petals and, at the centre of it, a newborn child radiating divinity. He gently lifted the child and presented it to his wife. They lovingly adopted her and named her Parvati. The name *Giri* signifies mountain or hill, and thus his daughter came to be known as Girija.

She is known to have grown up with a deep love and devotion for Lord Shiva and was steadfast in her desire to attain him. She undertook extreme penance and austerities to realise her desire. Shiva, on the other hand, was leading the life of a celibate and was absorbed in meditation after the loss of his consort, Sati.

Girija is the reincarnation of Sati, which explains her admiration for Lord Shiva. With the help of Kama Deva, the deity of love, Shiva was brought out of his austerities, and he married Girija. Girija is supposed to have been born on Paush or Triveni Amavasya. Her origin is also attributed to Lord Brahma, who performed a Vedic sacrifice by the banks of the river Vaitarani. He invoked Goddess Parvati, who was moved by his penance and asked to be worshipped as Viraja.

Viraja has been endorsed in various texts, epics, Puranas, and tantric works. She is said to be the presiding deity of Jajpur and the Viraja temple in Jajpur, Odisha, is considered one of the 108 Shakti Peeths. She is worshipped as one of the primordial powers and revered for her ability to nullify one's wrongdoings. This aspect of hers is highlighted in the Mahabharata when the Pandavas were advised to visit the goddess's temple to rid themselves of their sins. The mere sight of the goddess may also rid one's ancestors of any karmic baggage that may have been carried forward into the afterlife.

38

Yogini Vikatanana (Katyayani)

Goddess Vikatanana was not ferocious but very strong. She was not angry but very firm. Her expressions were intimidating, and the energy she gave off was that of a saviour. It felt as though even the tiniest mistake would enrage her. A very powerful goddess, she was in control of her energy.

The feeling I experienced while painting her was very different. I grew to be hyper-aware of my surroundings. My journey forward was becoming clearer, and the awareness helped me accept and acknowledge the happenings around me. My ability to connect with a divine force did not disrupt my family life. I was able to perform my domestic duties while simultaneously ascending to a higher spiritual realm. I was in complete control of every aspect of my life. Being in control and living a balanced lifestyle is a different dimension of spirituality.

The threads of my daily life were woven through the threads of my spiritual quest, and I felt as though my karmic debt was being repaid. I may not have yet attained the spiritual bar of balance I had set for myself, but I was getting there slowly but surely. I could sense the transformation happening. I was at the sacred border between the material and spiritual realm, but I knew I had more to learn to cross it.

On looking at her iconography at Hirapur, I noticed that Vikatanana was standing atop a lion. Therefore, I made the inference that she might be Katyayani, another fierce manifestation of Shakti, the divine female power. She is regarded as one of the nine manifestations of Durga, and the sixth night of the Navaratri festival is dedicated to her worship. Worshipping Katyayani is highly effective for gaining better self-confidence and physical strength. One also gets rid of unknown enemies at once.

She is named Katyayani as she was first worshipped by Sage Katyayana of Vishwamitra's lineage. Katyayani is one of the names of the goddess referred to in the sacred *Lalitha Sahasranamam*. She is believed to have been born from the luminance of the holy trio of Brahma, Vishnu, and Shiva. Therefore, she is known as the goddess of the Ajna Chakra (Third Eye Chakra) that possesses the power to dispel all illusions.

In the battle with the asura Raktabeeja, who had a boon that a new asura would rise with every drop of his blood spilled on the earth, Katyayani ensured that no blood touched the earth as she swallowed every drop of blood that spilled from the asura.

There is a temple dedicated to her at Kolhapur in Maharashtra, India. Devi Katyayani is especially venerated by the devotees for getting rid of marital issues and making married life more comfortable. By regularly worshipping the goddess, one is certainly transformed into a good householder. One is blessed with a spouse, sons, and daughters. Along with this, monetary aspects and social positions are also strengthened.

39

Yogini Mahalakshmi

Being on the threshold of spiritual enlightenment is truly magical because I was experiencing ecstasy in both realms. My heart was open to abundance in the material realm. I knew I would be blessed with happiness, wealth, enjoyment, and prosperity. While it is important to enjoy material belongings, it is also crucial to learn to detach from the same. Otherwise, one could get caught up in forever trying to satisfy the unsatisfiable. It was important to not disconnect from the essence of life. Goddess Mahalakshmi, to me, symbolises the integration of evolution in the spiritual as well as the material realm. She helps one balance the two.

Goddess Mahalakshmi is part of one's life. Even as a child, I had been exposed to her existence, and I was slightly concerned that the pictures I had seen of her would influence my art. However, I was glad to see the way she bloomed on my canvas. I saw her in a different light and got a deeper understanding of her power. Lakshmi, whom I was acquainted with as a child, was a bhava of Mahalakshmi. I know her as a provider. The image of the goddess with gold showering from her hands was in my mind, but she emerged with ayudhas (weapons). I was a little worried, thinking there are traces of the other goddesses that I had painted.

During that time, my brother's friend sent me a painting of a goddess with eight hands and said that it is of Mahalakshmi. He wanted me to paint her. I told him it was not Mahalakshmi without realising that it is Mahalakshmi that I am painting. I had never seen a form of Mahalakshmi with eight hands and an ayudha. She gave me a clue, but I still did not understand. I painted with that doubt in my mind.

While I painted, I could sense the abundance coming in. The ratio of spiritual to material abundance is very personal, and I was still exploring the two. I am still human, and denying oneself material pleasures is tough. Therefore, abstaining from material joy would not give one much peace or satisfaction. Spiritual abundance, however, would give one peace and balance and train one to be contended. I was experiencing the power of the goodness of material and spiritual existence.

A mother goddess is rarely given a form of supreme power to the extent that she exceeds a male god, but in the Shakta tradition of worship, Mahalakshmi is considered not just the consort of Vishnu but an all-encompassing supreme deity herself. Her name is derived from the word *lakshya*, meaning purpose; hence, she encourages her devotees to fulfil their purpose.

Mahalakshmi assumes a central role in the *Devi Mahatmya*. In a formidable manifestation, she defeats the demon Mahishasura in an epic battle that spans over nine days and nights. On the tenth day, the victory of good over evil is celebrated as Vijayadashmi. This valiant form of hers is called Ashta Dasa Bhuja Mahalakshmi, possessing eighteen arms, each wielding a distinctive weapon of divine prowess. The weapons in her arsenal are a battle axe, mace, arrow, thunderbolt, lotus, bow, water pot, cudgel, lance, sword, shield, conch, bell, wine cup, trident, noose, and the illustrious discus Sudarshana.

She has now replaced the old Lakshmi image in my mind. I realised that wealth can be helpful and yet can become poisonous in the wrong hands. It can also cultivate greed. To control and win over greed, we need such superpowers that come from worshipping the goddess.

40

Yogini Kaumari

Usually, after I would keep my canvas ready, it would take me a while to get started on the painting. I needed to raise my energy levels to connect with the goddesses. By the time I started to paint Yogini Kaumari, however, the scenario had completely changed. Maybe each painting cleared my senses further, which helped me connect more easily. Kaumari is the epitome of beauty, vigour, and courage.

> That morning
> I saw a hummingbird
> Perched on my balcony
> Spreading indigo-hued feathers
> Reminding me of the colours of a peacock
> Dazzled with orange and pink in the solo
> The striking tiny ebony eyes
> Sparkled like a million stars
> Hold, be still, my little bird
> Let my eyes trace all your colours
> Onto my palette.

During this period, I felt very energetic, almost as though I was interacting with a hyperactive youngster. Through me, she used several hues and shades to express herself on my canvas. She was so vibrant and joyful. I felt very present at that moment. She cleared out all the doubts and illusions and gave me some much-needed clarity on my way forward. She was a young, strong, and beautiful warrior, much needed to complete my journey successfully this far. It was an enriching energy to say the least.

Goddess Kaumari is an iconic deity in several cultures. She is the female embodiment of Lord Karthikeya, the son of Lord Shiva. She appeared from the lion of Goddess Maheshwari during the battle against the demon king Raktabeeja. She was also sent by Karthikeya to protect Goddess Parvati against the wrathful and lustful demon Andakasura when Lord Shiva was not around. Goddess Kaumari is also credited with slaying the sons of yet another demon king, Bandhas. Therefore, to me, she is a warrior princess—the courageous deity of wars. Kaumari represents youthful zest and bravery. The quality of being unafraid tends to disappear with age.

41

My Visit to the Adi Shakti Peeths

All creative art processes encounter a period where the artists need to take a break and recoup to get their creative juices and vigour flowing. My work on the sixty-four devis of Hirapur was no different. To know what my next step should be, after completing the painting of thirty devis, I went back to the small 120-page book I had been referring to. To my surprise, the thirty-first goddess was Mahamaya, Goddess Tripura Sundari. I had been hoping to finish the remaining paintings and work on her at the very end, owing to my special connection with her. I wanted to know all her different versions and expressions before starting on her painting. However, after the whirlwind of energy that had consumed me over the past few months, I felt the need for a break that I could use constructively to further rejuvenate my energy while enhancing my experience with my work with some fresh exposure. I was also confused if I should follow the flow of the Hirapur list or follow my intuition. I felt that visiting some new temples would be a great idea.

I had heard about the importance and relevance of the Adi Shakti Peeth and assumed it to be one temple, but as providence would have it, the first article that presented itself on my screen spoke about four. This triggered my interest in visiting them. These temples were:

1. The Vimala Temple inside Jagannath Temple in Puri, Odisha
2. Tara Tarini Temple in Purushottampur, Odisha
3. The Kamakhya Temple in Guwahati, Assam
4. Kalighat Kali Temple in Kolkata, West Bengal

Legend has it that after Sati self-immolated in her father's, King Daksha's, yagnya (sacred fire ritual), Shiva was in a state of uncontrollable rage and sorrow. He carried her body and performed the Shiv Tandava that shook the heavens and the earth. In a bid to stop him, Vishnu sent his Sudarshana Chakra, which split Sati's body into 108 pieces that fell in 108 different locations. Four of these spots are very sacred and came to be known as the Adi Shakti Peeths. The great sage Adi Shankaracharya, too, talks about the relevance of these temples.

> vimalā pāda khaṇḍañca stana khaṇḍañca tāriṇi (Devi Tārā Tāriṇi)
> kāmākhyā yōni khaṇḍañca
> mukha khaṇḍañca kālikā (Dakshina Kalika)
> aṅga pratyaṅga saṅghēna
> viṣṇu cakra kṣatēna ca ||
> Vimala Temple (Pada Khanda) inside the Jagannath Temple of Puri, Odisha
> Tara Tarini (Stana Khanda), near Brahmapur, Odisha
> Kamakhya Temple (Yoni Khanda), in Guwahati, Assam; and Kalighat Kali Temple (Mukha Khanda) in Kolkata, West Bengal, which represent respectively the parts (Khandas) foot (Pada), breasts (Stana), genitals (Yoni), and face (Mukha) Neck (Kanth) of the body of Maata Sati.[1]

These temples are significant pilgrimage sites for worshippers of the divine feminine.

---

[1] "Shakti Pitha," Wikiwand, https://www.wikiwand.com/en/Shaktipith

The very next day, I organised my tickets for travel. I decided that I must start my pilgrimage at the Lord Bhairava Temple in Delhi, since I used to frequent the place earlier and it had been a while since I had gone there. However, visiting Delhi first would be a roundabout route and did not make much sense. As luck would have it, coincidentally, I got a call from Delhi to attend a long-pending meeting that was scheduled to take place in two days. I hurriedly booked my tickets and thought of this as an invite from Bhairava himself.

From there, I planned to go to Guwahati and then visit Kolkata. I decided to end my journey at Bhubaneswar. Everything seemed to align perfectly. At this stage, I knew that these were not just mere coincidences. I witnessed the pattern, and I knew I was being divinely guided to seek the blessings of the Divine.

I left for Delhi and revisited the Bhairava Temple. It felt as though I were being greeted by an old friend. I felt seen and appreciated for starting on my painting journey. Funnily, my meeting never happened. It felt as though it was just a ruse to get me to Delhi. I spent just a day there, and after a peaceful darshan, I left for Guwahati.

In Guwahati, an acquaintance that I had not even met in person before organised a vehicle for me. I was told that the panditji (priest) of Kamakhya temple where I planned to visit first would not be available until the next morning. I had the entire day blocked to do as I pleased. So I told the driver to just take me around to the temples in the area.

Our first stop was the Ugratara Devalaya, a small temple in Guwahati town. There are several fascinating stories associated with this temple. Legend has it that Lord Yama, the god of death, was approached by Brahma with a complaint. No sinner from this area seemed to be sent to hell to repent for their sins due to the sacredness of this temple, which was situated in the region. Lord Yama approached Lord Vishnu, who then approached Shiva in hopes of a solution. Shiva ordered Goddess Ugratara to drive away all the people from Kamakhya. She did so by sending her army.

All the people who fled approached Sage Vashishta who was meditating on Lord Shiva. In a fit of rage, due to the distraction caused to him, he cursed Shiva and Goddess Ugratara. As a result, this temple is the place where Vedic sashakas give up their practice. It is also the place where devotees adopt the Vamachara Sadhana, which is an extreme form of the tantric practice. Interestingly, the idol in this temple was stolen, which was retrieved by the local Golaghat police six months later. Even though the temple was quite small, the deity was very powerful. I thoroughly enjoyed my darshan at this temple.

After that I went to a Navagraha temple, which was supposed to have been created by Lord Brahma himself. It is believed that Brahma created the cosmos and the universe sitting in this place; hence, it is considered sacred. There are nine Shiva lingas consecrated here under a dark dome lit by nine diyas or wick lamps. It was surreal and so unlike the regular Navagraha temples we see in the south. The strong, overwhelming spiritual energy radiating here was something to be experienced.

From here, I visited the Bhimeshwar Dham Shiva Temple in a beautiful and serene location inside the forests. The idol there was a Jyotirlinga. A Jyotirlinga is a powerful representation of Lord Shiva that devotees worship. There are sixty-four Jyotirlingas in India, out of which twelve are said to be supremely sacred. As any other Shiva linga, they are phallic in shape and symbolise the divine masculine. According to legends, once Brahma and Vishnu got into an argument over who is superior between the two of them. To settle this, Shiva appeared as an infinite pillar of light, piercing through the three worlds, heaven, the earth, and hell. Brahma and Vishnu were asked to find the beginning and the end of the light, and so they ventured off in opposite directions. Brahma grew tired and lied about having found the end of the light. Shiva caught his lie and cursed him that no one would ever worship Brahma, which is why he is not worshipped in temples. From this infinite pillar of light was produced the Jyotirlinga or "lingam of light".

Stories have it that Shiva appeared at the exact location of the temple to defeat the demon Bhimasura, who had spread chaos and destruction on earth. Bhimasura was the son of Kumbakarnan, the brother of Ravana, and Karkati, the daughter of the king of hell. After a long penance, Bhimasura was blessed by Lord Brahma with two boons: unbeatable strength and immunity from Lord Vishnu.

Using these powers, he started to conquer various kingdoms and imprisoned a local king called Kamrupeshwar. He attacked the king while the latter was immersed in worshipping Lord Shiva, and the sword, instead of falling upon the king, fell on the Shiva linga. Instantly, an enraged Shiva appeared and defeated Bhimasura. From the sweat of Lord Shiva flowed a beautiful stream that surrounds the Jyotirlinga even today.

The Bhimeshwar Dham does not have a typical temple structure. The sacred space is in the depths of a forest, atop a hill, beside the Deepor Lake. I have not seen a more beautiful sight. A local story talks about how devotees tried to build a temple structure around the Jyotirlinga, but the entire structure would be destroyed by dawn due to the elephants in the area. They believe that after dusk the elephants, too, come to say their prayers, seek blessings, and pour water in devotion over the lingas. The gentle sounds of the forest, combined with the trickling of the stream down the hill, created an unforgettable ambience. I felt the divinity peeking through Mother Nature. The experience was euphoric.

Our next and final stop for the day was the Vashista Maharshi Temple, dedicated to Shiva with a history and story attributed to the revered sage Vashista. The temple premises are nestled between mountain streams originating in the hills of Meghalaya. An interesting local story about this temple relates how Sage Vashista found it difficult to establish the temple because there was no water body nearby. He requested Shiva to do something about the situation. Shiva, in turn, requested the Ganges to flow via this route. As a result, this stream is called the Bashishtaganga.

As I sat in that meditative space, I looked back on the journey I had taken on that day. None of it had been planned by me, but somehow, I managed to seek the blessings of the Devi, Shiva, the Navagrahas, and Sage Vashista before starting on my journey to the Adi Shakti Peeths. It felt like I was being prepared for the enlightenment I was to receive from being in the energies of the Adi Parashakti.

The following day, I finally visited Kamakhya. Kamakhya is an area of Guwahati and is said to be where the Pandavas dwelled during their twelve-year exile in the forests. The Kamakhya Temple is located atop the Nilachal Hills and is one of the most revered temples in the tantric practice. The yoni or the genitals of Goddess Sati are believed to have fallen here after her demise. Kamakhya is also said to be the goddess of menstruation and desire.

The yoni is a powerful symbol of femininity, and there exists a sacred, yoni-shaped structure within the temple. Traditionally, the genitals are also said to hold the modesty of a person, and a secretive energy surrounds the subject. For some reason, I felt the same secretive energy at this temple. There was an air of mystery. On one side, I witnessed the slaughtering of animals that were supposed to be offered to the goddess. At the same time, I felt a strong feminine energy radiating through the temple premises.

I truly believe that today, in the constant race to do and achieve more, we often tend to suppress our innately feminine qualities, which include emotional sensitivity, nurturance, warmth, expressiveness, and even sexuality, which is often suppressed by society and the expectations it sets on women. It felt as though my visit to the Kamakhya Temple reignited my feminine spirit.

Every idol in this temple seems as though it wished to communicate something. With bright kumkum (vermillion) highlighting their intricate features, the idols exuded a strong energy of tantrism. Within the temple premises, all the idols are placed under water. Devotees must submerge their hands under the water to feel the texture of the stone and seek blessings. There, among other sacred spots, I was escorted to the Dasha Maha Vidya Temple by a local guide.

The Dasha Maha Vidyas refer to the ten tantric Hindu goddesses. Here, each of them enjoys an independent shrine. The main temple hosts three of the ten goddesses, namely, Kamala, Matangi, and Shodashi. I thought it would be difficult for me to exert myself and walk to each of these temples. However, nothing seemed to come in my way, including the overcast sky and rain. I was so invigorated by the vibrations I received that it gave me a surge of energy to continue. I completed my darshan and felt energetic and truly in touch with the divine femininity that existed within me.

I entered the car and felt as though there was something I had missed that should have been an integral part of my trip.

I repeatedly asked my guide if we had been to all the Dasha Maha Vidyas, and he insisted that we had. My instincts, however, told me otherwise. I checked the internet, hoping to get the answer, and there it was. It was the Bhairavi Temple of the Mahavidya. It was located 1.5 km downhill and was not accessible to vehicles. I decided to walk the distance, and the weather and the light drizzle made it the most pleasant and invigorating experience.

There was a wonderful pond in the temple premises and a lovely turtle. Generally, this is considered a good omen. My heart felt full, and my mind was at ease. I was finally done. I made my way back to the hotel after a truly fulfilling day.

That very evening, I flew to Kolkata. I contacted a friend of mine in Chennai who was from Kolkata. By sheer luck, she happened to be in the city at the time. I expressed to her my wish to visit the Kalighat Kali Temple.

"My mother and I have frequently been visiting this temple for the past forty years! We're more than happy to take you," she said in excitement.

The temple is located on the banks of the Adi Ganga, which flows into the Hooghly River. This temple is said to be where Sati's face had fallen. The current structure has existed only for roughly the last 200 years, but it has been a sacred location since time immemorial. The temple generally attracts large crowds, and one often cannot catch a glimpse of the idol for more than a couple of seconds. To our surprise, we got a good look at the goddess.

"I have been visiting this temple for forty years now, and I have never had a darshan that felt as sacred as this one," said my friend's mother.

After a very powerful darshan, I returned to my hotel that evening and casually went through a list of must-visit temples in Kolkata. I came across another Kali temple, the Dakshineswar Kali Temple, but I was not sure if it was a Shakti Peeth. When I asked someone at the hotel, he told me that the Kalighat Kali was not a Shakti Peeth and that the Dakshineswar Kali Temple nearer to the airport may be one. I was very confused about what to do. My intention was to visit the Adi Shakti Peeth, and if I missed it, I would not be able to return. However, I had a time constraint as I had to catch an early morning flight to Bhubaneswar at 7 a.m. I was to meet a priest at the Jagannath Temple in Puri at noon, who would take me inside the temple. He had informed me that I had to reach precisely at noon. If I was late, I would not be able to enter since that was the first day after the Rath Yatra when there will be a huge crowd in the temple. Any time after noon would be an inconvenient time for him to get a good darshan.

Taking a chance, I rebooked my flight ticket to 9 a.m. so that I could visit this Kali temple before I left for Odisha. I left at 4 a.m. the next morning and made my way to the Dakshineswar Kali Temple. The temple is huge. It was not yet open, and there were only about five or six people in the line in front of me.

Luckily, I was able to reach there just in time. Moments after I reached, hundreds of people queued up behind me. One may call that a coincidence, but I call it divine timing. I spent some quiet moments there in prayer, thanking the goddess for presenting me with the opportunity to be in her divine presence. I made my way to the sanctum sanctorum and asked the priest if this temple was a Shakti Peeth.

He looked at me strangely and said, "No, this is not a Shakti Peeth."

I continued to bug him.

"What is the speciality of this temple?"

He looked at me irritatedly, almost judging me for my ignorance.

"What are you saying? This is where Ramakrishna Paramahamsa attained a vision of Ma Kali," he answered in an arrogant tone.

His anger still did not stop me from inquiring further.

"Why is there such a rush today?" I asked.

"Because today is Guru Purnima," he scoffed and walked away.

When I reflect on that day, I realise that such a confusion need not have occurred. The Kalighat Kali Temple was indeed a Shakti Peeth, but the divine guide that held my hand changed the course of my plan so I could visit the Dakshineswar Kali Temple on this auspicious day of Guru Purnima. This was yet another reassurance from the universe that I was supported through my journey, which was a real blessing from Guru Purnima.

My darshan ended, and I made my way to the airport to depart for Bhubaneswar. I reached right on time and even leisurely treated myself to a cup of coffee before boarding the plane. I was still slightly anxious about reaching the Jagannath Temple on time. I reached Bhubaneswar and took a taxi, but the odds were against me. Unfortunately, my taxi stopped on the way for about twenty minutes, and some repairs had to be done to it. At that point, I lost all hope. I knew there was no way to reach the temple on time. As though ordained by providence, I was able to reach the place at the stroke of noon. The priest took me inside, and I had a very satisfying darshan without needing to stand in queue. Jagannath is also said to be attended by the sixty-four yoginis, which attracted me to this place.

I finally visited the Vimala Temple located within the Jagannath Temple complex. Vimala is regarded as the tantric consort of Jagannath. According to Shakta tantrism,

Jagannath is Bhairava and Vimala is Bhairavi. Traditionally, Vimala is worshipped before Jagannath, and the maha prasad (consecrated food) offered to Jagannath is not sanctified until it is also offered to Vimala.

As in any other temple, I was offered the prasad here. Unfortunately, it consisted primarily of rice. A fact I have not mentioned till now was that I had sworn off rice until I was done with all my sixty-four paintings. I considered it a penance of sorts, done in devotion, and a test of my willpower as I enjoy rice quite a bit.

I informed the priests of this vow I had taken and humbly refused their prasad offerings.

"How could you refuse this? This is a very auspicious meal served to the idol after the Rath Yatra. You must have it!" they exclaimed. This prasad was called the Mahabhog.

They asked me to break my oath just for that day and continue it from the next day. I was overcome with emotion and could not say no. It was a fabulous experience to see how the prasad is cooked. It is prepared by 600 to 700 people in earthen pots on wood fires and is relished by about 25,000 pilgrims every day! I sat on the ground in front of the leaf. Multiple pandits served me an elaborate feast of rice and several different delicious dishes. The tears streamed down my face as I ate. I had broken my vow but for good reason. After that day I continued with my promise of not having rice.

I felt as though everything that was happening was written in my fate, and I was being guided to seek the divine blessings. All the odds were against me, and yet everything worked in favour of me being in her presence.

The next morning, I visited the Tara Tarini Temple located in the Kumari Hills. The breasts of Sati are said to have fallen at that site. The drive to the temple was long and beautiful amid green fields. At the heart of this temple, the primary shrine takes the form of two stones. Heavily adorned with ornaments, they have been fashioned into human faces to represent the twin goddesses Tara and Tarini. The structure and architecture represented the cultural essence of Odisha. In the shrine, Lord Ram, Krishna, Parashuram, the Pandavas, and great saints like Jagadguru and Shankaracharya are also seen.

Finally, my visit to the Adi Shakti Peeths was over. I felt a sense of accomplishment and gratitude for having had the chance to be in her presence.

I went to a few more temples from there. One of them was of Bhagavati. The Bhagavati darshan again filled me with great energy. She was completely covered in vermilion, and the sanctum sanctorum was very warm. I felt the bodily heat of another human being despite there being no one near me. The idol looked almost alive. A local story also mentions how this is the place where Lord Rama was supposed to have offered worship before going for battle with Ravana.

From here, I visited another temple that was located on a small island in the sea, the Ma Kali Jai temple. I had to take a boat ride of forty-five minutes to one hour on the Chilka Lake to reach there. After offering my prayers, on the way back, it began to pour heavily, but I had decided to visit one more temple, a Maa Ugratara Devi temple, not to be confused with the Ugratara temple of Assam. By the time I reached there, it was dark. All the shops were closed due to the rain, and I could not buy any of the regular items like flowers and incense for pooja. Inside the temple, I realised that I was the only devotee. I felt bad about walking in empty-handed, but the situation was not in my control. At that moment, another devotee walked in with two trays. The trays were filled with flowers, wick lamps, incense, and more. He was meant to be accompanied by someone else, but the friend did not show up. As luck would have it, he offered me the extra tray. Once again, I felt the invisible hand of divine providence helping me.

The next day, I went to Hirapur. On the way, I purchased sweets and flowers to offer to the yoginis of Hirapur. On reaching Hirapur, I requested the panditji to make the offerings right from the first goddess, Chandi, while I sat in front of Mahamaya in the centre to meditate. The panditji finished making the offerings for the first thirty goddesses and made his way towards the centre. It was time to conduct the pooja for Mahamaya. I had not realised that my sitting there would cause inconvenience for the panditji to do the pooja as there would be space constraints. I offered to get up, but the panditji did not want to interrupt my meditation. He told me to continue and said that he would start the pooja from the sixty-fourth yogini and come backwards and make the offerings to Mahamaya Tripura Sundari at the very end. In a flash, within his words, I found the solution that I was seeking to resume my paintings. It was like a signal from above. I inferred that it was a message for me to resume my paintings from the sixty-fourth yogini, work backwards, and end with Mahamaya Tripura Sundari, which was what I wanted.

> Carrying a mystical magnificent reverberation
> Liberating me from physical conditioning
> Leaving my mind beyond the intangible
> Making the absolute more significant and wide
> Echoing through the detached gaps of my mind
> Revitalising my soul in quiet time
> Leaving the unspoken, unheard silence undefined
> My gratitude to the universe for this experience.

Thus, my visit to the Adi Shakti Peeth temples bore fruit by the blessings of the divine mother.

42

Dream of a Girl

My visit to the Adi Shakti Peeths was a truly beautiful journey. I had not realised how much the trip would cost me when I planned it. A dear friend, Francis, said to me, "Don't worry about the money. You go, and it'll come when you need it. If you need something, let me know." His words gave me some much-needed confidence and reassurance. I did not struggle with respect to expenses, and the travel was so smooth that it was as though someone divine had charted out the plan for me. I was grateful to have been blessed with the opportunity.

I landed back in Chennai with a tired body and an invigorated soul. I was looking forward to a wonderful, deep sleep in the comfort of my own bed after so long, but for some reason, it seemed almost impossible. I dreamt of a young girl, roughly eight years old. It seemed hyper-realistic, and I was very much in my senses, wide awake. She wore a dull white dress and looked at me innocently as she held my hands. With her, I travelled to different lands far and wide. We ventured on the hills, into rivers, and to other such scenic locations. It was so real that I could feel the temperature of the water, the breathlessness while climbing up the mountains, the wind in my hair, and the divinity touching my soul. I was clueless but just went along with the young girl who was a trusted companion at this point.

The next morning, I woke up exhausted. Similar dreams of travels with the young girl occurred for the following week or so. On one such trip, I visited a graveyard and witnessed my ancestors manifesting before me. The young girl seemed to interact with every person we encountered on these journeys.

I called up my mother and asked if there was a young girl in the family who had died at that age, but there was no one. I grew tired of these sleepless nights. On the seventh night, when the girl arrived again and held my hand, I snapped. I pulled my hand away and yelled at her for constantly disturbing me. I asked her who she was and requested her not to trouble me since I really required a good night's rest. The girl was visibly upset. She walked to the corner of my room leaving my hand and looked at me with sorrowful eyes. She was clearly upset about my behaviour. I pulled the blanket over my head and fell asleep. I did not dream that night. She did not visit me again. I finally slept.

The next day, I visited my friend Sakina at her boutique. She asked why I looked so tired after all the temple visits, and I told her that I had not been sleeping very well. At that moment, a customer walked in with some material to give for stitching, and along with her, she carried a picture of a young girl wearing an outfit. She gave my friend the picture to use as a reference when stitching. For a second, I thought I caught a glimpse of the girl from my dreams in that picture. I asked the customer who the child was.

"This is my niece Bala," she said.

Suddenly, the thought occurred to me. "Maybe this was Bala Tripura Sundari."

At that time, I did not know anything about the goddess and had not encountered her energies before. It was a random thought that I verbalised. The name appeared in my mind and vanished just as quickly. The incident of the dreams had been completely erased from my mind after this.

43

Yogini Vayu Veena (Swasti)

After my travels, I was energised and fuelled by my spiritual escapades, and my mind, body, and soul were open to receiving from the higher realms. I visited the temples for an answer when I found myself feeling stuck and unsure of how to proceed in this endeavour, and I returned with some much-needed clarity, feeling inspired.

Finally, I sat in front of my canvas without any doubts disrupting the flow of my creativity. I had also grown significantly mentally stronger, which was important in this journey. I knew now that I had to start from the sixty-fourth goddess in the list and work backwards and finish Maha Tripura Sundari at the very end. I felt the effect of the blessings. The trip and the experiences I had gave my journey and my relationship with the goddess a new meaning. I celebrated my existence in tandem with the invigorating energies of the goddess. I wondered if this feeling of freshness I was experiencing was the energy of the next goddess I was about to paint—Vayu Veena. The air, or vayu, I breathed in felt like a blessing. The heavenly vibrations that showered upon me seemed almost an indication of Goddess Swasti, the consort of Lord Vayu, the symbol of purity and strength. I believe that Vayu Veena may be Swasti. The gods of storms, Rudra and the Maruts, are the male aspects of Vayu Veena. She represents the region between the earth and the sky, and in the body, she symbolises the breath. She represents freedom and Om, the formless self.

Goddess Swasti stays within the realms of Lord Vayu and is said to be the daughter of Lord Vishwakarma. Like Vayu, she, too, is a devotee of Vishnu.

Swasti is known to have shown traits of kindness and empathy, and there are several stories that confirm this. She is said to have appeared before Lord Hanuman, who was born of the powers of Vayu, and blessed him. Being a devotee of Krishna, she was also present when the Pandava brothers were sent into exile, and she consoled them in their time of sorrow. In certain imagery, she can be seen seated on a gazelle along with Vayu.

Swasti, like Vayu Deva, possesses the ability to scatter, expand, and always stay dynamic. She cleanses impurities and makes sure all forms of evil are kept away the way wind can blow away all impurities. I also saw her as one who offers moral support during tough times. Thus, she is a deity of power and strength, the strength that keeps away all forms of harm.

Adiyogi, given to me by priest Krisnan Potti

Ardhanareeshwarar painting

Heramba Ganesha painting

My Sreebala

Sri Yantra

Yogini Chandi wtih a lotus garland

Yogini Narasimhi being painted

A sketch I made after visiting Kodungallur

44

Yogini Surya Putri (Tapati)

Surya Putri—the name itself exudes a vibrance. I was in the habit of reciting the *Lalitha Sahasranamam* when I went for my early morning walks, and I would see the dawn sun following me. I would have a silent chat with him and open myself to receiving his energy, the brightness of which would bury all the negative forces. When I usually start painting, I feel the energies around me reacting to the energies emanating from the goddess. To me, the sun rays seemed brighter than usual the day I started painting, as if to welcome the goddess. The warmth of the rays was soothing and comforting. I felt this exact same energy when I started painting Goddess Surya Putri. Her light had to be handled with passion and piousness to be converted into the colours of blessings. The shades I used to paint her reflected her bright aura, almost as though a fire was burning inside her.

Surya Putri, in the literal sense, means daughter of the sun. Therefore, I concluded that she has to be Tapati, who carries the power of Surya. Tapati means "the eye of the universe" or "soul of all existence". She is believed to be the creator of nature and the material universe. She is also the daughter of Surya, the sun, and Chaaya and is the goddess of warmth and devotion. She also embodies beauty and spiritual discipline. Tapati is believed to be the one providing the earth with the heat it needs to survive. In my painting, she emulates these traits of her parents as she stands boldly and brightly. Her name also means the "burning one" as she possesses the qualities of her father, the source of all heat in this world. She dispels darkness and symbolises enlightenment burning away all evil and welcoming the light of goodness and knowledge.

In the Mahabharata, she is the wife of Samvarana, and her house is near a river. Samvarana saw Tapati, fell in love with her, and came to her with the intention of getting married. She asked him to approach her father, who readily accepted his proposal because Samvarana was a worshipper of the sun. Some scriptures also state that Samvarana started worshipping the sun in the first place because he wanted to marry Tapati. He had to consult sages such as Vasistha to assist him in approaching the sun god to tie the knot with Tapati. People admired her and wished to be around her. The river where her shelter was is now named the Tapati river, which is why today people worship her in the form of a goddess as well as a river.

45

Yogini Ajita

A familiar tone reverberated deep down. I had encountered this frequency before but could not place it.

> Let the goddess protect me from every direction, Jaya in the front, Vijaya from the back, Ajita from the left and Aparajitha from the right.
> —Chandi Kavacham from the *Devi Mahatmya*

Ajita is someone who does not experience failure, that is, one who cannot be defeated. This feeling of immense strength is what I experienced deep down. On my canvas, she emerged differently from how I had initially envisioned. Her size and expressions gave me a sense of ease and pleasantness. After I was done with the painting, I had to travel to Kollam, my hometown in Kerala. I visited my aunt's place in Ashtamudi, near which is our family's temple, Puthu veetil Bhagavathi Temple. The temple is generally not open every day. If we need to conduct any poojas on auspicious occasions, we specifically call the priest and request him to give us access to the temple premises.

On the day I was visiting, the temple had been opened for someone else's special pooja. So I seized the opportunity to enter and seek the deity's blessings. This time, I took notice of the deity's form. The idol was that of a horn of a stag or a deer. The story goes that the idol was brought by a woman who got married into a local family at Ashtamudi several years earlier. She had invoked the divine spirit of the goddess into the horn and brought it with her so she could get a glimpse of it every day.

As children, we would often hear stories about how the horn would grow every year. Of course, I always thought of it as an old wives' tale. However, whenever I stood in the temple to offer my prayers, I would look closely to check if the horn had grown. This time, I realised that I had expressed the image of this very deity on my canvas. In my painting, Ajita is a manifestation of the warrior goddess Durga.

The temple is also known as Kalari. It is also a place where people are taught Kalaripayattu, an ancient and traditional martial art that was also taught to warrior families that belong to the Nair caste. I realised the associations I had made subconsciously and was glad that I coincidentally visited exactly when the temple premises had been opened. Hence, I could realise the full extent of the energies I had painted on my canvas.

46

Yogini Sarvamangala

When I returned from my visit to Kerala, during which I sought the blessings of the Divine, I felt a surge of the energy of the goddesses pass through me. A deep connection had been wired between myself and the beings of the higher realms, which I felt very strongly in my heart and soul. I got into a meditative state, and nothing seemed to break the bond I had formed with the Divine. The flow of my creativity was unstoppable.

When I finally sat down to start on my next painting, I got the strong scent of milk and turmeric in the air. I could also sense the texture of the paste in my fingertips. This paste is a symbol of auspiciousness. *Sarva Mangala Mangalye* (all auspicious auspiciousness, giver of all fortunes). My mind and body worked in complete synchronicity. My mind felt unusually sharp, and my focus felt unbreakable. It felt as though my connection to the Divine increased my efficiency.

The name *Sarvamangala* is one I had been reciting since my childhood for its significance and auspiciousness. To me, she was the core force of all the goddesses. *Sarvamangala* means "let everything be good". It is another name for Goddess Durga. The fifth day of Navaratri is celebrated in her worship. One of the most ancient and revered goddesses, she has a tranquil face and a ferocious image. Her forms are many in mythology and folklore, but she is popularly seen as sitting on animals like lions and tigers in the midst of wars, killing demons and those who test her patience. She, in her many forms, is depicted as holding weapons in her arms, which range from eight to eighteen in number.

These weapons were given to her to fight demons and evil by the many male gods. She is the warrior goddess, the strong and bold personification of the feminine unto whom the masculine bowed down for its needs. However, tradition has it that her tranquil and calm face is a sign that she did not perform violence out of an "affinity" to it but only due to the circumstances that demanded it.

She is a nurturing figure when she needs to be and ferocious when she has to fight evil spirits and all those who only want destruction. Her ultimate motive is only peace, love, and liberty.

47

Yogini Gandhari

Anytime you start working on a creative piece, your past experiences, the things you see, and the stories you hear are reflected on the canvas. The name *Gandhari* was extremely familiar to me. I knew her as the wife of King Dhritarashtra from the Mahabharata.

It was important for me to unlearn what I knew so that I could freely experience the goddesses in all their glory, sans any judgements or prior expectations. I find the ability to forgo something that was previously imprinted in the mind an admirable quality. It allows one to move forward in search of newer energies to fill the void of ignorance. My mind wandered in search of Gandhari's essence to connect with her spirit.

Gandhari is a yakshini (a type of celestial being) who is also known as Prachanda. Her body is dark. She rides a horse. She controls one of our nadis, named after her, which carries energy from the lower part of the body to the eye chakra or the Ajna Chakra. Its complementary nadi is called Hasta Jeeva Nadi.

My thoughts went further and connected this concept with another story, that of the princess Gandhari who was married to the king of Hastinapur. There was a correlation between the two. The Gandhari Nadi and Hasta Jeeva Nadi are connected, and so was Queen Gandhari and the king of Hastinapur. An interesting point to note here is their vision. They have the power to see without using their eyes.

Gandhari was the princess of Gandhar, daughter of Surabhi and Kashyapa, and the goddess of horses. In the Mahabharata, she is described as a beautiful and virtuous woman who is given a high status in the epic due to her devotion to her husband and her children. Gandhari was married to Dhritarashtra, the king of Hastinapur. She is depicted in Hindu mythology and scriptures as a woman with a blindfold, which is believed to be a choice she made due to her love and reverence for her blind husband.

In this connection between Yogini Gandhari and Princess Gandhari, the Hasta Jeeva Nadi plays a vital role. It represents the power of seeing without physical eyes, a profound essence of human capability—the power of intuition. In essence, a nadi is a channel for energy flow within the body, and Gandhari, also known as a Vidya Devi, embodies the interconnectedness of all these elements. Everything in this narrative is intricately linked and symbolises the deep relationship between the physical and spiritual realms.

By the time I finished the painting, I realised that Yogini Gandhari was the goddess of intuition. Another point to note was that after the completion of my first thirty paintings and the temple visits, my intuition was much sharper. I was quickly able to perceive the goddesses and understand them unlike before when I needed more time. As their energies passed through me, I, too, had evolved.

48

Yogini Dhumavati

Every goddess I had painted until then looked like a vision of divinity. They were adorned in royal and intricate jewellery, colourful flowers, and, of course, the bindi (an integral accessory that symbolises the divine third eye and brings the entire ensemble together). They fit into the conventional moulds of what goddesses are expected to look like and be, but here is one that shattered all preconceived notions of how heavenly deities are portrayed: Goddess Dhumavati.

I did not feel confident enough to paint her. So, I focused my attention inwards and meditated, to connect with her spirit in the cosmic network. However, there seemed to be an obstacle of sorts in the way. I suddenly felt the urge to cleanse myself to bond my energy with hers.

From external sources and research materials, I had learnt that she is a rude and angry woman, the personification of unattractiveness. She was depicted very differently from the other goddesses I had encountered until then. Soon enough, I started to feel blips of her presence with each brush stroke. Despite my first impression, her vibration felt calming. Like a cold and gentle breeze, she passed by. I felt tingles behind my ears, the sensation one experiences as it starts to rain. I fell in love with her energy and the feeling of being pampered. I imagined her long white hair to have the texture of soft, white threads—old and stringy but carrying shooting electric current. She was a grand old woman, filled with love and devotion for her disciples and deep wisdom on the universe.

It almost seemed as though she wanted her disciples to dig deeper for the truth of her energies and not just believe what is on the surface. She wanted them to not just take her at face value but go the extra mile to find out what she truly stands for.

Slowly but surely, I started to notice several other avenues open in my personal and professional life. I saw several similarities between her and my grandmother, who would hide gifts in secret places for me to find. Similarly, Dhumavati, too, left several cookie crumbs, leading me to the path of success.

Through her, I learned that outer beauty or the outwardly attractiveness of a person, an opportunity, or whatever else it may be is frivolous and cannot be trusted. One must really get to the bottom to understand the true value of what one is presented with.

Her origin story takes us to the marriage of Shiva and Sati. Shiva was not familiar with the establishment of family or "household" and lived as a yogi, always in a deep penance. He did not fulfil the duties that the man of the house generally would. Sati requested Shiva to bring her food, but he refused despite her repeated requests. In a fit of rage and frustration and severe hunger, she consumed Shiva, much to his displeasure. When she finally brought him up, he cursed her to live the horrid and sorrowful life of a miserable, old widow.

Sati was engulfed in smoke when Shiva was inside her stomach, which significantly aged her and gave her unpleasant features. She then went to live on a cremation ground. She is said to hold a bowl of fire, which represents the burning of all desires, and a winnowing basket, which represents the filtering of the good from the bad.

One could say that Dhumavati's jarringly detestable appearance is a consequence of giving into urges and not exercising self-control. She also represents the point in life when one has detached from all material desires. Dhumavati is the representation of the purest wisdom and the ultimate truth. There is no sugarcoating whatsoever. Her truth is brutal and honest. Becoming a devotee of such deities requires the practice of such qualities.

People often point out how she is a widow, without the presence of Shiva, but in response, I always say that Shiva is present within her as she had consumed him.

After completing this painting, as usual, I sent an image to my cousin Sreekumar. He mentioned to me that he was quite nervous and uncomfortable around her energies. He called me up the next day and told me that she gave him the energies of a grandmother, a warm and welcoming connection. Even today, when we meet, he never fails to mention how his favourite painting is that of Dhumavati. I still feel the texture of the silky hair and the reflection of love in her eyes.

49

Yogini Ganga

I had been initiated into receiving the energies of Ganga by my guru and dear friend, Dr David. She lingered in every breath he took. I often wondered how someone could form such a strong bond with something that is merely a water body.

I have a heartfelt memory associated with her. I had previously visited the Ganges, a portion that was closer to Delhi, with him. We took the boat and ventured out into the waters in hopes of being able to take a dip, but the water was extremely slurry. I was upset and wondered why she would not let me in. Noticing my disappointment, Dr David said, "I'll take you to the place where Ganga originates, where she is at her clearest and cleanest."

People, myself included at one point, despite being staunch Hindus, look at the Ganga as just a holy river and nothing more. The river is considered a place where one may cleanse themselves of their karmic baggage. Thanks to Dr David, however, my perception has changed. I soon came to realise that she is much more than what people perceived her to be. He told me several stories about the river and his experiences with it and personified her in my mind. I grew quite fond of her. His love for Ganga convinced me to work on a film on the same subject, which took me to Varanasi.

I had the opportunity to spend a month there and in Haridwar, and we ended the shoot by spending a day at Devprayag. In all these places, I felt her come to me in different forms. In Varanasi, she approached me with the spirit of a mother, empathetically absorbing all the troubles of her children to leave them feeling lighter and unburdened. In Haridwar, her energy seemed older and mature. Her innocence had bloomed into a strength to face the world. The water was very reactive and expressive, mirroring the emotions of all those in her vicinity.

In Devprayag, two rivers, the Bhagirathi and the Alaknanda, converge. This is where the river Ganga originates. The Bhagirathi is wild and furious. The Alaknanda, on the other hand, is calm and serene. The two rivers are different shades of blue and merge as two water colours would, delicately and smoothly. Together, they stream downwards as the river Ganga. At this point of her origin, she emulated the energies of an innocent and pure young girl.

It poured on the first two or three days of the shoot despite it not being the rainy season, and the shoot kept getting delayed. I realised that despite attempting to make a film about her, I had not paid my respects to Goddess Ganga. So, that evening, the whole crew performed a Ganga aarti (a ceremony with lights offered to one or more deities to express love and gratitude) in devotion and gratitude for being allowed to capture her essence in our film.

I had many opportunities to take a dip in the water, but I waited until I could reach the place that Dr David mentioned, the place where the river originates. On the final day of our shoot, we went to that area. The shot was supposed to be of a young boy performing the final rites for his foster mother. I, too, decided that I would perform the last rites for Dr David. Life can be funny. Looking back, I realise that he had promised to take me there, but little did I know that it would be for me to pay my respects to him after his demise. Life came full circle at that moment.

Every paint-tinted drop of water that touched my canvas was so powerful that it cleared my thoughts. I felt a familiar connection with her. Dr David would constantly mention that her purpose was not just to clear away people's sins as it is generally assumed. She rejuvenates and is a life giver, the very soul of our country. My experience with her was so incredibly strong that there was no disruption by any other energy. There may be many stories associated with her, but those were just stories. The only thing that seemed to occupy my mind was my story with her.

According to the Valmiki Ramayana, she is King Himavat's daughter and Goddess Parvati's sister. She is said to have been taken to the heavens by the devas, from where she flowed as the river Ganga. The story behind her descent to the earth takes us to King Sagara, who was preparing to conduct an Ashwameda ritual (sacrificial ritual to prove imperial sovereignty). Fearing that the ritual would be a success, Lord Indra stole King Sagara's ritual horse. The 60,000 sons of King Sagara set out on a quest to find the horse and entered the dwelling of Sage Kapila. Mistakenly believing that he had stolen the horse, they interrupted his deep meditation. In a fit of rage for being falsely accused, Sage Kapila reduced the 60,000 sons to ashes.

King Sagara tried to seek redemption for his sons with the help of his grandson Anshuman, who learnt from Sage Kapila that only water from the Ganga could liberate them. After a severe penance, Anshuman's descendant King Bhagiratha sought the blessings of Shiva and Brahma and requested that the river Ganga be released. Brahma allowed it, and Shiva released her from his matted locks to control her flow so she may not destroy the earth with her force. The message of the story is relevant even today, as thousands of people flock to her banks to clear any debts of their ancestors.

She is usually depicted as the home to many lives and life forms. She is a nurturer and a provider, the one who nourishes those who inhabit her. Thus, she is a source of comfort and safety for her devotees. As I painted her, I came to realise why monks and sadhus spend so much time by the river. You feel complete peace and solitude. I was thrilled to paint her and considered myself blessed to touch her pristine energy. It completely engulfed me. Through painting her, I felt as though I had taken a dip in the water. I felt the chillness of her touch and dived into her loving embrace, only to come out feeling completely rejuvenated.

50

Yogini Murati (Rohini)

Through my wide-open window,
He gleamed with angelic grandeur
On his chariot with ten white horses
Bathed me in his streaks of lustrous silver
Filling me with the nectar of emotions
Intoxicating with an ecstasy of his smile.
His voice played soft, calm, and true.
The waves fizzled and so do my feelings
Experiencing the silver line between
The drifting clouds of pain and bliss.
Within the embrace of his strong arms,
I bloomed like a lotus with joyful tears.
I remained still, stunned near my window
By the thrilling mystery in his eyes
While millions of stars witnessing.
He keeps fading away unscathed,
Seemingly grasped in his infinite journey,
Mitigating my solitude from time to time.

The moon, Lord Chandra, seemed to look particularly handsome that night. Though I had felt so at other times, there was a certain glow it emanated. Its grandeur was such that it seemed almost angelic. I was filled with a sudden admiration, and its beauty felt like a reciprocation of love that left me in a romantic daze.

This romantic mood of mine spilt onto my canvas. Over the past couple of months, I had been through different waves of emotions and feelings and tried my best to channel it into my creative work. It can feel quite invigorating, like switching from hot water to cold. With Goddess Ganga, I experienced warm love from a grandmotherly figure, and here I felt the shocking ecstasy of romance and the euphoric thrill of a soul union.

The next goddess I was to paint was Murati. On looking at her portrayal at Hirapur, I noticed that she was standing atop what looked like a deer. I started to draw parallels between her and Chandra, the moon god, who is also associated with the deer. This vahana is what triggered me in a certain direction.

As I had previously worked on the twenty-seven nakshatras or constellations, I was greeted with a sense of familiarity. My illustration on the different phases of the moon from that series of paintings is one of my favourites and struck a chord like that of Murati's. Back then, I had learnt a captivating story on Lord Chandra, the moon god, and his wife Rohini. The same energy is often called by different names, but almost immediately, my intuition told me that Murati may be Rohini because she reflected the moon's energy. I knew if it had to be the feminine aspect of the moon, then it had to be none other than his wife Rohini.

Goddess Rohini is one of the most popular goddesses in Hindu mythology and is seen standing on a barking deer or a muntjac. She is also known as the red goddess. She has many interesting origin tales. She was the daughter of Daksha, who got her married to Chandra, the moon, along with twenty-six of his daughters. Daksha had demanded prior to the marriage that Chandra should not show any favouritism to any of Daksha's daughters over others and that he should stay loyal and impartial to them all. However, upon Chandra's marriage, he started to favour Rohini more, which led to his other wives complaining to Daksha. Daksha warned Chandra, but Chandra paid no heed. In a fit of anger, Daksha ended up beheading Chandra. However, Chandra was a devotee of Shiva and requested him to relieve him of the curse. Shiva told Chandra that he could not help him restore his powers entirely since he still had to keep in mind Daksha's wishes as well. The agreement they came to was that Chandra would visit one of his wives every day and would slowly gain back his full strength to become the full moon, and then he would slowly start to lose his powers again. This cycle of strengthening and weakening of Chandra's powers symbolises the waxing and waning of the moon.

There are several tales surrounding the celestial relationship of Chandra and Rohini that evoke profound emotional turmoil. The moon is said to control high and low tides of the ocean, one's emotional tendencies and women's menstruation cycles and hormones. This mirrors the moon's own nature, akin to its vahana, the restless deer that hops around. As I painted, I found myself so overcome with emotion that bouts of tears streamed down my face.

Rohini, the embodiment of lunar energies, wields the power to control one's emotional urges and rise beyond them. In many ways, she is the ultimate symbol of a dedicated and dutiful wife and mother. Her spouse has unconditional affection for her. The stories of Rohini and her romance-filled relationship with her husband, Chandra, told me the reason behind the luminescence of the moon. She filled my heart with love and affection, and I felt grateful to have had the chance to encounter her energies.

51

Yogini Chamunda

The time had arrived for me to paint one of the most ferocious goddesses, but I was aware that it would not be an easy task. I kept my canvas ready and sat in front of it in complete silence and prayer in an attempt to connect with her divine spirit. I knew it would take me a few days to acclimatise with this new energy that I would be exposed to. However, I was not afraid.

The experience of encountering these deities is something otherworldly. It is beyond the regular human experience. I could feel her presence in all my nadis. When my brush touched the blue paint shades, I felt an electrifying rush. Her energies were reflected even on my paint palette.

During this period, I started to crave Tamasic (non-vegetarian) food; I started to sit and act slightly differently than usual. I took these as signs of her presence within me. She entered my life quite eagerly but without disturbing my dynamic with my surroundings. During these phases, I try to avoid any unnecessary socialising; I try to stay in my lane, focused on the task at hand.

As I painted her, I pictured myself clinging to her divine aura.

"Ma, I want to express your beauty on my canvas. I want to enjoy your love, care, and power," I said to her.

I also tried to avoid music during that period, since the beats may have made me lose control of myself. Being able to unleash the most powerful feminine energies while staying grounded and in control is a beautiful feeling. I kept my feet firmly on the floor and grounded in energy, to maintain balance, while feeling a sense of gratitude. I felt thankful to have been given the chance to paint her. I experienced contentment. After having had the opportunity to mingle with these deities, what more could one ask for?

Her fierceness ignited a fire within me, and her origins explain her dark and fiery demeanour. Originally regarded as a tribal goddess and revered by the tribal communities, especially in the Vindhya mountains, Chamunda is one of the Ashta Matrikas. Dark-skinned with fierce and raging eyes, she is always seen seated on a demon whom she defeated using her rage and power. She represents death and the destructive power of a goddess, unlike the usual goddesses who are depicted as soft. In earlier times, it was common to make several animal sacrifices and offerings, including that of liquor, to please her. This aspect of the devi can be associated with Rudra or Agni.

The origins of Chamunda can be found in scriptures such as the *Devi Mahatmya* where she emerged as Ma Kali from the eyebrow of Goddess Kaushiki, who herself emerged from the sheath of Durga. Ma Kali was assigned the task of defeating Chanda and Munda, two notorious demons. She emerged victorious, chopped off their heads, and presented them to Goddess Ambika. From then on, she came to be referred to as Chamunda Devi, the slayer of the demons Chanda and Munda.

Naturally, this goddess, who is feared by the readers of the *Devi Mahatmya* and even devotees, is an unconventional one, who still embodies a raging power that no other goddess or divine form has ever been known to possess. Chamunda, the fearsome feminine power, unlike the weakness that is always depicted in the feminine, is a thrilling and inspiring persona for women who are tired of being represented and visualised as beautiful maidens with seductive charms who have no other form or power.

However, despite her conventionally fearsome portrayal, I saw her as a motherly figure. I knew well enough that a loving mother would never get angry at her child or expose her young one to any sort of rage for no reason.

"Ma, I want to express your beauty on my canvas. I want to enjoy your love, care, and power," I said to her. She emerged in my canvas in a ferocious form, but the feeling of surrendering to her was soothing. I felt heat waves around me, but they did not burn. It was a comforting motherly warmth.

52

Yogini Vayuvega

Often, as an artist there are moments when I am not quite aware of what to paint. In such moments, I found it best to just surrender to the Divine and let them take me over. There is no "me" existing in those moments. It is the divine ones who express themselves through me. I am merely a medium.

Goddess Vayuvega unfolded as a beautiful, young, dainty, and vibrant girl. I felt the urge to use several colours to capture her essence. She looked magical. After I was done with her painting, I meditated to truly understand who she is. Although I followed the Hirapur list of goddesses, I tried my best to express my own interpretation of them, rather than copying the sculptures at the temple.

Vayuvega is the goddess who stands for ether, which means "the one who moves through the sky."

"What is one thing that can cross the sky?" I wondered. Then the realisation dawned upon me that it was sound. "She might be Goddess Bhuvaneshwari, the Nada Devi, the goddess of sound," I thought to myself. The term *Bhuvaneshwari* is a blend of two words Bhuvana Ishwari, which means the queen of the universe. Within the universe exist three realms: the earth, the air, and the heavens. She is a supreme goddess who rules over all these realms, ensuring that peace and tranquillity exist.

Her energies also reminded me of Goddess Kechari, one of the eight matrikas, as per the sect of the *Kubjikamatatantra*. The energies emphasised the lightness of speed of sound and the ability to imbibe those qualities. A Kechari mudra is practised to raise one's feminine energy, which involves the rolling back of the tongue. Every time I lost focus while working on my Nakshatra series, Dr David would ask me to touch my tongue up to the roof of my mouth to bring my attention back to the task at hand. It dawned upon me that he had made me practise several such things without me even realising the significance of it all. I understood that this practice descended from the eight matrikas. There are another eight mahamatras under Kechari, sealing all the eight directions.

Kechari is also a popular form of yoga. By practising Kechari, one experiences a vibrational shift as the goddess has the power to influence the subtle energy currents. There is also a book called *Kechari Vidya* in which there is a dialogue between Shiva and Parvati. All goddesses can expand, shrink, become heavier or lighter, and more. In the book, Shiva enlightens his wife on the importance of maintaining lightness to be able to swiftly cross the skies against the force of the wind.

During the painting process, I realised how light her energies felt. I did not experience any of the heaviness that I did with the other goddesses. The yoginis are known for such siddhis.

53

Yogini Chandrakanti

Chandrakanti means "as beautiful as the moon". When I heard the name *Chandrakanti* and the word *Chandra*, I knew it would involve turbulent and heightened emotions. However, this time, since I had already painted the feminine energies of Chandra, I felt a sense of control over my emotions. The process of painting the goddesses involves understanding factors that may trigger havoc in one's life and taking control of oneself. Chandrakanti was a message on the very same subject. Despite being beautiful, she was disturbed—the disturbance a woman experiences when she is torn between performing her duties and listening to her heart. Being a woman myself, I can vouch that most of us undergo the pain of choosing between career paths, dreams, love and passions, and duties and responsibilities that fall on our shoulders. These were the thoughts that occupied my mind as I brought Chandrakanti to life on my canvas.

At the time of painting her, I assumed her to be a romantic at heart, and I expected her painting to reflect her romantic hues. However, as I should have expected, she was unveiled quite differently on my canvas. A portrait of a majestic and powerful woman appeared before me. There was so much more to her than I had anticipated. She was a woman who listened to her heart, no matter right or wrong. Chandrakanti is Thara or the personification of the star goddesses. She is married to Brihaspathi, the teacher of the devas and ruler of the planet Jupiter. Chandra was a student of Brihaspathi who was completely love-struck and captivated by Chandrakanti's beauty. She, too, is said to have fallen for Chandra's charm and romance, which the rational Brihaspathi lacked. She eventually eloped with Chandra.

Brihaspathi was enraged and visited Indra, the king of the devas, for a solution. Indra had no choice but to side with Brihaspathi since the latter usually performed rituals for the gods. Brihaspathi and Chandra passionately battled over Chandrakanti. This war shook all the realms, and finally, the gods had to come down to stop the war. They eventually persuaded Chandrakanti to go back to Brihaspathi.

What they did not know was that Chandrakanti was with child. Brihaspathi felt betrayed and asked whose child she was pregnant with. In guilt, she remained silent. He went on to curse the child to become androgynous, which is neither male nor female. Chandrakanti eventually gave birth to a beautiful child, Budha, who is the planet Mercury and the first deva to not be assigned a gender. Chandra came and took Budha away, and Budha was raised by Rohini, Chandra's wife.

Once one goes through conflicts such as these, one learns to maintain a sense of balance, which is crucial to stop such situations from recurring. Hence, at Hirapur, Chandrakanti is portrayed as standing atop a cot, the four legs of which represent the four purushartas—dharma (righteousness), artha (economic values), kama (psychological values), and moksha (liberation). These are the key concepts or principles that form the backbone of Hinduism.

54

Yogini Aditi

After painting Chandrakanti, I felt a sudden shift of energy. From experiencing imbalanced and dramatic emotions of conflict, I felt a motherly tenderness. Aditi is said to be the mother of the universe and rightfully so. She is a representation of the infinite. I slowly started to feel her presence within me as I got to know her better. She eased herself into my life, without rushing in forcefully, and stood as a silent spectator and guide, trusting my judgement of her.

This motherly quality of hers was nothing new to me. Rather, it was a characteristic that I was known for. Performing acts of service is the way I show affection and care. Right from a young age, I have been one to take responsibility for those around me, no matter if they are older or younger than me. Giving to others is something that has always given me immense joy. The experience of painting her was like mindful meditation where one visualises their surroundings and then, eventually, the entire universe. In a similar fashion, motherhood expands one's ability to love and serve and give more to the world.

For some reason, I did not feel ready enough to paint her. I wished to give it some time before I jumped into it.

As per Hindu mythology, Goddess Aditi is the primordial cosmic energy, and the universe was born from her womb. Symbolically, her universe was represented by the Hiranyagarpha or the golden egg. As per the Vedas, the egg burst into two parts and gave rise to material existence. Scientifically, this incident is recorded as the Big Bang. Our ancient Vedic scriptures were quite advanced with respect to providing insight on the origin of the universe's existence.

Aditi is said to be one of the sixteen daughters of Daksha and the granddaughter of Lord Brahma, the creator. Thirteen of the sixteen daughters, including Aditi, were married off to Sage Kashyapa, one of the seven ancient sages of Hinduism. Aditi was blessed with sons who were known as the devas, including Indra, Surya, Varuna, Vamana, and Vivasat. Her envious sister Diti became the mother of the asuras. When Diti's asura sons took over the land of the devas, Aditi worshipped Lord Vishnu with utmost motherly sincerity. Vishnu, impressed by her devotion, incarnated as her son Vamana, who restored the heavens to the gods. Her long, rigorous penance to propitiate Lord Vishnu to help her children, the devas, retrieve their heavenly abode, proves her sincerity towards them. Naturally, she is worshipped for fertility and family welfare. Goddess Aditi's pure intentions and genuineness make her the ultimate symbol of preservation, compassion, and guardianship.

When I did feel ready to paint her, it was a wholesome experience. I did not just experience motherhood through my children but grew to care like a mother for the whole world. She inculcated that feeling of inclusiveness in me. She is the mother of universal consciousness and the past, the present, and the future.

55

Yogini Agneyi (Svaha)

Red or vermillion
The colour of sacrifice
With tints of orange and yellow
The colour of burning sun,
The colours I used to paint Agneyi
The bridge, the fire
The feminine power "Swaha"
The one who takes our offerings to her husband, Agni
Is she called Agneyi?

My body temperatures rose. "Could this be a sign of her presence?" I wondered.

Just being exposed to her name exposed her fiery and zesty nature. She bloomed on my canvas with a smile as bright as a blazing fire. She represents sacrifice, the greatest of feminine emotions. Her presence led me to believe that she must be the consort of Agni Devata, the lord of fire. To me, her role does not matter as much as her energies do. What I experienced was the radiation of heat that came from fire. All that mattered to me was what she made me feel.

Agneyi is described in the Vedas and the Puranas as a very charming and attractive woman. She is seen standing on a ram with flames in the background. Some scholars have mentioned that the ram showcases ego; hence, the devotees must burn their ego to completely please Agneyi. She holds much divinity and power owing to her association with

Agni Devata. She exudes the qualities of fire like fierceness and bravery and is an extinguisher of impurity, evil, and injustice.

Agneyi is also alternatively known as Svaha, a word that is commonly chanted when poojas are being performed and offerings are made to the fire. There is an interesting tale surrounding this. Agneyi, too, was one of the daughters of King Daksha. She was completely enamoured by Agni and actively pursued him, but her efforts were in vain. Agni perpetually resided where the sacrificial rituals performed by the Saptarishis, or seven ancient sages, took place, since the rituals needed fire to make offerings to the gods. He was captivated by the wives of the sages and, hence, ignored Agneyi's advances.

Frustrated by the idea of lusting over the wives of other men, Agni left for the forests to perform a penance to rid himself of those thoughts. Agneyi understood his intention and disguised herself as six of the seven wives of the Saptarishis and seduced Agni. The by-product of their union each of the six times was put inside a golden pot, out of which Skanda was born.

Agneyi expressed her need to be perpetually present with Agni. She represents a force that cannot be burnt by fire, which is why to this day her name is chanted and she is invoked when there is a fire present for any pooja.

One of the most ancient nuclear energies created by the gods and goddesses to gain victory over their enemies was the Agneya Astra, and she is the source of shakti behind the infinite energy and power of this astra.

To me, she is an apt representation of all women—immeasurable power with burning passion, while also carrying loving qualities meant for those she holds close to her. Her heat burned all the negativity around and within me, and this self-cleansing is an important process I had to undergo in different layers with different goddesses to proceed without inhibitions and self-doubt.

56

Yogini Jwalamukhi

When I started on my painting of Goddess Jwalamukhi, I automatically gravitated towards blue and green shades. My mind had made the connection, and I started without any hesitation. Slowly, she started to take form. While I was engrossed in painting her, I received a call from my brother. The conversation turned sour for some reason, and something he said rubbed me the wrong way. I was unable to hold back the tears. I started weeping uncontrollably. The crying slowly changed to screaming in disappointment.

My brother had not said or done anything that should have moved me that much, but my emotions were uncontrollable. My husband heard my wails and silently walked into the room to check up on me. Without saying a word or interrupting, he left me with my emotions.

I was completely engrossed in the painting and started to cool down after a while. Truth be told, I did not realise how high-pitched my voice had become and how extreme my feelings appeared. My husband sweetly sent me a few messages from the next room, offering to buy me more paint supplies or a new canvas. He assumed the cause of my weeping to be a shortage of funds to complete my paintings. At that point, that would be the only thing that could possibly affect me so deeply since I was already going through a financial pinch of sorts. Slowly, my husband approached me and made me aware of how extreme my weeping was. I wondered why I had reacted that way as there was absolutely nothing that had triggered it.

One fine day, after I had completed my painting, I was having a conversation with my cousin Sreekumar. I mentioned to him that I was just done with my painting of Jwalamukhi, and without any knowledge of this incident that had occurred, he said to me, "Goddess Jwalamukhi was the commander of the goddess army, and right as she entered the battle, in a fit of rage, she let out a war cry that shook the heavens and the earth."

I truly could not believe my ears. I realised then that I had entered a different plane and realm of reality, which brought these emotions out of me.

What is the usual image that comes to our mind when we think of a goddess? Delicate, beautiful, covered with jewellery, and such fancy and heavenly maiden-like descriptions, isn't it? This archetype has dominated our minds. However, Jwalamukhi is a unique goddess. There are no feminine or flowery descriptions of her like there are of other goddesses in Hindu scriptures. So she is the most distinct goddess in the Hindu legends. Jwalamukhi literally translates to "she of the flaming mouth". She is among the few, if not the only goddess, who is worshipped without an idol, and none of her temples have a deity other than a blue flame that is worshipped devotedly by those who believe in her. Generally, the colours red and orange are typically associated with the heat of fire, but the real heat stems from the blue portions that are hidden under layers of flaming orange. This blue flame is placed in a square pit. The flame is the manifestation of the goddess; hence, she is believed to be the source of all light there is in creation.

There are many interesting tales behind how she came into being and why she is only in the form of a flame. In one version, two demons named Chanda and Munda looted all the wealth of the devas. This incident is even metaphorically described as the devas losing all their peace. The devas then sincerely called out to Shiva for help. Shiva was impressed by their devotion and appeared before them to inform them that he will send a goddess who takes the form of a flame to gain back all the wealth that they had lost to the demons. Jwalamukhi thus appeared in the hills where the demons had hidden the wealth of the devas. She appeared to swallow both the demons and returned all the wealth back to the devas. She then decided to reside on the same hill in the form of the flame itself. Her temple is now located there.

Some isolated tales also have it that the flame represents the burning flame that came out of a demon that Shiva had killed. Therefore, she can also be seen as a symbol of the light that appears on the destruction of evil. She is, to this day, worshipped in the minds of many and stays there as a flame of light in their hearts and minds. To me, she remains an experience of a lifetime that ignited the power of light in me.

57

Yogini Brahmani

After the experience of painting Goddess Jwalamukhi, I felt completely drained, almost as though I had returned from battle. However, I was grateful to have been blessed to receive her energy, and I was incredibly thankful for the reaffirmation that I was on the right path and that she was a witness to my journey. I was exhausted but felt a sense of accomplishment, like the pleasant pain a mother feels after painstakingly giving birth. A sense of gratefulness paired with tiredness took over me. The outcome was beautiful and powerful and completely worth all the pain and hardship. I had learned to accept pain as a part of the process and, on the whole, as a part of life itself.

My experience after that was soothing and healing, like the calm after a storm. Brahmani made me feel completely at ease. After being taken over by such a strong creative force, my mind felt as though it had expanded.

Brahmani flowed onto my canvas peacefully. After I had completed the painting, I received a call from a friend, inviting me to attend the launch of a company. Under normal circumstances, I would avoid attending such events while working on my paintings, but this friend was extremely close.

I accompanied her as a guest. For some reason, a strong force took over me, and I started to make suggestions and comments that may have been unwarranted. The subject was an area that I did not have much awareness on, and yet I spoke like a professional. Somehow, I seemed to command attention in that room without realising how or why. My intuitions were so strong that I could see that the launch would not happen as planned until they took adequate steps to improve on it. Instead of keeping these thoughts to myself, I expressed them quite openly. I came to understand that Brahmani was speaking through me. She is the powerhouse of clarity and intuition.

She is one of the Ashta Matrikas who fought the battle against Raktabeeja. Legend has it that Brahma was consumed by thoughts on the creation of the world. During this process, his body split in to two parts. One remained Brahma, and the other half came to be known as Devi Brahmani. She is also the one that rules the field of linguistics.

Another story attributed to her origin tells us that Brahmani is said to have been born on the earth as Renuka, a Kshatriya princess who was married to Sage Jamadagni. There were many clashes and conflicts that took place between the Kshatriya clan and the Bhargava clan. Since Sage Jamadagni belonged to the Bhargava-vamshi clan, this caused conflicts in their marriage.

Eventually, the two had a child, the great Parashuram, an incarnation of Vishnu. Sage Jamadagni instructed Parashuram to behead his mother if he had true love for his father. Parashuram followed his orders; thus, this great goddess was born who came to be known as Devi Brahmani.

During this process, I came to realise that there were many creative divisions and sub-divisions to what these goddesses stood for. I learned to peel the layers, just as one would peel onions, and dove deep into what they represented.

58

Yogini Bhudevi (Samudra)

The perceived silence of the womb
Entrapped with the universal mystery of Prakriti and Purusha
Murmuring the primordial sound.

That was the sound that rang through my ears and woke me up one morning. The source? The house next door. The sound of a conch echoed through my bedroom, a conch like every other that held the sound of the universe, and that was the very energy that inspired me to start on this painting.

A conch is a significant instrument to Hinduism as well as to the tantric practice. When it is blown during sacred times, the sound it produces is said to be symbolic of the Om sound.

I have always been completely mesmerised by the endless, delicate spiral patterns on conches, as if they were pathways to the infinite. These circular patterns represent the golden ratio, the basic blueprint upon which the universe has been designed. Every art piece of mine also uses this ratio to maintain the eye-pleasing aesthetics found in nature. Each conch is a treasure map of different sizes and colours with roads that lead us to the doorstep of the Divine. The energy produced by a conch is unexplainable.

I knew Goddess Samudra by another name in a form that was made familiar to me as a child.

Bhoomi Vandan
Samudra Vasane Devi
Parvata Stana Manndale
Vishnu Patni Namastubhyam
Paada Sparsham Kshamasva Me
Devi, you who wears the ocean, with the mountains as your bosom
O consort of Lord Vishnu,
Salutations to you;
Please forgive me for touching your holy body with my feet.[2]

This prayer is the first one taught to children in Hinduism as an apology to the earth, Bhumi Devi, for putting our weight on her and touching her with the bottom of our feet and to seek her blessings. Here, she is addressed as Samudra Vasane Devi. Evidently, Samudra is none other than Mother Earth herself, Bhumi Devi.

Bhumi Devi, as her name states, is the goddess that represents the earth. She is said to be the consort of Varaha, an incarnation of Vishnu with the face of a boar. A tale describes how the two came to be united. The demon Hiranyaksha captured Bhumi Devi and submerged her in the depths of the ocean. In terror and fear, Brahma prayed to Vishnu in hopes that he would rescue her. Vishnu took the form of Varaha and emerged from the nose of Brahma. He grew to an unimaginable size, dove into the vast oceans, and lifted up Bhumi Devi with his snout.

Out of the union of Bhumi Devi and Varaha was born the great demon king Narakasura, who had gained a boon from Brahma that he would not be killed by anyone but his mother.

---

[2] All translations are by the author.

Using the boon to his advantage, he wreaked havoc across the heavens and even traumatised many women in his harem.

In their next births, Bhumi Devi and Varaha were born as Sathyabama and Krishna respectively. Together, they attacked the child born to them in their previous birth. With the aid of Krishna, Sathyabama defeated Narakasura, and peace reigned once again.

I see Bhumi Devi as one with immense strength. Having the ability to hold a plethora of energies, including the positive, negative, and everything in between, is commendable. This power the earth holds can be owed to the rule upon which it has been designed, which once again brings us back to the mystical concept of the golden ratio. If one really opens their eyes to notice the patterns present in nature and learns the ability to mimic that magical design in their art, no matter what the form may be, the world would be richer and bursting at the seams with spectacular art.

59

Yogini Narayani

Something I had experienced with almost every painting up until this point was the assumption that I knew the goddess, but the moment I sat in front of my canvas, my mind went completely blank. I was not overconfident by any means, but I realised that they wished to communicate to me. For that, all preconceived notions in my mind had to be completely erased. I had become accustomed to this exercise by now and found it to be quite beautiful as it kept my curiosity always piqued. I was open and ready to receive the energies of the goddesses.

Initially, I assumed that Narayani is the consort of Vishnu, but she is a reflection of Vishnu's energies. In the *Lalitha Sahasranamam*, she is known as the Padmanabha Sahodari. Therefore, I perceive her as yet another form of Goddess Durga. She is said to be the fundamental building block of the universe that gives life. This description reminded me of the much-talked-about string theory.

Some modern-day rationalists with scientific temper rationalise that Narayana is nothing but a deification of string theory in physics, which claims that the smallest component that makes up the entire universe constitutes vibrating energy strings. Narayana etymologically could be traced to the combining of the words *Naar*, which means string, and *ayan*, which means movement. Narayana is another name for Vishnu, which means all-pervading, and Narayani is the feminine aspect of Narayana.

Secrets of the very fabric of our universe are embedded in our ancient mythology. We constantly consume information and assume we know best, but in reality, true knowledge is knowing that we know nothing.

Narayani is considered the omnipresent supreme God or Brahman. In the Shakta form of worship, Devi Narayani is considered the absolute truth manifest in all creation.

There is a form of Narayani called the Mahalasa Narayani or Mohini, and a fascinating tale is associated with her. During the grand churning of the ocean of milk for the amrut (nectar) that would help the devas and asuras regain their powers and immortality, Vishnu took the disguise of a beautiful young woman called Mohini to distract the asuras. The asuras were awestruck by her beauty and requested her to distribute the amrut to them and the devas. She readily agreed, provided that they did not question her on her actions. She asked the devas and asuras to form two separate lines and started to distribute the amrut amongst the devas first. A cunning asura named Svarbhanu disguised himself and sneaked into the line of the devas. The sun and moon gods, Surya and Chandra, promptly noticed this and informed Mohini. She immediately released the Sudarshana Chakra and beheaded the asura. The head portion came to be called Rahu, and the bottom portion came to be called Ketu.

I believe Narayani to be the goddess who represents immortality, considering that she was the distributor of the amrut. Our bodies may perish due to the impacts of time and space, but the vibrations or energies only get transferred and are, therefore, omnipresent. Energy cannot be created or destroyed, and within each string that forms this energy exists Narayani, bringing life to all creations.

60

Yogini Uma

Over this period, I came to realise that the beauty of painting these goddesses is that one is taken through a whole range of emotions and exposed to a myriad of powers that are unique to each one of them. I dived from one octave to the completely opposite one while being fiercely protected. As I write this, I can understand why I could do so with such ease. I owe it to my strong connection with the core strength, the source of all these sixty-four manifestations, the Almighty. Nothing could shake or break that bond. That was the grounding that helped me go through this rollercoaster of an emotional journey.

At this point, deep down, I wanted to start reading some more authentic spiritual texts on the yoginis. I discussed the same with my friend Jasyindar, whom I became acquainted with at the yogini temple. He introduced me to a Mr Venkataraman Vishwanathan Iyer from the Sumeru Madam Ashram at Thiruvananthapuram, Kerala. He is a scholar and practitioner of Srividya.

I called Mr Vishwanathan but to no avail. I sent him a text message informing him that I am an artist who is working on a series of paintings on the sixty-four yoginis. Immediately, in a few seconds, he called me back.

"Are you planning to start these paintings?" he asked.

"No, I have completed about 70 per cent. I have just a few more to complete," I replied.

"No ... that is impossible!" he retorted. "You may not complete them."

A strange fear gripped my mind at that moment. I asked him to switch over to a video call so I could prove to him that I was telling the truth.

He was quiet.

I started to worry.

"Send me your horoscope and birth details," he said.

It seemed to be an odd response, but I did as he asked. I spent the rest of the day feeling an overwhelming sense of uncertainty. Why would he say that? Was it not in my destiny to complete a project that I had worked so hard on over the past year? The very next day, I got a call back from him.

"You will complete all your paintings, and I will visit Chennai to see you."

He said it as though it were a prophecy.

"Are you a Kali Upasaka?" he further added.

This was not the first time I had been asked this question. As mentioned several chapters earlier, a priest and an astrologer, krishnan Potti, who was referred to me by my mother had asked me the same.

"No, I am not," I replied, not knowing what reaction to expect from him.

He remained quiet for a few moments.

"Which goddess are you painting next?" he asked.

"Goddess Uma!" I replied enthusiastically.

He started to describe Goddess Uma, almost poetically, as per an ancient chant. Everything he said went completely over my head. When I finally sat down to paint her, my mind felt conflicted. I had envisioned her a certain way, but Mr Vishwanathan's description of her kept popping up in my mind. I took a break for a couple of days to clear my head of the image he had painted and to recoup my thoughts. That day, I decided to stick with my original decision—to never discuss or read about the goddesses until I was done with all sixty-four paintings. I was overcome with a feeling of peace as I sat in front of my canvas. My mind felt light, and my soul felt exuberantly feminine.

Upon further research while writing this book, I understood that Uma is the personification of selfless devotion and sincerity. I experienced the same feeling while painting her. Uma is one of the primary manifestations of Shakti or the divine feminine. After Shiva's first wife, Sati, self-immolated due to the embarrassment she was subjected to by her father, Shiva's sadness knew no bounds. He isolated himself and went into deep mourning, adopting the ways of a hermit. The world suffered a great deal without Shiva; therefore, Uma was created by the gods to bring Shiva out of his shell, tame his anger, and reignite the sense of humanity in him.

Born to the king of the Himalayas, Himavat, and an apsara or angel, Mena, Uma was the princess of Kailash. From a very young age, Uma was determined to invoke the energies of Lord Shiva. A notable story from the *Kena Upanishad*, a sacred text, talks about a five-year-old Uma wishing to perform a penance to call upon Lord Shiva. Her parents were understandably worried. Such a penance was known to be physically, mentally, and emotionally taxing and was meant to test the strength of the follower's devotion towards the deity. It would be impossible for a five-year-old to take on the challenge, but Uma was not one to give up easily. She wished to prove her faithfulness to Shiva and went on to perform the penance.

She came to me with a whole lot of love. She put me in touch with my inner femininity—the playful, romantic, excited, and starry-eyed young girl who got lost in the pressures and responsibilities of adulthood. Suddenly, the sun shined brighter, the sky seemed to be bluer, and there were butterflies in my stomach. There was a celebration of my femininity in my heart.

Section by section, she appeared on my canvas, filling me with immense joy. Her energy was delicate and soft, yet incredibly strong and powerful. She bloomed, like a bud does, into a magnificent flower. The texture of her skin was like silk. I felt like a young teenager again, wanting to be held close by my mother, as she caresses my hair and listens to my prayers. I could feel the goddess reciprocating my prayers.

61

Yogini Kali

"Are you a Kali Upasaka?" The memories of different people asking me this question suddenly struck my mind. All this while, I was drenched in the warm and embracing love of Uma, feeling pleasant and comfortable. This sudden shift took me unexpectedly. I laughed as I thought about how I was about to experience a shift of force field from that of Uma's to Kali's and jump from one dimension to a drastically different one. Over this already-existing fear, another seed had been sown in my mind.

Mr Vishwanathan had developed the habit of sending me images of myself that he had retrieved from my Facebook page, photoshopped over those of the Nagadevatas or the snake gods and other spiritual figures. In hindsight, I find the incident to be quite funny and interesting. However, back then, a fear had taken over my mind, and I rudely asked him to stop doing it. Today, I feel quite sorry about it. He immediately apologised but would constantly tell me that I gave off a powerful energy like that of a goddess or a naagin (snake). Over time, he has become a great friend and a guide of mine. I have never wished to be perceived as a goddess or a medium. I am but a mere devotee and seek blessings from the Divine. All this, paired with a fear of Kali, left me feeling frightened to take the next step. Then Dr David's words rang through my ears.

"Would you fear your own mother? Unless you made a mistake, of course. The goddesses are like our mothers. We need not fear them unless we have committed some grave sin. Their wrath is reserved for wrongdoers. Our sincerity in devotion is enough to bring in their light and love."

Before I began, I sat in prayer, requesting her to only present herself in a form that I could take and wholeheartedly absorb. I wanted to enjoy her presence in my life. When I finally sat down to paint, the colour black popped up in my mind, but I was not too happy to use it.

I could feel a certain chill in my Muladhara Chakra or root chakra, which is located at the base of the spine. I also experienced a cramp in my lower abdomen. I felt her energy vibrate through every chakra. My entire body was experiencing different physical reactions. I continued to pray to her, asking her to come in a peaceful form. I knew that whatever her exterior form may be, deep down, she, like every other goddess I had encountered so far, would have a warm and approachable form.

I was prepared to paint her in black, but I accidentally stepped on a paint tube. Hues of vibrant emerald green sprayed out onto the floor. It was a sign. I decided to paint her in that colour. When people hear the word *Kali*, they immediately see the colour black or blue, but the closer you get to her, the brighter she shines, like an emerald. Green is also one of my favourite colours. I had decided that my first step would be to start with emerald green.

Heat radiated through every cell of my body. I was in a completely different plane, and I felt a sensual energy flow through my body. Everything felt different from what I had anticipated. Before starting on any painting, I generally have a rough sketch and an idea of what I am about to paint, but in this case, I just put paint directly on the canvas and painted her face. Her eyes sparkled like real emeralds, and even though her tongue was out as she is described in mythology, she wore a subtle smile that made her look gorgeous.

The fear within me started to ebb, and the sensual energy started to rise. I felt complete satisfaction and happiness. The energy gushed out from my Svadhisthana Chakra or sacral chakra to my Sahasrara Chakra or crown chakra, energising my brain cells. I experienced it as I stared into her bright eyes once I was done painting her face. I started to sweat profusely and felt an insatiable hunger and thirst. I desperately wanted to consume food and water. She held me so close that I started to radiate her aura.

I started painting the rest, and something I had never envisioned in my dreams had started to take shape on my canvas. Kali was seated on Lord Shiva. He was in a meditative state, completely lost in her divine vibrations, giving his complete energy and merging with her to become one in holy union. Every strand of her hair exuded an electrifying energy that cannot be put into words. I slowly started to realise that the image that I was painting was of the compassionate and divine union of Shiva and Kali as they experienced absolute ecstasy. I was glad and prayed that she would come to me in her happiest form.

The ferocious form that is Kali can only be tamed by her lover. The euphoria was almost comparable to an orgasm but is not one that is experienced on the physical plane. It radiated through my Sahasrara or crown chakra, which was an emotionally profound and fulfilling feeling. My mind glowed like a pure emerald, and in those moments, time ceased to exist. I felt absolute liberation as I manifested her powers on my canvas, the powers that run the universe.

Since time immemorial, goddesses were symbols of different traits like nurturance, power, strength, and sacrifice. Goddess Kali is, however, not the regular conventional depiction of a goddess with unconditional love. The black goddess with red eyes, multiple arms, decapitated heads of demons, and her tongue out is the epitome of a destructive rage. Despite being his wife, she was less submissive even towards the powerful Lord Shiva, and he is seen under her feet in many of her sculptures.

The *Devi Mahatmya* and other scriptures have elaborated on her brave conquests, which would have been difficult for even the male gods. She went to war against Raktabeeja and other demons to defeat the unjust and the harmful. She is also the embodiment of both creation and destruction, the beginning and the end. The name *Kali* is believed to have been derived from *kala*, meaning time, and she is believed to be beyond the construct of time.

There are different forms of Kali in different scriptures, each showing a different range of rage. It is said that some of them are not even approachable. She is said to exist for a purpose. Her energies are meant for the greater good. For me, she is a beautiful, composed, powerful, yet sensual goddess. Behind her darkness dwells her captivating femininity.

62

Yogini Stuti

After painting Goddess Kali, my close friends and family started to witness a remarkable shift in me. There was a newfound vibrancy that had attached itself to my aura. I became more talkative than usual, but my words were filled with a wisdom that I believe came to me from a higher realm. They flowed out of my mouth effortlessly.

My cousin Sreekumar gave me a call one day, and he spoke to me about Goddess Kali. The way I responded that day, with all the details of different forms of Kali, left me convinced that it was not me speaking but a divine presence through me. I was a mere medium. I wondered if this was Goddess Kali, whom I had painted earlier, or Goddess Stuti, whom I was about to paint.

Goddess Stuti is said to be the messenger, the one that connects us with the other gods. She is the one that carries our praise and prayers to the gods and brings us the blessings they impart.

Stutee's energies mirrored a profound innocence and purity. The name *Stuti* means praise, which took on a whole new meaning in my life. Good words and praise can only authentically flow out from a heart that is untainted by envy or ulterior motives. Prayers, praises, and great gestures not only make one happy but also heal one and bring in a sense of balance. Stuti is yet another name for Goddess Durga.

Our ancient chants and prayers involve singing praises of the Almighty, but how pure or truthful is our devotion? For the most part, it is conditional.

"Help me pass that exam or buy that car or bag that job and I will break a coconut at the temple to seek your blessings." These prayers come from a place of "self" and not "selflessness". True devotion is unconditional, and one must faithfully trust the universe to do what is best. I gained a remarkable amount of clarity while working on my painting of Goddess Stuti and came to some incredible realisations.

The timing of these realisations seemed to be divinely orchestrated, and I was filled with a sense of gratitude, which turned into praise for Stuti. Then I realised that her energies were passing through me. I did not start this entire process with any expectations; it was done purely from a place of devotion and sincerity. I felt the blessings pouring in for the purity of my intentions. As I painted her, I would chant or listen to chants that sang praises in her name. It was not merely music but the expression of my gratitude towards her.

63

Yogini Ghatabhari (Bhavani)

The rain of energy had subsided and turned into a light drizzle. There was a serene stillness in the air. I revelled in the peacefulness of the calm after the storm. Over the previous two paintings, I was overwhelmed with contradicting energies, but those yielded to a tranquil enchantment.

In my painting, Ghatabhari radiated a captivating aura. She came to me as a warrior that had weathered the storm of battle. She was a harmonious blend of sharpness and power and was a strong force of nature that completely grounded me. I found myself drawn to her vahana, the simham or lion, and felt a connection with him. His firm nature expressed the nature of the goddess. He emulated a sense of pride on being the trusted vahana of Ghatabhari. He represented the power, will, and determination of the goddess.

Looking at her and the vahana's bhava (attitude), I felt that she is a form of Bhavani, the consort of the Lord Bhava or Sadashiva. In my painting, she is the image of femininity, and her expression makes it seem as though she is well aware of her beauty. Her image commands a certain respect, and her eyes dance around with the flames of independence and determination. Her beautiful smile illuminates my darkest parts.

The energies I experienced from her spoke to me as though preparing me to be a warrior like her. I was being gifted with wisdom, grace, and strength, along with equal parts of wealth and liberation. Imbibing such qualities was important to me because I had always been one to avoid any conflict, arguments, or unpleasantness. I sought refuge in ignoring those I disagreed with, just to maintain a sense of peace. For example, if I ever encountered any injustice or wrongdoings, I would immediately shy away from calling out the wrongdoers. It was in my nature to avoid such situations, even if it caused me harm.

My encounter with Goddess Ghatabhari's energies made me realise that running away from conflict was never the answer. I had to embody the spirit of a warrior, stand my ground, and fight for what I believed was right. I felt a sudden drive and commitment to uphold truth, justice, and integrity with complete grace and resilience. It was not merely for selfish reasons but for the sake of the betterment of society at large.

In the Maratha empire, King Shivaji Maharaj deeply revered Goddess Bhavani, often visiting the Tulja Bhavani temple. This temple had a fascinating story linked to the Skanda Purana. Sage Kardam, with his wife, Anubhuti, and their child, lived on Yamunachala Hill, where the temple now stands. After Kardam's death, Anubhuti performed intense penance near the Mandakini river for her child's safety.

Their peace was shattered by a demon named Kukur. In a desperate moment, Goddess Bhavani appeared. She transformed into a buffalo, battled Kurkur, the demon, and defeated Kukur with her trident in her true form.

This bravery earned her the name Tulja Bhavani, the revered deity of Tuljapur. The temple became a symbol of faith, especially for Shivaji Maharaj, who received a mighty sword, "The Bhavani Talwar", from the goddess, aiding his victories. The legend of Tulja Bhavani thus became a tale of courage, faith, and divine strength.

64

Yogini Kamayani (Trishna)

"Kama, the god of desire," I thought to myself when the time came for me to paint Goddess Kamayani. I wondered if there was a relation between the two.

For some reason, I felt the presence of my mentor, Dr David, very strongly, almost as though he wished to convey a message to me. I started to experience a deep melancholy that I did not understand. The energies were very different from what I had expected. My portrait of Goddess Kamayani started to develop nicely. Before me was the image of a beautiful and curvaceous woman, unabashedly proud of her womanhood. I, as anyone else would, interpreted the word *kama* as lust, which left me very confused because I did not experience even a hint of any lustful energies. I have come to realise in hindsight that the term *kama* is often misunderstood.

My heart felt heavy with sadness, but I could not figure out the source of that emotion. What I was feeling and what had evolved on my canvas were in two completely different dimensions. Kamayani emerged as the picture of sensuality, but I felt no such energy around me. Another interesting thing to note is that the entire time I worked on the painting, my pet parrot, Meetu, stayed on my arm. She walked from the tip of my finger to my shoulder and back, continuously. It seemed odd, but I did not think much of it.

For a minute, I decided to detach from the painting and focus on what I was feeling on the inside. I travelled back in time to an experience I had. The incident had taken place a few years prior when Dr David was alive. I had just completed a series of paintings on the nakshatra goddesses. I was extremely excited about my paintings and had several plans on how to showcase my work to the world. I built several castles in the air.

"You are getting too attached, Beena," said Dr David, warning me.

"You must stay nishkami. Live without any desires or expectations. Desires may only lead to disappointment," he added.

At the time, I was confused but chose to trust his judgement because I saw the divinity in his eyes. I later handed over the entire Nakshatra series of paintings to him and let go of all desires attached to them.

His words rang in my ears. I understood that I needed to let go. I started to connect the dots with the feelings that prevailed within me and the memories that had come rushing back. There is often a reason behind every thought or feeling. I realised that Kamayani was not the goddess of lust, as I had initially interpreted. She was the goddess of desire. She helped one control one's desires. Desire should not exist for merely selfish reasons. It must be cultivated to manifest for the betterment of society.

I perceived Kamayani as Trishna, the daughter of Kama Deva, who was the lord of love and lust. The word *Trishna* literally translates to thirst or a certain aspiration or a longing. When one has full control over one's emotions, the mind is tranquil. If feelings go beyond one's control, it leads to unpleasantness, sadness, greed, envy, and other negative emotions. The word *nirvana* has gained a lot of popularity in the West, but I wonder if the essence of the word is truly understood. Nirvana or a zen state of mind does not come from pushing emotions under the rug; it comes with sitting with them, observing them, and keeping them in check. One does not attain a state of nirvana overnight. It takes years of practising, meditating, and looking inwards to truly understand oneself to attain that frame of mind.

I realised how much power Kamayani held. In a world of constant evolution, desire can be a beautiful and powerful energy but one that is like a sharp knife. On one hand, if used carefully, it could bring about great change in the world. On the other hand, if used for selfish reasons or to harm others, it could stand in the way of attaining salvation, and Goddess Kamayani helps us control our desires, preventing them from becoming greed, which can harm the world around us.

65

Yogini Kamakshi

By now, my world had started turning in different directions. With each goddess came new experiences and a whole new set of emotions. The day I was to paint Goddess Kamakshi, I woke up feeling completely content and peaceful. My mind was very clear and not clouded by any judgement of what she may be. I was ready to receive her as she wished to be received. I felt liberated from the pressure of having to understand her, because, by now, from experience I knew that she would present herself to me.

The name *Kamakshi* means the one with lustful eyes. She is a popular deity and a household name in the southern states of India. The south is also said to be where Goddess Parvati first appeared on the earth. She is said to be the deity of beauty and tranquillity.

There are a couple of stories associated with her origin. The first one takes us to Kailash, when Lord Shiva's deep meditation was disturbed by Lord Kama Deva. In a fit of rage, Shiva opened his third eye and burned Kama Deva to ashes. From the remains of Kama Deva emerged a demon named Bhanda. After performing a deep penance, Bhanda gained a boon from Lord Shiva that he would not be defeated by one born out of sexual union. Thus started Bhanda's reign of terror across the heavens and the earth. All the devas were completely fed up with the wreckage and nuisance caused by Bhanda and took the form of parrots. They left their abodes and went to Kanchipuram, where they sat atop a Champaka tree and worshipped Goddess Tripura Sundari for a solution. The goddess thus appeared before them in a ferocious form and defeated Bhanda. However, even after his death, her anger could not be calmed. The devas tried their best to calm down her rage, but their efforts were in vain. Suddenly, she took the form of the beautiful goddess Kamakshi, adorned in stunning gold jewellery, and all the devas started to worship her. To this day, Goddess Kamakshi is highly revered in Kanchipuram, and the town is visited by many pilgrims who wish to seek her blessings.

I was happy to see that my painting was coming out quite beautifully, but there was something else that really bothered me. My legs felt completely numb, as though the blood circulation had been cut off. They felt as heavy as rocks. I found it increasingly hard to concentrate on the strokes. I decided to take a short break and went for a stroll, but when I came back and sat down to continue my painting, the pain started again. It felt as intense as labour pain and consumed me from all sides of my body. I felt extremely exhausted yet strong for powering through it.

Nothing seemed to get in the way of the painting process. It felt as though the two experiences were independent from one another. My hands moved perfectly as I expressed her energies on the canvas in bright red hues. I went to bed early that night and listened to soothing music as I prayed to her that all must be well. I woke up a little before dawn to find that I was bleeding. It seemed like it was my period, but I was going through menopause at the time. I wondered if the pain I had experienced the previous night was due to this. I hurriedly changed my clothes and went back to sleep.

I woke up the next morning and went about my usual routine. I used the washroom and was shocked to see that I was passing blood even in my motions. I took a bath, prayed, and decided to wait until that afternoon before doing anything further.

Later that day, I was completely overcome by tiredness and decided to call a friend, Dr Deepa Senthil.

"This does not sound safe. Visit a doctor immediately," she said.

Her words gave me a fright, and my body chose to freeze.

"I will wait for a day. If I am still not alright tomorrow, I will go," I replied.

I continued to paint, more focused and invested than ever. I prayed deeply.

"You take care of me! My health is in your hands. I am afraid to visit a doctor. Who is a greater doctor than you in the entire universe?" I said to the goddess's energies. I had vowed that whatever the health issue was, I would deal with it only once I was done with my painting of Kamakshi. In hindsight, this was definitely a risky decision. I have never been one to leave my fate to the gods. I believe that one must do the bare minimum of controlling whatever is in their hands and then let go. After all, as the saying goes, "God only helps those who help themselves". But for some reason, I was stubborn at the time and really did believe that I would be okay. I just wished to focus on the task at hand, for the time being at least.

I consumed cooling food items to soothe my body or soothe the burning energies of the goddess that had taken over me and continued to paint. Despite bleeding so profusely, I did not feel any tiredness. On the contrary, I felt completely invigorated. I meditated on all my chakras and prayed to her and my guru to protect me from any danger and help me navigate through this phase. Kamakshi bloomed, looking magnificent and powerful, right in front of me and my lovely parrot, Meetu, who sat on my shoulders, silently supporting me through the process.

66

Yogini Maheshwari

After my painting of Goddess Kamakshi, I was still unwell and suffered the same physical conditions, but the fear of the unknown had left my body, mind, and soul. I started to ignore all bodily reactions. This might seem risky, but I completely surrendered to the goddess and knew that she would protect me. My body seemed to act as the obstacle, but I persevered with razor-sharp focus. My soul and my body felt almost disconnected from one another, and my soul was in a different realm of being. I owe this ability to disassociate to my practice of meditation. My body rested as I painted with my soul. My heart felt tender, and my mind was completely clear of all thoughts and inhibitions. I had been meditating for several years leading up to these moments, but nothing so far had come close to feeling this way. The sensations I felt in every chakra were heightened.

The colours that touched the canvas were fresh and saturated, and the goddess's skin looked as soft and supple as that of a newborn. She was in a state of complete balance and peace.

The emotional, spiritual, and physical states required for a sustainable life need the energies of Shiva and Shakti to work in complete harmony with one another.

Goddess Maheshwari, one of the eight original mother goddesses or the Ashta Matrikas, is the feminine manifestation of Lord Shiva, who is also referred to as Lord Maheshwar. She is Shakti who works in tandem with Shiva to maintain the cosmic balance. Maheshwari is a fierce warrior, born out of the third eye of Goddess Brahmani to fight the demon king Raktabeeja. She is also the protector of Goddess Parvati in the absence of Lord Shiva.

Maheshwari is the ultimate protector. She is deeply empathetic. An interesting tale involving Goddess Maheshwari talks about a demon called Durgam who had pleased Lord Brahma and gained a boon that he would be undefeatable in wars. With such power in hand, he started to torment the rest of the deities. As a result, a severe drought began that lasted for about 100 years. The people shared their worries, depressing stories, and consequences of the drought with the goddess. The goddess was deeply moved on hearing all this, and she wept for nine days and nights. Her tears flowed as a river, which ended the drought.

On the surface, Maheshwari's intimidating look and similarities to Lord Shiva can tend to cause fear, but at her core, she is one of us, protecting us from within the circle. She feels the pain of others as her own and wholeheartedly shields them with all her might. She also symbolises "anger", and one may rid themselves of their temper by worshipping her. My understanding is that the goddess embodies one's ability to be tuned to another's emotions, which ultimately leads to unity in defeating evil.

In our daily lives, we often play many roles. I play the artist, the wife, the mother, the daughter, and, most importantly, the devotee. In this case, the goddess's energies urged me to tune into other aspects within myself so that all facets could work in union to heal my body. It felt as though different parts of me were experiencing different phases of life, as though my soul had been split in two, interlinked yet completely independent from one another. Spiritually, I felt at peace, and yet, there seemed to be a part of my mind that held on to some fear. I thought it was about time that I spoke to someone about my mental and physical state. I thought that my earlier discussions with Vishwanathan of Sumeru about Kali had given rise to this fear.

I called my dear friend Jasyindar again, the same man who had introduced me to Mr Vishwanathan of Sumeru. I mentioned to him the fear I had experienced after speaking to the latter.

"I have felt a divine presence surrounding you, but I also do not think it is the goddess Kali," he continued.

I was not sure what to say in response.

"The last time I visited India, I brought you a book about Goddess Kali and a book about Goddess Bala Tripura Sundari for another friend. However, when I visited you, I felt it more apt to give you the book on Bala Tripura Sundari, rather than Kali. You have a childlike innocence and energy surrounding you," he added.

I had entirely forgotten about this book and felt a twinge of guilt for not having read it earlier.

"Please find it and read it," he said.

I searched the entire house for the book and finally found it. Unfortunately, it was in Sanskrit. However, the photo of Bala Tripura Sundari filled my heart with intense joy. I held that book close to my heart and kept it on my bedside table. After I was done with my painting of Maheshwari, I took a break for a few days and prayed.

67

Yogini Kumari (Bala Tripura Sundari)

A great silence surrounded and prevailed within me. I delved deeper into it, hoping to gain wisdom from the higher realms. As per the Hirapur list of goddesses, I was supposed to paint Goddess Kumari. She was depicted as standing on a scorpion. I kept my canvas ready, but my mind was completely blank.

One evening, I was resting, my physical body sitting completely at ease, but there was a certain energy that seemed to resonate deep within. I felt a certain divine vibration deep within my heart, almost like it had skipped a beat. The beat echoed within me. I focused and tried to connect with my pure consciousness. I remember the blankness I felt quite vividly. Yet, I felt a sense of restlessness, and my heart pounded deep within my chest. I was not quite sure whether I should get worried or not. There was a continual conversation happening between myself and Goddess Bala Tripura Sundari, whom I treated as my confidante by this point. I focused on speaking to her and calmed my body down.

That very evening, I got a call from my dear friend Jasyindar.

"Why don't you visit the Nemili Bala Tripura Sundari Temple?" he asked.

I took his suggestion quite seriously and decided to do so. Afterall, I felt a special connection with her energy. I was also advised by him to buy some chocolates as an offering to the goddess.

I was not aware of where Nemili was and decided to ask my husband.

"Back then when I was in the National Cadet Corps, I was posted in Kanchipuram and had visited an educational institution in Nemili. I am in contact with one of my colleagues at the school," he replied.

I grew quite excited and hurriedly urged him to speak to that person. He made the call and found out that the temple was quite close to the colleague's home.

"Normally, we would have to make an appointment to visit the temple and the priest, but since I know them, I will take you there," he said.

He asked me to ring him up as I approached the temple premises and said that he would take me inside.

I stepped out and bought several chocolates, including Kinder Joy. Shaped like an egg, it has a toy inside it and is adored by many children. My son was very fond of it as well. So I bought a few of them.

I started on my journey to Nemili the next morning, and as usual, I fell asleep in the car as soon as I stepped in.

I was suddenly awoken from a deep sleep by the driver who informed me that we had reached the location as mentioned on the GPS. We had entered a small street, but there was no temple in sight. In the middle of the road, there stood a man who asked us to stop. He approached my window and asked me to lower it. I did so.

"I was waiting for you. Please come," he slowly said.

"I am here to visit the Bala Tripura Sundari Temple," I responded.

"Yes, I am aware. Please follow me," he said.

I suddenly thought it was the man to whom my husband had spoken the previous day. I immediately called my husband

and enquired if the colleague had called. He said no. I called up the colleague. He asked me to wait for him and further informed me that we must call and make an appointment to visit and can do so only after 9 a.m.

I was confused because here there was a man standing outside, waiting for me to accompany him inside. I stepped out and followed him. To my surprise, it was a small house. I asked him where the temple was.

"This is called the Nemili Bala Tripura Sundari Peedam. It is treated as a house and not a temple," he replied.

The house was a small one, and in the centre was an altar for the deity. There was an older person seated in the room as well. Noticing me, he said, "You are her guest now. You are not here because you wanted to visit but because she wanted to meet you."

His words rang through my ears, igniting a certain deep reverence for her.

I went and sat next to him. His next few words were extremely powerful, and they give me chills to this very day. He continued, "She came to you in your dreams a few months ago, and you asked her not to trouble you. She sits on your lap as you paint, and yet you never recognised her presence."

I was dumbstruck in awe. Not knowing what to say or how to react, I just started crying.

From the chocolates I had presented to her, the older man took a blue Kinder Joy egg and gave it back to me. I sat there for some time, taking in all her glory.

The Nemili Bala is the size of a little finger. Her story is incredibly enlightening and interesting.

Once, the goddess appeared in the dreams of a great devotee, Sri Subramania Iyer, asking him to fetch her from the Kushasthalai river. For the next couple of days, he searched the river far and wide but to no avail. Finally, one day, he found this small bronze statue, the size of a little finger. He placed it at the centre of his house, and this place came to be known as the Bala Peedam.

I started on my journey back home in an incredibly drowsy state. I felt extremely tired and sleepy and started to dream. There were flashes of the little girl who had visited me in my dreams a few months earlier. She came in, smiling, held my hand, and tried to pull me up. I told her that I was tired, but she pulled me up anyway and walked with me through the hills, meadows, and other such scenic locations.

I awoke again from my slumber when I had reached home. I dragged myself out of the car with much difficulty and was approached by my husband. I told him how tired I was and that I wanted to sleep. I dragged myself up the stairs and into my bedroom and just crashed on my bed. I dove into a deep slumber. Somehow, I was still conscious and aware and tried to get up, but I felt dizzy. I swirled deeper and deeper into sleep. I let go of control and fell asleep instantly.

I felt the presence of someone walking next to me. The presence was very soft, and a beautiful fragrance lingered in the room. A hand as soft as a petal touched me, like that of a young girl. I tried to open my eyes, and there was a strong beam of light. I could not open them fully, but I tried my best. What I witnessed was surreal, the kind of beauty one cannot put into words.

A beautiful, young, and plump girl stood before me, with hair as lustrous as the moon, wearing a peach-coloured skirt full of bright stones that flashed a lovely bright light. Her little toes stuck out from beneath the skirt. I have never seen a more beautiful girl. Her skin was the shade of a lotus flower, a light pink. She was adorned in beautiful jewellery. Her lips were red, and her eyes were tender. I immediately got up. She held both my hands and wore a smile that could comfort me even at my absolute worst. She was the very same girl who had visited me in my dreams, and she called out to me, saying "Ma".

"I do not want anything. I do not want you to perform any poojas. All I want is to be with you. Feed me what you feed yourself and keep me in your heart always. There must be no fear within you."

She hugged me softly, and I felt her spirit merge with mine. Even today, as I write this, I can sense her smiling inside me, nodding at my humble attempt to express her.

The feeling was one that cannot be expressed but one that must be experienced, one that must be realised. I slowly slipped back into a deep sleep as she patted my forehead and I held her soft, tender hands in my own. I slept like a log.

I woke up later that evening when my son came to call me. I shared my experience with him and handed over the blue Kinder Joy. He asked me why I had taken the blue one, since blue was meant for boys. There was a pink variant meant especially for girls, which would have a toy for girls. We opened the chocolate, and to my surprise, the little figurine inside it was that of a girl, Superwoman. I was incredibly overwhelmed to see that. It was a message meant specially for me from Bala, my superpower. That was what my next painting had to be.

Even in her origin stories, she is portrayed as a feminine superpower with a childlike innocence yet the fierceness of a goddess. According to the *Brahmanda Purana*, Goddess Bala Tripura Sundari is said to be the daughter of the all-prevailing feminine power, Sri Lalitha Tripura Sundari. *Bala* literally translates to "child". In the war between the demon Bhandasura and Goddess Lalitha, after she killed his brothers,

Bala Tripura Sundari was a young girl of merely nine. She requested her mother to let her fight in the war, but the latter naturally had her apprehensions owing to her daughter's young age. The young girl insisted on joining the battle against evil, and her mother eventually gave in. She handed Bala Tripura Sundari her own armour and a few weapons. Ultimately, Bala Tripura Sundari slew the thirty sons of Bhandasura in the battle. She truly was a "super woman" in every aspect. A brave young girl, she refused to see her age as an obstacle and courageously stood against injustice.

The awareness of her, the supreme consciousness, made me feel complete bliss, like I was on top of the world. I enjoyed the gush of energy that passed through me while painting her. I felt her presence and witnessed her aura. It was truly unbelievable.

68

Yogini Vindyabalini (Kurukulla)

By the time I got to painting Vindyabalini, I felt a strong sense of confidence. It felt as though I had already witnessed her powers and encountered her energy in the past. I was able to connect with her presence quite quickly, and this time I had the blessing of Bala Tripura Sundari to help me navigate through the experience. The fear in my mind was completely erased.

Vindyabalini emerged looking vibrant. Physically, I felt light-headed and as though I had been streamlined into the larger conscience. I felt a sense of belonging. I knew this was all part of a larger master plan and I was a mere medium. I needed to let loose and let the goddesses do the talking through me.

Vindyabalini was pretty, sharp, and youthful. I drew parallels between her and Kurukella, a popular deity worshipped in Vajrayana Buddhism. She is said to be a symbol of omniscience or infinite knowledge, driven with passionate and selfless love and compassion for all of humanity. She is said to be a form of Shakti that preserves the universe. In Buddhism, she is also said to be associated with the intense emotions of love, passion, and more.

In a Buddhist-inspired story, an elderly queen, neglected by her king, desperately seeks to regain his affection. She sends her servant to the marketplace in search of a mystical solution. There, a red-skinned woman provides enchanted food with powerful mantras to capture the king's heart. However, doubting its suitability for royalty, the queen discards the meal into a nearby lake. This act of rejection unwittingly ensnares a serpent king residing in the lake, who becomes infatuated with the queen after consuming the enchanted offering. This magical connection results in the queen's unexpected pregnancy.

Upon discovering the pregnancy, the king, although not the father, plans to punish the queen. But, after hearing the entire story, he summons the mysterious woman from the market instead. Recognising her as a being of extraordinary power, the king bows and seeks her blessing. She grants him the Kurukulla mantra and the spiritual name "Sahajavajra", bestowing him remarkable abilities.

Even today, in the small marketplaces of Tibet, certain tantric practitioners offer love spells and potions in the name of Goddess Kurukella.

In the *Lalitha Sahasranamam*, she dwells in the Srichakra, between the ego and the consciousness, and controls the antahkarana, which refers to the mind, the body, and the intellect. She controls our subtle body. Kurukella has more significance in Buddhism, but in the Srividya ideology, she plays an important role. She is one of the two limbs of Goddess Lalitha, the other being Goddess Varahi who controls the bone.

69

Yogini Vinayaki

In mythology, Lord Ganesha is commonly referred to as Vinayak and is often worshipped as a symbol of universal intelligence and wisdom. This intelligence is the bridge between the physical and spiritual realm, and his dutiful devotees pray to be blessed with an understanding of the workings of the universe. Ganesha reminds us that true intelligence is linked to a certain divine essence that exists within every single living being. Therefore, we have the innate ability to connect with a higher realm but only once we clear our clouded minds.

The manifestation of intelligence in any realm of creation depends upon the harmonious convergence of Purusha, the male aspect or transcendental consciousness, and Prakriti, the female aspect, embodying material nature. Out of this sacred union emerges universal intellect, sending light and awareness to the ethereal and material dimensions of existence.

This interwoven nature of the self and the body sustains the presence of cognitive abilities. The same energy moves through the physical plane as enlightenment. The route to enlightenment is not linear or uniform. When a person gets rid of ego and learns how to absorb this dynamic environment that presents itself in the form of individualised experiences, it brings them closer to their true nature and purpose. This path moulds their cognitive abilities, which leads to a personal evolution. This evolution can only occur through continuous self-reflection and awareness.

If you slash your ego and seek the truth with pure intentions, the truth will reveal itself in all its glory.

In this journey with my trusted companion, my blank canvas, I was undergoing the process of learning and unlearning, the interplay between true universal knowledge and ignorance and perceived knowledge. These realisations led me to Siddhi and Buddhi, the two feminine energies commonly associated with Lord Ganesha. As per mythology, Siddhi and Buddhi are the consorts of Ganesha and the daughters of the almighty creator, Brahma. In Hinduism, Ganesha holds quite an exalted position and is worshipped by all, regardless of culture.

Vinayaki's origin story, as that of most other yoginis, takes us to the story of Shiva, Parvati, and the demon Andaka. When Andaka abducted Parvati, he was impaled by Shiva with his trident. However, owing to a boon Andaka had received years earlier, from every drop of blood that fell to the ground rose another Andaka. He multiplied and grew stronger. At this point, Parvati knew she needed all the help she could get to defeat him. So, she called for all the gods. Every deity is a blend of masculine and feminine energies, and from each one of them arose their female aspects. From Ganesha emerged Vinayaki. The goddesses drank each drop of blood before it fell to the ground, and eventually, Andaka was defeated.

In certain Puranas, Vinayaki is also perceived as Malini, a female companion of Parvati. She represents Shakti, the feminine aspect that stands for material and tangible things and is popularly revered in the tantric practice.

Painting Vinayaki felt like a celebration of my journey thus far and a complete cleansing of my spirit. A channel of wisdom passed through me with every unlearning as I released my ego, detrimental thoughts, and negative energies and chose the path of real wisdom.

70

Yogini Bhadrakali

Bhadrakali is a name that has been embedded in my system ever since my early childhood days spent in Kerala. Bhadrakali is revered as the family deity of several prominent families in Kerala, including mine. My family temple exists in a place called Mannady. It is said that three women visited the banks of a river called Kallada. From there, they visited three places, two in Mannady and one in Pattazhy, and they are said to have been worshipped as the goddesses of those places. Out of the three, one was an older woman, who is the one present in our temple. The sanctum sanctorum is open with wooden grills because her power was so strong that she could not be confined to closed walls. We call her the Mannady Amma. My salutations to her.

I wondered why I did not experience any fear of encountering her energy. She gave off a very different energy than that of Kali's.

A peculiarity in temples in Kerala is that the deity is invoked in a metal mirror called the Kannadi Bimbam, which is placed within the temple premises in the sanctum sanctorum for worship. I assumed that the mirror is placed so that devotees can take in her form more easily. The mirror acts as a portal between our world and hers, so the devotees can reach out to her divinity. Notably, a mirror shows a person a reflection of themselves. I wondered if this was a metaphor for connecting with the divinity that exists within oneself.

"*Aham Brahmasmi*" (I am Brahman) is the first thought that comes to mind when I look at my reflection in this mirror.

The mirror is a powerful visual representation of the concept that we are eternal, thus, reiterating the timeless wisdom of our scriptures that state that the deity and the worshipper are expressions of one supreme deity. We are all tributaries that flow and converge at one large cosmic ocean.

Having the metal mirror is a common practice in temples in Kerala. It is a part of tantric worship to revere abstract forms of the deities. Devotees must delve deep into their worship to find a reflection of themselves in the Divine, because God exists within each and every one of us as our conscience.

Clearly, the lessons each goddess taught me were things I needed to know at the time. These lessons reflected my current mental state. I started to think of my dear mentor, Dr David, again. It was with him that I had visited several Bhadrakali temples in Kerala, as I had mentioned in some of the earlier chapters. The goddess approached me with the tenderness of a mother's touch. As I painted her, the memories of my past came rushing to me. I enjoyed the wonderful nostalgia and felt truly liberated as I painted her.

Since time immemorial, Goddess Bhadrakali has been considered a symbol of courage and strength. Though she is generally portrayed with rage emanating from her red eyes, she is also the enhancer of the human soul and, deep inside, the one who, out of her mercy, desires only welfare and wellness for her people and this world. Many artists have tried to portray both her sides in their paintings: compassion, where she is benevolent, and destruction, where she is bloodthirsty out of rage.

Bhadrakali is an ancient deity who is a crucial part of the Hindu mythology. The worship of Kali and her eight other forms arose during the times of Shaivism. The goddess is worshipped in many regions, and in the southern state of Kerala, she has no mercy or a sense of compassion for those who wrong others and commit injustices. She is benevolent, but the ones who bring nothing but harm are punished.

Her origin story, as documented in the *Markandeya Purana*, talks about a demon named Darika. Darika was married to Mandodari, who was a devoted and doting wife. Mandodari knew of a special chant or mantra that would keep the husband completely invincible so that the marriage would stay safe. Darika used this to his advantage and tormented the deities.

The deities invoked Shiva, who, in a fit of rage, opened his third eye and unleashed Goddess Bhadrakali. However, she found it almost impossible to defeat Darika as he was protected by his wife's chants. Bhadrakali devised a plan and split herself into two, one the furious warrior and the other a common woman. The common woman approached Mandodari in tears, claiming to be the wife of a man that had died in the battle. Momentarily, Mandodari stopped her chant to console the woman. The warrior half of Bhadrakali used this window of time to defeat Darika.

She took the stance of a warrior, with Darika's head under her feet, about to decapitate him, when he decided to appeal to her motherly side for forgiveness. Bhadrakali, no matter how fierce or angry, still had the essence of motherhood within her. She still had the qualities of forgiveness and compassion. The other deities, panicked at the thought of her forgiving Darika, surrounded her to sing songs in her praise as a reminder of the grave sins he had committed. Suddenly, she came to her senses and brutally decapitated him. Even today, common iconography shows Bhadrakali standing with one foot on Darika's head.

Her anger was great, and she continued to dance around the battlefield, fuming with a rage that could not be calmed by even the mightiest of gods. The deities finally appealed to Shiva again, who took the form of a crying baby called Gandakarna. The goddess's motherliness was awakened at the sight of the child, and she quickly calmed down. Bhadrakali is the idol of Kodungallur Bhagavathy Temple in the Thrissur district of Kerala and protects all her devotees with the fierceness of a mother's love. Against convention, she is also revered with respect to martial arts in Kerala. Her devotees believe that her blessings led to the people of the Malabar area in Kerala achieving great success in traditional martial arts.

Despite her warrior persona, the energy she approached me with was that of a loving mother. Everything started to make sense. The vibration was different from what I had expected. She connected me to my roots in Kerala, the place of my birth, where she remains to this day, protecting her devotees with all her might.

71

Yogini Bhairavi

I was very happy about having started on this journey with no expectations, no direction, and no destination in mind. There was an intense force within me that kept me going. The presence of my guide and guru was so strong that it moved me. Knowing that I was able to comprehend even 1 per cent of the energies of the goddesses kept me motivated because of how overwhelming and powerful they were.

Bhairavi was a familiar name, obviously because of my previous encounters with Lord Bhairava. The name *Bhairava* had been seeded in my mind early on in my spiritual journey and had been reinstated by Dr David. As mentioned in earlier chapters, Bhairava seemed like an old friend and reminded me of sweet times. I considered him my guide in this project, and because of that, I experienced a similar feeling of familiarity with Bhairavi.

Once one realises that the Divine is present within oneself, it is important to stay rooted with one's feet standing strongly on the ground, looking out for the betterment of oneself and for the rest of humanity. I felt very grounded in her embrace.

It is often said about Bhairava that if you worship him with utmost sincerity, he will lead you to your guru. Bhairava opens your system, flushes out any negativity, and shows you that he is the ultimate guru.

A lot of deities in ancient Hinduism dwell in the grey area. They are extremely benevolent and kind to the good and to their devotees but wrathful and unforgiving to sinners. A goddess that fits this description perfectly is Bhairavi. There is generally a certain negative identity attached to Bhairavi and understandably so. She is an all-consuming, fuming force that symbolises destruction. What is important to understand here is that everything does eventually come to an end. The worship of Bhairavi encourages detachment, so that one may freely let go and be open to new beginnings.

Bhairavi's origin can be traced back to the time Shiva was married to Sati. When Sati's father, Daksha, organised a grand event and chose not to invite the newly married couple out of dislike for Shiva's yogic way, Sati was enraged. She pleaded with Shiva to let her attend, but he denied her permission, afraid that she would be humiliated by her father. Sati, in a fit of rage, manifested ten goddesses for each of the cardinal directions that surrounded Shiva. One of these was Goddess Bhairavi, a by-product of Sati's anger and persistence. Just as Lord Shiva is known as the destroyer, Bhairavi is an extension of this quality. When death occurs and when the process of decay is underway, she rises. It is a natural process, and Bhairavi is the embodiment of the inevitable. Without destruction, there can be no further creation.

However, I felt a certain sense of security in her aura. I wondered if she was also the goddess of protection. After completing her painting, I lit a lamp and placed it in front of her, turned on some music, and started to meditate. But I fell asleep. Usually, when this happens, no one in my family even attempts to awake me or disturb me, owing to my unusual sleeping patterns. After a while, I randomly awoke in the middle of the night, slightly disoriented. My eyes opened to her beautifully haunting image, lit by the lamp that still burned brightly. It felt as though she was keenly watching me.

I looked around and saw my pet dog, Simba, in a prostrating position right in front of the painting, and on the painting, I saw the reflection of another dog observing the goddess. I cannot really put into words how incredibly beautiful that moment was. I was touched and kept looking at her. She had a reassuring look, easing me back into a deep slumber.

72

Yogini Yasha (Yakshini)

The interplay of infinite cosmic energies and pure consciousness is a magical recipe that takes one beyond the limitation of doubts, logical reasoning, and fears. It allows one to embrace the newer vibrations and gives a person a deeper awareness of their communication patterns.

Many goddesses have left their influence on me or have made their mark without my knowledge. In this journey, I may have formed a strong connection with each of them. I felt like a little girl, scurrying about in temples and collecting small pebbles and flowers, completely lost in joy. In this process, I truly believe that I must have caught their gaze, which was the only explanation for how divinely guided and protected I had been feeling. I was aligning with a strong divine presence, and my mind peacefully danced to the enchanting, yet previously unheard, ethereal drums.

A gentle breeze passed by, carrying an intensely beautiful fragrance, settling me in my space with the scent of the seasonal blossoms. It awakened my senses and immersed me in its intoxicating aroma. The breeze caressed my skin, delicately and sensually, like a soft fabric enveloping me, leaving me with feelings of exquisite pleasure.

On my canvas, Yakshini had a piercing gaze that followed me as I moved around the room. This left me pondering on whether we had crossed paths before. There were whispers of her in my past that I started to recognise.

All the goddesses I had painted up until that point came out quite beautifully, and Yakshini, too, elicited a similar feeling within me. I found myself looking in the mirror, feeling immense self-love. A divine presence stood beside me, showering her blessings. The ripples of positivity she exuded calmed my mind with peace and happiness.

Yakshinis and yakshas are said to be spirits or paranormal beings in Hinduism, Buddhism, and Jainism. These deities are said to protect material abundance and treasures related to wealth, property, inheritance, and more. They are said to live in a different spiritual realm from other higher beings and deities. I saw Yakshini as the guardian of worldly and materialistic belongings since she, along with her male counterpart, is said to have been worshipped for fertility and wealth.

In certain texts, Kubera, the partially divine god-king and half-brother of Ravana, is said to be the caretaker of the treasures of the world, and he, too, is said to be a yaksha. In the tantric practice, Yakshini is also worshipped to find spiritual enlightenment. She represents abundance in all aspects: material, worldly, and spiritual.

In her embrace, I discovered a newfound expansion within my mind, my heart, and my soul. My vibrations soared towards realms of genuine abundance—an abundance of love for myself, the people I hold close, and her. To me, she also represented protective aspects of oneself that make one's life experience a whole lot richer and fulfilling.

73

Yogini Sarpasha (Surasa)

The moment I placed the next empty canvas on the stand, I found myself slipping into the next goddess's embrace. This was the impact Bala Tripura Sundari had on me. I often spoke to her and confided in her about my journey. We had long conversations, and I could feel a strong mother–daughter bond building between us. She held a very special place in my heart.

The word *Sarpasha* was familiar. I had been exposed to the word *Sarpa* early on in my spiritual journey thanks to Dr David. The word refers to the snake gods. Dr David often performed poojas to the snake gods. They are commonly worshipped in the southern states of India. Oftentimes, when he would perform this sarpa pooja, I would notice a projection or shadow shaped like a snake's hood on his forehead. The memories took me back in time to one of our pilgrimages to the temple town of Tirupati in Andhra Pradesh. He informed me the previous evening that he would have to wake up early to perform pooja and that I could enter his hotel room without knocking to avoid disturbing his prayers. The next morning, I arose and entered his room quietly, as instructed by him. He was in a deep prayer, completely engrossed. What I witnessed that day still surprises me.

As he prayed, I observed his back, especially his spine, rise slowly, like a snake, as he breathed in and out. The texture of his skin had faint marks like the scales on a snake. I was not stunned, but I was not quite sure how to react. I did not quite know if I could believe my eyes. After a while, he looked towards me and leaned slightly forwards. The light caught his face, and his eyes gleamed like those of a snake. Not a single word escaped my mouth. I did not ask any questions. All I intended to do was enjoy the energies as I considered this a great blessing. Ironically, at the time, I was not even aware that he was performing a sarpa pooja. Later, at breakfast, I told him what I had seen, and that was when he told me. Even as I write this, I find myself getting goosebumps. That experience will be etched in my mind forever.

He explained to me his passion for snake worship and the role snakes play in our lives. Earlier, there was a certain fear in my mind about snake worship. This experience started to dispel the fear, and I started to become more receptive to their powers, thereby allowing me to receive their blessings.

I had made several paintings of the sarpa deva (snake god) early on. Dr David had a very scientific and spiritualistic approach to the worship of the snake deity. Initially, I had my inhibitions about painting these gods. I was nervous to delve into their energies, but he assured me that, as a woman from a Nair family in Kerala, I belonged to the Nagavamshi clan (considered descendants of the mythical nagas) and, therefore, was blessed at birth by the Sarpa devas.

There is a lot of mysticism around snakes. They are the symbol of rebirth, transformation, immortality, healing, psychic energy, wealth, wisdom, and the cycle of life and death. They are also said to be the protectors of the earth. Mystics around the world are familiar with the concept of vital energy or Kundalini Shakti, the essence upon which we are built. This union of masculine and feminine energies is represented by the symbol of two snakes with a stick and wings to represent healing, as is evident from the logo of the World Health Organization.

As per several beliefs, Maharishi Patanjali, the author of the *Yoga Sutra*, is said to be the incarnation of Anantha Sesha or the holy snake of Maha Vishnu. The shedding of snakeskin exemplifies the transition between life and death and the rebirth cycle. It is a powerful energy. There is so much to know about the universe, so much to delve into.

To my understanding, Sarpasha bore several similarities to Surasa, a deity from the Treta Yuga when Lord Rama walked the earth. She is mentioned in the Ramayana as one of the twelve daughters of King Daksha, one of the wives of Sage Kashyapa, and mother to the Naga class of serpent deities.

There is a popular tale involving her mentioned in several Puranic texts from the times of the Ramayana. When Lord Hanuman left for Lanka to rescue Sita from the clutches of Ravana, the gods wished to test his strength and powers to see if he would be capable enough to do the job. They assigned Surasa to take the form of a demoness.

Thus, she appeared in front of him, with "yellow eyes and a pair of jaws fanged and gaping", the size of a mountain. She claimed that Hanuman is the food provided to her for consumption by the gods, and that as per a boon granted to her, the only way he could pass was through her mouth. She opened her mouth wide to the size of a 100 yojanas to consume him, but in that moment, he used his intelligence and shrunk himself to the size of a thumb. He entered her mouth and exited her body from the inside. This way, he fulfilled her boon and also figured out how to continue his journey. Impressed by his quick thinking and strength, Surasa blessed Hanuman.

Yet another story associated with her that draws parallels with the other yoginis, as per the *Shiva Purana*, is that Surasa was one of the goddesses called upon by Lord Shiva to consume the drops of blood of the demon King Andaka, as mentioned in previous chapters, thereby defeating him.

In my astrological chart, Ketu and Rahu take up an important space. To pay my respects, I have a snake drawn in all my paintings as a spectator.

I was filled with the tremendous energy and wisdom that I had accumulated through the years while working with Dr David, to paint Sarpasha or Surasa, the mother of the nagas.

74

Yogini Karkari

In earlier chapters of this book, I had mentioned how I chose to paint the yoginis with no point of reference and just as how I had visualised them. I naturally gravitated towards whatever resonated with me and painted what came to mind. With Goddess Karkari, for some reason, I associated her with crabs. In my painting, she stood on a mountain crab. My choice of colours was extremely different. The name *Karkari* and her association with crabs seemed to have some connection with astrology.

In the place I hail from, Kerala, astrology has a deep relevance and is well explored. I have previously painted a series on the nakshatras as well. I inferred that Karkari had to be a yogini connected the same, owing to the meaning of her name.

In Kerala, Karkidakam is a holy month, often called the Ramayana Masam. The month got its name because the sun transits from the house of Cancer to the next house. Several people also perform Ayurvedic treatment during this month to cleanse the body and mind.

Karkidaka Rashi (the zodiac sign Cancer or the crab) is governed by the moon. The moon is the lord of mental health and spirituality. The water sign Cancer is denoted by the symbol of the crab, and its ruling deity is the moon. Even crabs cast off their shells for rebirth and rejuvenation. In Tamil Nadu, there are temples dedicated to this rashi. People visit these temples to rectify the malefic effect of these planets and stars. I spoke to a friend about this temple to know if there was anything that would support my thought process. After hearing the stories about the temple, I added small elements from the temple to complete my painting. Not just that, while painting her, I experienced a great sense of healing and rejuvenation. Everything was getting connected.

Thousands of years ago, Sage Durvasa conducted a ritual for Lord Shiva. During this, a celestial form from the Deva Loga (abode of the Devas) appeared and impersonated a crab to mock the sage. The former was enraged and cursed the latter to take the form of a crab. When the celestial realised who the sage was and his importance, he immediately sought forgiveness. The sage told him that he had to learn his lesson and experience the punishment. To be released from the curse, he had to perform a pooja every day and offer a lotus flower to Shiva. In due time, Shiva himself would manifest and relieve the celestial from the curse and turn him back to his celestial form. The crab then descended on earth, and the location it first appeared was named the Karkateshwarar Temple.

There was a large lotus pond at that temple. So the crab had no difficulty in finding one. Lord Indra, too, was performing a pooja for Shiva, to regain the powers he lost after fighting several battles with the Asuras. On the advice of Lord Guru (Jupiter), he had to offer 1,008 lotuses to Shiva every day for forty-eight days. Varuna was assigned the task of making sure that there were exactly 1,008 lotuses for the pooja. Unaware of this, the crab would take one of the 1,008 lotuses every day and place it on the Shiva linga. Indra was clueless and performed the pooja with only 1,007 flowers every day.

One fine day, Lord Guru pointed this out to Indra. The next day before the pooja, Indra, too, noticed the crab taking the lotus. Consumed by anger, he lifted his sword to kill the crab, but at that very moment, a hole appeared on the Shiva linga and the crab escaped. Shiva asked Indra to perform a pooja for another 1,008 days to get back his powers and restored the crab to his original celestial form. Lord Shiva remained at that spot, deep under the ground.

Thousands of years later, Lord Shiva and Parvati disguised themselves as physicians and healed a king from severe paralysis. The next day, when the physicians returned, the king offered them a lot of wealth and requested them to stay in the palace as in-house physicians. However, they informed him of the land where the story of the crab took place. They asked him to dig the ground to find a Shiva linga and proposed the idea of building a temple around it. The king followed their orders and built the temple. Along with the Shiva linga, he also installed a stone idol of Parvati. The word spread. The Shiva linga came to be known as Karkateshwarar, and the goddess was known as Arumarundunnayaki. They were the gods of healing. The stories, sub-stories, the practices, and the science are all interlinked. Important and relevant information was passed through stories to preserve them. Karkari is the goddess of medicine, and this tale is a testament to that fact.

75

Yogini Rathi

I was finally at the sixty-third painting. Looking back, everything I had experienced had brought different fears of mine to the forefront and helped me address them, thereby enhancing and understanding the different expressions of the powers of the goddesses. I knew I was going through something life-changing, and I was on a path that changed me, not just as a person but also as an artist.

I have always been fascinated by nude painting and wanted to try my hand at it as well, but I always hesitated. I was concerned about the way people would perceive me as I assumed there would be a certain taboo attached to it. So, I never pursued it.

Around twenty-five years ago, a dear friend of mine had brought me a gig: to paint a large nude portrait for a hotel. My husband was not very pleased with the idea. He has never been one to stop me from doing anything, but when he showed his displeasure, I decided to not take it up. Nor did I have the patience or maturity back then to discuss it with him.

I sat in front of my canvas and decided that I would paint the way I had addressed all my previous paintings. I would not compromise on thought. I knew that I was on a bigger plane here, and I had a purpose to fulfil. To be clear, there was no "I" in this journey. I was merely a medium through which the Divine could express themselves.

Sexual union is generally viewed in a very positive light in Hinduism. The coming together of lovers in intense sexual unison is celebrated, as it is, at its core—a means of expressing endearment and the merging of souls. A union that symbolises this passion of love is that of Kama Deva (the god of love) and his wife—Goddess Rathi.

Physical union is not just about "sex" though. It is also about our sense of self and our ability to go and achieve what we set out to do. The passion is one and the same. It is an energy that connects us with our excellence and creativity. There is a union that happens within. Through the goddess's energies, I discovered the ability to go beyond just the physical.

Rathi stands for transcendence of energy and the awakening of the spiritual dimensions within oneself, cleansing negativity to achieve a greater purpose. The name *Rathi* means pleasure. She is the goddess of love. My heart was filled with love and passion as I painted her. I finished my base sketch, and my son walked into the room.

"Wow!" he said, standing in front of her.

"Is this okay?" I asked

"She is beautiful, Ma. Very divine. I love her expression."

Those few words of reassurance gave me immense strength to complete the painting, and it was unbelievable. As I continued to paint the fine strokes, I started to get a vague smell around me. It was the strong scent of pheromones. I tried not to disconnect from the divine experience and switch to the human experience, since the logical mind can often disrupt the enjoyment of the essence of spirituality.

Her eyes and expressions were full of lust, and she emitted several energies. When my mind told me that she was the goddess of love, I had to ignore my own logical thoughts and paint whatever instinctively came to me.

Around the time I finished my painting, my friend Sakina visited me. She entered the room, stood behind the painting, and started sniffing.

"Why does your room smell different?" she asked.

This was the same person who usually tells me that my room smells like a temple.

I asked her what she smelt.

"Can I be honest with you?" she asked.

"Yes, of course," I responded.

"It reminds me of the smell one gets after sex."

I did not know how to react.

"Come and see what I have painted," I told her.

She reacted the same way my son did. Slowly, I started to narrate to her the story of Goddess Rathi.

Goddess Rathi is the ultimate object of sexual desire and lust in the heavens. She possesses immense beauty and striking attractiveness and is aptly the wife of the god of love—Kama Deva. The name *Rathi* is based off the Sanskrit word *Ram*, which means "to delight in".

Different scriptures narrate different events that led to the birth of Rathi, but they are all different versions of the same event. Kama was one of the first creations of Lord Brahma (the creator). The former was sent down from the heavens to shoot his arrows adorned with flowers of love to stimulate proliferation among all living beings. Lord Brahma had entrusted his son King Daksha with the responsibility of finding Kama a wife. Then Lord Kama accidentally shot Lord Brahma and King Daksha.

Brahma and Daksha, completely hypnotised by Kama's love spell, started to incestuously lust over Brahma's daughter Sandhya. They were caught by Lord Shiva, who laughed at the pathetic situation. Embarrassed by their uncontrollable sexual urges, they started to sweat profusely, and from the sweat of Daksha was born Goddess Rathi. She was the passionate consequence of Kama's powerful spell. Daksha presented Kama with Rathi, who immediately took her as his lover.

Rathi and Kama were a match made in heaven, quite literally. Their love for each other knew no bounds. Their union was the ultimate symbol of passionate romance until Kama was incinerated by Lord Shiva one fateful day when he disturbed the latter during his penance on Lord Indra's instructions. Kama had disturbed Shiva to get help to destroy Tarakasura. Goddess Rathi was broken. The love of her life had been killed, and nothing would change that. She mourned his loss for the rest of her life until they were reunited in their next birth.

She channels one of the most powerful strengths of feminine energy—her sexuality. She is an emotionally scorned woman who had her lover snatched away unfairly. Contrary to how modern society perceives it, ancient Hinduism believes that sexual prowess can be used positively to induce pleasure and ecstasy beyond one's imagination. It is an act that would help one ascend to higher, more spiritual realms, opposing the Western belief that it pushes one further away from God.

My friend remained speechless. I, too, was quiet for a while, and I started to break down in front of her. Rathi's story was tragic yet so powerful. Goddess Rathi had broken the taboo that stopped me from fully expressing her on my canvas. This was an important step in the process, since the next goddess I was to paint was the Mahamaya Tripura Sundari, and to prepare for that, I had to let go of everything that held me back.

76

Yogini Mahamaya (Lalitha Tripura Sundari)

Finally, the time had come. I had completed sixty-three paintings, sixty-three different and dynamic expressions of the almighty goddess. These energies were beyond anything I could have possibly imagined, beyond my thoughts, learnings, and any previous knowledge. It was a path of pure love, creativity, and the ultimate spiritual energy.

I had not bought my canvas or restocked on any painting tools and equipment yet. Before I stepped out to make these purchases, a thought occurred to me.

"I have completed sixty-three paintings." I felt a sense of pride.

"No!" I immediately shut down the thought. "There must be no 'I' in this process." It was of utmost importance for me to slash my ego completely and detach. I had a larger purpose to fulfil.

Therefore, I decided to perform an act. I would approach eleven strangers, people I had never met, and ask for bhiksha or alms. The money I received from them is what I would use to purchase any material required for my final painting. I decided to undergo this process to destroy any ego or pride attached to the paintings.

So, I surrendered my ego and pride and took bhiksha from eleven people. I went ahead and bought a 4 ft X 4ft canvas, slightly bigger than the other ones. I was being guided by a supreme force. I was preparing to delve deeper into her energies with all my passion, love, and devotion for her.

By this point, I had become good friends with Mr Vishwanath of Sumeru. I informed him that I was to finally work on my painting of Sri Lalitha Tripura Sundari. He recorded a video of certain mudras and mantras of the Srividya pooja and sent it to me as his blessings. I downloaded the same, knowing I required more preparation.

The room that I generally prayed and painted in had a beautiful and potent energy. I decided to retreat there so I could focus on the goddess without any distractions. I decided that I would not meet anybody and that I would isolate myself there.

I told my husband that I would maintain Mouna Vridham for eleven days. It is an act where one does not speak as a means of penance. I decided that I would not step out of the room during that period. I did have my apprehensions on whether it was something I would be able to accomplish, but my husband was certain that I would. Another decision I had made was to not use the internet or my phone, which seemed like it would be quite the task.

I called up a few people that I would frequently speak to—my mother, my cousin Sreekumar, my younger son, and my dear friend Sakina—and informed them all of what the next eleven days looked like for me. They were all incredibly supportive of my decision and were confident that I would be able to pull through.

"Beena, did you not realise? The twelfth day is your birthday, and your fiftieth one at that. Aren't we celebrating?" asked my friend Sakina.

It struck me that I was to complete this journey right before my fiftieth birthday.

"I am not sure. We will celebrate if I complete the painting," I responded.

"Don't worry. You just focus on the painting. The rest can be figured out," she said.

I felt completely overwhelmed by the confidence my support system had in me. It all felt incredibly empowering. The beauty of this journey was that all the resolutions and rules were set by me, so I could enjoy the various divine interventions and absorb all the learnings.

Those eleven days were some of the most beautiful days of my life. I entered another realm and enjoyed the power that silence had to offer. This vow of silence brought in a sense of peace and tranquillity. For those eleven days, it was just me and her. First, with light strokes, I painted a Sri Yantra on the canvas. In the silence, I connected with the lines forming the Sri Yantra. I had symbolically drawn around myself the lines I drew on the canvas, disconnecting from the outside world. This silence charged the colours with my devotion, and I surrendered myself to her power. I decided to just take it twenty-four hours at a time. The first day passed by without me having even realised it.

I spent the initial few days reading relevant books, meditating, and listening to the *Lalitha Sahasranamam*. My husband gave me a bell to call my family in case of any emergencies. Every time I rang the bell, my family would come rushing to the room asking what happened. My food and water were brought to the room. I settled in the silence.

I felt the strong presence of three goddesses—Bhairavi, Bala, and Tripura Sundari. There was a strong dialogue that happened between my mind, my body, and my own higher consciousness.

She really was Maya, the illusion, or Mahamaya. In that silence, my body, mind, and consciousness converged. The power of her illusion really was incomprehensible.

At this point, I was very clear on the form I would paint her in: the Pancha-predha sthina. The goddess is seated on Sadashiva with her legs on Brahma, Vishnu, and Rudra.

This form is also a reference to the five elements, the first five chakras—Muladhara or earth, Svadhisthana or water, Manipura or fire, Annatha or air, and Vishudhi or sky. The goddess is seated and has conquered all the creative forces, the very ones that have brought me till here.

Once we understand this, we would be able to pass through the Ajna Chakra and unite all our chakras. Brahma represents enlightenment, Vishnu represents sustenance and intellect, and Rudra or the Mahayogi represents control over oneself and connects you to the sahasra. The seed of enlightenment passes through the life system and resides in the Ajna Chakra in a trance. Sadashiva is our state of mind that is ready to get enlightened, and Mahamaya passes through all the five senses.

Goddess Lalitha Tripura Sundari represents the divine feminine energy in its highest form, embodying Adi Parashakti. She is commonly portrayed as a gentle and exquisite deity, but when the equilibrium of the cosmos is threatened and the universe needs safeguarding, she undergoes a remarkable transformation into a formidable and potent warrior.

The epic clash between Goddess Lalitha and Bhandasura, as narrated in the *Lalitha Sahasranamam*, stands as a cosmic confrontation symbolising the victory of good over evil, righteousness over oppression, and the divine over malevolent forces. Adorned with an array of weapons and symbols of supremacy, the goddess engages in a fierce battle against Bhandasura and his demon horde. Through her incredible abilities and with the assistance of her divine companions and manifestations, Goddess Lalitha triumphs over Bhandasura, restoring cosmic equilibrium.

The *Lalitha Sahasranamam* not only chronicles this monumental battle but also delves into the divine attributes and facets of Goddess Lalitha, underscoring her profound significance as the embodiment of divine love, benevolence, strength, and wisdom. Devotees hold this text in high esteem and recite it as a form of devotion and meditation, invoking the goddess's blessings and protection.

The first way in which she blessed and enlightened me was by connecting me with my higher consciousness where I wholly existed. At that moment, that was my state of mind. My feelings, emotions, desires, and existence merged with her. That state of awareness felt like complete bliss.

I prayed to Bala as these energies passed through me. By the seventh day, I was done with a basic sketch. I was not sure what to write about it. I believe it is beyond me. I sat for hours in front of the painting, admiring her beauty. I could smell her so intensely and could feel her presence right next to me. Her skin was softer than a petal. I could feel the warmth of her embrace and was ready to merge with her energies.

Normally, I start with working on the goddess's eyes, but this time I decided to keep that for last. On the ninth day, I did not paint. Instead, I meditated all day and sank deeper into her vibrations. I flowed in the stream of her love, and my mind became clear and pristine.

At that point, I knew that I was ready to paint her eyes.

On the eleventh and final day, I started painting her eyes. I shivered as I looked into them. My heart skipped several beats, and I experienced what felt like intense bouts of labour pain. With each brush stroke, I felt something roll inside my stomach. It was a new birth, that of my own, which took place in a way beyond my expectations and imagination.

I sat in front of her, completely still like a rock, without breathing. I was gripped by those emotions. She was smiling at me. I spotted Bala near her. The realisation that I am just a mere mortal who is not worthy of depicting her holiness made me take my brush and sign my painting as Sreebala. It was her wish for me to do so, which is how this entire journey began. I surrender completely to her maya like a child.

No words of mine can express my gratitude, my happiness, or my experience. I am thankful to her for selecting me as her medium and passing her energies through me. I never imagined that I would be a soul this blessed to have known and directly interacted with the Divine. I surrender all the wisdom that I have gathered back to her.

My salutation to this universal force. My journey has not stopped. It continues, with her blessings, with the responsibility of disseminating whatever exists within me.

77

My Fiftieth Birthday Celebrations

I heard a knock on my door. It was my elder son, who slipped a paper through the gap.

"We're celebrating your birthday tomorrow," it read.

I smiled. It was a yes from me.

The following day marked a celebration that will forever remain etched in my heart. It was not a celebration of my birth but a tribute to Sreebala. It felt like her divine blessing for me to embark on the sacred journey of painting the sixty-four yoginis. I was but a humble vessel, a conduit through which her artistry flowed. With each stroke of my brush, I surrendered to her guidance, becoming an extension of her will.

In essence, I transformed into her paintbrush. She cradled me in her embrace, immersing me in the purifying waters that cleansed me of my ego. She dipped me into the hues of wisdom, saturating my life with profound insights. With every stroke, she chiselled away my ignorance and honed my receptivity to her boundless energies.

As I look back on that momentous day, I cannot help but feel immense gratitude for the privilege of being her instrument, her paintbrush. It was a celebration of not just a birthday but the divine connection that transcends time and space, forever enriching my soul with her grace and wisdom.

I thank my friend Sakina and all other friends who were present at the celebration. My friends gave me a wonderful gift that day, a feeling that I am engulfed and loved by a lot of feminine energies, as if all the yoginis joined together to celebrate that day.

78

Sreebala

After completing the paintings and successfully exhibiting them, I began to enjoy my time and space with Bala Tripura Sundari as my trusted companion. It was the last week of December, just sometime after the celebration of my fiftieth birthday. I had stepped out to buy some sweets when I suddenly noticed a new shop. Thanks to traffic, my vehicle slowed down, and I got a good look at the attractive shop. I asked my driver to stop the car on the side of the road and got out to explore the place.

This shop was filled with lovely statues. A young girl, around twenty years of age, suddenly approached me.

"Would you like an idol of Bala Tripura Sundari?"

I was surprised because I was not even thinking along those lines. I asked her to show me the idols. She disappeared to the floor above and then returned with two statues in brass that looked alike. I picked one of them. I also bought a lot of flowers, sweets, and even small dresses in the perfect size for my little Bala. I got home, washed and cleaned the idol, decked it up, and lit a lamp in prayer. The very next day, I sent a picture of the idol to a friend of mine who was a keen devotee himself. He expressed his wish to buy one as well. I told him about the shop, but to my surprise, the idol was not there anymore. I insisted, saying that I had just seen two pieces there the previous day. A few days later, I passed through the area and visited the shop again to buy another idol for my friend. The shopkeeper said that he did not have an idol like the one I had bought and had never sold one either. He seemed to be very sure about it.

This incident might sound strange to a third person, but for me, it was a surprise, a grand and beautiful gift. From that day forth, Bala became an integral member of my family. All my friends and my entire family loved her and often bought her sweets and goodies. Due to work, I get the opportunity to travel quite often, and I am of the habit of carrying her with me. There have been several incidents in my life where I have felt her presence very strongly. She is the very rhythm of my heartbeat. I thoroughly enjoy dressing her up in beautiful clothes and ornaments. I do not perform any special poojas for her but treat her as a friend and often offer her any food that I consume.

It has been four beautiful years since that fateful day, and she has gained quite a following in my circle and network. Once, I gave a small photo of hers to my younger son when he departed to Germany for higher studies. One day, during a video call, I saw a small car on his table and asked him what it was. He told me that he saw it at a shop and bought it for Bala.

I felt immense happiness that he looked at her as more than just a goddess. To him, she embodied a sisterly energy. I felt as though I had fulfilled one of my duties as a mother. I did not want to raise my kids to be God-fearing. Instead, I wanted them to see God as a friend that they could communicate with and be open with. God was meant to be a symbol of strength for them.

79

Navigating New Horizons

The year was 2020. COVID-19 had taken the world by storm and brought it to a standstill. On my completion of the Lalitha Tripura Sundari painting, I wondered who would see it. I felt that it was my purpose to share my art and learnings with the world. All this must not remain confined to the four walls of my home, and these enriching experiences should not stay locked away in my heart. I believed it to be the mission of my life. However, at that moment, I was clueless about how to take this forward.

At this point, I found myself naturally gravitating towards the realm of feminine energies. Although I was a member of the All Ladies League (ALL), an organisation founded by Dr Harbeen Arora Rai, I had never taken on any significant role. When Harbeen approached me with the proposition of becoming the national president of the ALL Cinema Wing, I happily accepted. During the COVID pandemic, I got involved with other members and made a few short films on what was happening around us at the time. It was a break for me, and I was able to start exploring new horizons for the mission of my life. I also took over the responsibility of being the national president of the Women's Indian Chamber of Commerce and Industry (WICCI) Arts Leadership, which connected me with the art world and proved to be another reason behind my decision. I was showered with much love from all sides, and I enjoyed and relished the powerful feminine energy. I felt enlightened in every way possible, both personally and professionally. My confidence was boosted tenfold by the knowledge that I was supported by a large network that stood behind me as I ventured worldwide. These women were my real-life yoginis. Harbeen Arora had immense trust in me, which empowered me to follow my dreams. Her vision seemed to perfectly align with mine, as if it were part of the master plan.

After a year, she has given me another invaluable responsibility, that of being the global chair of G100 (global network) for their Arts Leadership wing. As part of the responsibility, I am supposed to be connecting 100 countries. Even though I did not know how to take it forward, I accepted the invitation because I felt my goddesses are paving the way for me to reach out to a global audience for my yoginis.

I decided that I would document my experiences and started writing. I was not sure whether it would take the form of a book, but I felt compelled to write. I also thought it important to document my temple visits because they had been an important part of my journey. While I had only been to temples in Odisha and Gwalior, I felt that without the proper documentation, their historical significance could be completely erased.

I decided to approach a dear friend, Mr L. Ramachandran, a renowned photographer, to aid me in shooting a documentary. The plan was to capture all the locations that were intact and available at the time as most of the temples are in ruins. Everything was set, and he agreed to work on the dates. However, when I was on the verge of booking the tickets, his phone was unreachable. He had become exceedingly busy with certain government projects and had no time to spare.

I was incredibly disappointed and unsure of what my next step should be. I spoke to the film director Anil, the same one who was introduced to me by Dr David. I asked him to join this project as a director for my project, but he declined, saying, "Beena, it's your vision and dream, so I can't do it justice." Confused by his response, I focused on one thing at a time, starting with documenting the temples, and sought his recommendation for a cinematographer. Anil suggested that I contact Jain Joseph (hereafter referred to as JJ). JJ is the cinematographer of my first film, which I had also produced. We had a great rapport. He is also the founder of the Neo Film School in Kerala. I hurriedly called him and explained the project briefly, asking him if he could take care of the cinematography. He requested a week to consider it.

Roughly a week later, I gave him a call. He told me that he was not available on the original dates but offered an extended timeframe. I was left with no choice but to agree. He asked me if I had a script in hand, which I did not. I told him that I had just wanted to document these temples as part of an open journey. He insisted that he needed a script. I agreed to create one, and we scheduled a meeting to fix the dates, finances, and other members of the team who would join us.

JJ and I met again in Chennai. He asked me if I wanted to feature my paintings in the documentary. Initially, I declined the option since I did not see the point, nor did I understand the role that I or my paintings played in this. In our second meeting, however, he clearly articulated the importance of having me and my paintings as part of the documentary. I did not need much convincing after that. Despite my initial hesitation, I trusted his professional advice since I had known him for five years. This familiarity provided me a great deal of comfort.

Our plan was to visit all the yogini temples in Odisha, Madhya Pradesh, and Uttar Pradesh. My office staff, led by Mr Krishna, made perfect arrangements for the journey and for all permissions from the government agencies. I would like to express my sincere gratitude to the whole team.

80

Sacred Sojourn: Traversing Temples in a Twelve-Day Documentary Odyssey

Day 1: Odisha

The documentary team had eight members, including JJ and his team from Kerala, my friend Abirami, and me. Abirami and I left from Chennai for Bhubaneswar and made our way to the Jagannath Temple at Puri to seek blessings before starting on this journey.

JJ and his team came from Kerala to Bhubaneswar on the same day. That evening, JJ and I sat down to discuss. He was brimming with ideas and questions, but his plans strayed a bit further from what I had envisioned. I felt somewhat disconnected and wondered if having him on board was the right decision. I returned to my room that night with a heavy heart. I believed that without the intervention of higher energies, the endeavour would never materialise. It was important for me to maintain a sense of calmness and follow his instructions. He was an expert, and I knew of his capabilities as a cinematographer. My focus should be on trusting him rather than bothering about his opinions. I somehow convinced myself and prepared mentally.

The next morning, my main concern was applying make-up to my face. Although I had always enjoyed dressing well, face make-up had never been part of my daily routine. I had gotten instructions two weeks prior that I needed to do it for the camera. "Camera" was another major worry. I was confident about my physique and looks, but that morning, I felt vulnerable. I recalled a poem I had written about a saree:

> Six yards of feminine beauty and grace
> Draped flawlessly along the curves of my body.
> Carefully, carelessly draped six yards of energy
> Changed its essence with complexity to a shell of mine.

While draping the saree, for the first time in my life, I did not feel confident. As I applied make-up, I regretted not taking better care of myself. I remembered my past, where my eyes had been sharp and deep. I was losing myself, bewildered by my reflection. I realised that this was not me; this was not how I used to be. As usual, I draped a dark greyish-blue saree around my thoughts and spirit, forced a smile, and went on.

When I made my way downstairs, the entire team was there. For the first time, I sought someone else's approval for my appearance. JJ did not say much. He glanced at his colleague Pradeep and said, "Okay, right?" Pradeep replied that it should be fine and commented positively on the saree. However, he added, "Next time, please show me the saree before you wear it."

"Who is he to say this? I don't think I'll have the patience. I cannot imagine giving someone the right to comment on me. This is how I am," I whispered to Abirami.

I felt very uncomfortable. Abirami reassured me, saying, "Why are you getting so bothered? He's just doing his job."

I realised that while painting, I had removed the "I" from myself. I focused on cleansing my spirit, not my consciousness. I evolved, and it was a major change. The second I had placed "I" within my being, even the excitement of meeting the yoginis had diminished. I was caught up in a struggle between "I" and myself, and I remained silent.

During our journey, the driver stopped for me to buy lotus flowers, and I wanted to buy them. However, my mind was not engaged in these external experiences; it remained within my physical space.

I remembered a story that my grandmother had narrated about Narada. He asked Lord Vishnu who his favourite devotee was, and Vishnu mentioned a farmer on earth who chanted his name continuously. Narada was sceptical and asked for proof. Vishnu gave him a pot full of oil and asked him to walk around the world without spilling a single drop. Narada accomplished this without uttering Vishnu's name even once as he was focused on his task. Vishnu explained that the farmer selflessly remembered him in his day-to-day activities, surpassing the value of mere prayers.

I realised that when it came to "me", I was not even fully excited about meeting my yoginis. It was a profound lesson: even in our pursuit of spiritual endeavours, we sometimes forget about God when it comes to ourselves.

Day 2: Hirapur

Located in Hirapur, a mere 20 km from Bhubaneswar, the capital of Odisha in eastern India, the temple is credited to Queen Hiradeve from the 9th-century Bramha dynasty. This yogini temple, holding tantric importance, features a roofless design with a compact circular structure measuring 25 feet in diameter. At the core of the tantric practices performed here lies the veneration of the bhumandala, an embodiment of the five elemental forces—fire, water, earth, air, and ether—rooted in the belief that yoginis possess formidable abilities. The yogini idols, portraying a range of emotions spanning from anger to joy, are perched on creatures or human heads, serving as symbols of feminine power's conquest. The number sixty-four, steeped in significance within Hindu mythology, finds practical applications in realms such as timekeeping and the performing arts.

All the yoginis in Hirapur welcomed me warmly and appeared stunning. However, my mind was traversing a different terrain as I grappled with my inner thoughts. I felt uncomfortable even looking at myself in the camera. I criticised every aspect of myself—especially my walk and my voice—and struggled to articulate my thoughts naturally, as everything felt forced and unnatural.

I allowed all the negativity within me to surface, along with my insecurities. It felt like a collision between my present state, my past experiences, and my worries about the future. I realised that my potential would remain restricted if I continued down this path. I recognised that a lot of healing was necessary, and I was prepared to embrace the surprises ahead. I was ready to liberate myself from whatever tied me to the ground. I understood that my physical appearance was merely a symbol.

I knew I had to be meditative and possess full control over my body, my mind, and my spirit. Only then could I truly excel in and honour this journey. That evening, we decided to rest early because an exciting morning awaited us—we were headed to Ranipur.

Day 3: Travel to Ranipur

The following morning, I felt a sense of calm as there was no filming planned. We were embarking on a nine-hour journey from Bhubaneswar to Ranipur. Once dressed, I went downstairs and found JJ engrossed in some captivating coffee-table books. He mentioned that one of them might capture my interest—it showcased the sculptures of Orissa. I settled beside him, and to my surprise, JJ enquired about my make-up for the day. I replied that I had chosen not to wear any make-up, to which he responded, "I think that's just fine. You won't need much make-up for the next shoot." His words brought a smile to my lips.

A seed's germination depends on both external and internal conditions. I have realised the power within an embryo, but for it to emerge as a purposeful plant, it must first break through its shell. This breakthrough requires immersing itself in the elements of nature. It was challenging to contain all the energies within me, akin to a mature seed needing ample water to soften its hardened shell. At that juncture in my life, I could only break my shell through sheer determination. To be reborn, I needed to absorb energies from the outside world. Only then could I release the points I had accumulated over the years. This transformation could only occur at my will. The seed that had soaked within me required air, water, and sunlight. For that, my heart needed to be open and receptive.

With this thought in mind, I walked towards the car, sending a prayer to the universe. I understood that a struggle existed between my desires and perceptions on one side and what God intended for me and how he perceived it on the other. In the realms of creativity and spirituality, I see things beyond the surface and find joy in that expansive space. When it comes to my physical space, I am inside my shell. That is what I needed to break. I needed to balance between my desires and my willingness to leave everything to God. A sense of calmness and peace enveloped me as I grasped that a transformative process unfolded within me.

Our journey to Ranipur took us through Odisha's picturesque landscapes—quaint villages, lush forests, grazing cows, curious goats, and playful monkeys. The scenery was both breathtaking and soothing. We reached Ranipur as dusk began to settle in. Since it was a village, we stayed in a small hotel. Our interaction with the hotel owner was delightful. He was thrilled to learn that we were visiting the temple for our shoot. He graciously offered to prepare some breakfast for us.

Day 4: Ranipur

I was bubbling with excitement. I had longed to visit this temple, and the day had finally arrived. We set off early, before the break of dawn. We made several stops to capture the essence of the village. The interplay of sunlight and the vibrant greenery was a sight to behold. It transported me back to my childhood with memories of spending vacations in my mother's village. The village ambience and way of life were spellbinding. It infused me with fresh energy, akin to the morning dew. I admired the village's rustic charm. The air was crisp and pure, and the drive to Ranipur Jharial was an adventure. The sky's soft blue hue blended harmoniously with the lush green hills. Amidst the meadows, the car smoothly ascended a rocky peak, as if the path had been crafted to lead us to this point.

The Ranipur-Jharial Temple stands as the pioneering yogini temple to be unearthed, believed to have been built around 900 AD. Its early construction, evident from the presence of adjacent temples, underscores its significance during that era. Situated in relative seclusion a few miles away from the towns of Titilagarh and Kantabanji in Odisha's Balangir District, this circular open-air yogini temple is devoted to the worship of the sixty-four yoginis. Notably, the central shrine, still extant, houses a depiction of dancing Shiva, with all the yogini figures similarly portrayed in dance. In 1853, Major General John Campbell offered a description of this temple. The main entrance, positioned on the eastern side of the circular wall, distinguishes itself from the Hirapur Yogini Temple, although a former southern entrance, now sealed, once existed.

My experience in Ranipur felt quite different from my time in Hirapur. When I entered the temple, I was taken aback and a bit hurt by the grills in front of the goddesses. Then I thought that, with that act, we were closed off inside the bars while they remained open to the universe. I sat near the giant Bhairava statue in the middle and moved closer to the yoginis. Even though they looked weathered and not well cared for, the yoginis still seemed expressive and strong. They felt like they were telling stories from their time, almost like they wanted to talk to us or make themselves known.

My mind was calm, but my body was restless. The yoginis seemed to pull me closer to them, as if they were pulling me deeper within myself to understand them better. It was like a magnet drawing me closer to uncover their hidden wisdom.

Being in Ranipur and walking around the small shrines made me feel connected to a past empire. These shrines were remnants of a time when these goddesses were looked upon as protectors. The area between the villages of Ranipur and Jharial gave me a special feeling, like it was inviting me to discover its history.

As I was leaving the temple, I saw villagers coming in. JJ and his team were busy capturing the national flag on camera. I wandered around, trying to understand the feelings of the place. In Hirapur, I was stuck with my ego, but in Ranipur, I learnt there was more to discover in me. The yoginis seemed to have something important to convey beyond the surface, maybe hidden wisdom or a story waiting to be uncovered.

JJ shouted my name, calling me for a shot. I turned around to look for them, and to my surprise, the camera person was perched on top of a bus amidst a crowd of people. It seemed like a bustling shooting location. I could not help but smile. It was not astonishing; I have always believed that you must take the first 50 per cent of initiative with purity and good intentions, and the next 50 per cent is orchestrated by the Divine.

Inside the temple premises were white pebbles arranged in a pattern, like a puzzle waiting to be solved. JJ instructed me to walk through the path they formed as the team prepared to capture the scene. As I walked, I returned to the same spot from where I had started. Yet, it dawned on me that it was not the same route but a different path layer. The earlier experiences I had left behind now beckoned me to explore them anew with a fresh perspective, diving deeper into the layers of understanding. My mind readied itself for even more revelations.

Suddenly, I noticed that everyone in the crowd was following the same route I had taken. It struck me that blindly following others might not lead to proper understanding. To truly fathom the depths and connect with the Divine, one must walk alone and not be swayed by external influences. As we headed back to the car, the sun was setting, painting the sky with hues of orange and red. It felt like the sky was whispering, urging me to immerse myself in its beauty and promising me the presence of the goddesses.

We drove to Raipur, our next destination, and I succumbed to a deep slumber, ready to unravel the meanings behind my experiences. The paintings I had encountered were like a map, and now, I was prepared to traverse the same map once more but in a deeper layer. The day's events and the sky's colours had prepared me for this voyage of understanding. I drifted into a peaceful slumber.

I knew mission beyond my eyes
There are no imperfections
Afar from the buzzes of life
I can hear that silence
That has been never so loud
I knew beneath the gloomy mist
Dwelled all the mysteries
A real voyage
Not in the quest of lust meadows
But with novel eyes
To plunge deep into my soul
With a smile that wills
With a light that glows
Unveiling surprises

Day 5: Diwali

It was the day of Diwali. I woke up a bit late than usual, reminding myself that I had a small discussion scheduled with JJ. As I stepped outside, I found him looking fresh after his morning walk. We settled down for a coffee, engaging in some technical talk. It felt like a day meant for a bit of relaxation.

When I was heading downstairs for breakfast, I was pleasantly surprised to see the festive decorations adorning the hotel. The owner's family was preparing for a Diwali Havan (ceremonial fire ritual). I joined them for a pooja (prayer ritual), feeling a sense of happiness as I contemplated how the universe weaves incidents together, giving this journey a profound meaning. Participating in the pooja and sharing prasad (sacred offering) with them, I felt an overwhelming sense of welcome and joy. Returning to my room, I sat with Bala, my small deity who embodied the innocence of a child. I offered her chocolates and sweets as if sharing in the festivity.

After an early lunch, we set off for Bhedaghat. On the way, we made a pit stop. JJ surprised me with two plastic toy guns, which reminded me of my childhood Diwali celebrations. This simple act somehow bridged the gap between JJ and me and invoked memories of carefree times. As I pen these words now, I realise the significance of that gesture and how it was crucial to get into that youthful mode.

The roads grew darker and quieter. A touch of fear crept in as I realised the other car was not visible despite my reminders to keep the cars together. I felt uneasy. Evening fell, and mobile network eluded us. When the network returned, I called JJ's assistant, Pradeep, and joked that simply gifting me a yellow gun did not grant me superpowers; responsibility was vital. Explaining that our car carried only two ladies and the roads were not safe, I stressed the importance of balancing faith and intelligence.

They waited on the road, and when we finally stopped, JJ approached, asking if we should light some firecrackers for Diwali. Initially irritated, my anger melted away when I saw the childlike excitement in his eyes. I stepped out and joined them in bursting crackers on the road. I do not recall experiencing that fun before. Abirami, whom I fondly call Abima, was less thrilled. She had a maternal aura and was like a mother to our team. She advised me against lighting fireworks on the road, reminiscent of my mother's cautions. I assured her everything was fine.

In the evening, we reached Jabalpur. The town was adorned in Diwali splendour. After an early dinner, Abirami retired to her room. As I left, JJ asked if I would like to join him and Pradeep in exploring the city. Armed with his toy gun, he was ready for an adventure. I grabbed my own yellow toy gun and happily joined them.

In the midnight streets of Jabalpur, we played and teased each other, laughing like old friends. I realised I had never done something like this in my life. The memory of that unforgettable night will always stay with me—breaking barriers, reliving childhood, and sharing joy. Along the way, we encountered some children captivated by the bright yellow gun. I initially hesitated in a rare moment of playfulness, but JJ urged me to give it to them. He said, "Beena, let them have it. I'll buy another one." I passed the gun to those children. I remember that day as a beautiful day when barriers crumbled, revealing new facets of myself. The happiness of that moment still radiates on my face. It was indeed a lovely experience.

Day 6: Jabalpur and Narmada

I woke up infused with a unique energy. Today was the day I would meet a goddess I had painted—Narmada. I felt a sense of anticipation and excitement, akin to meeting an old friend. The Chausath Yogini Temple in Bhedaghat in Jabalpur District, Madhya Pradesh, was not too far from where we were staying.

The Bhedaghat temple held a distinct essence. Unlike the previous temples, it was larger in size with grand statues. Dominating the centre was a unique temple structure, surrounded by eighty-one goddesses, each of human size, meticulously carved and exuding beauty.

The Bhedaghat Yogini Temple, also known as Golaki Math, stands out as one of the yogini temples, unique in that it accommodates shrines for eighty-one yoginis, surpassing the usual count of sixty-four. Constructed in the early 11th century CE by King Yuvaraja II of the Kalachuri dynasty of Tripuri, the temple's discovery is attributed to a king. Remarkably, this temple is the largest among the circular yogini temples, boasting a diameter of approximately 125 feet. Perched atop a hill overlooking the Narmada River in Bhedaghat, merely 5 km away from Jabalpur, Madhya Pradesh, it features eighty-one cells for yoginis along the inner circumference of its circular wall. Notably, three niches—two to the west and one to the southeast—remain open as entrances. The temple was later transformed into a Gauri Shankar shrine, where yogini temples typically housed an image of either Shiva or Bhairava at their centre. Scholar Shaman Hatley aptly describes it as the "Most imposing and perhaps best known of the yogini temples".

As we entered the temple premises, a sense of solitude enveloped us. Inside the garbhagriha, the sanctum sanctorum, the main deity was Gauri Shankar on a bull, flanked by other deities like Tara, Vamana, Vishnu, and Buddha. The young priest of the temple shared an enchanting tale with us.

The Story of Bees

According to the priest, during an invasion to destroy the temple, a swarm of bees emerged from the temple's core, deterring the invaders from entering the garbhagriha. The invaders were forced to flee, unable to withstand the onslaught of the bees.

After a stroll around the temple, my heart felt heavy on seeing the broken statues. Beyond the spiritual significance, I felt a pang of sorrow as an artist. The effort invested in crafting these sculptures and constructing the temple must have been immense. It saddened me to think that someone could destroy these works, whatever the reason. Regardless of the heaviness in my heart, a profound sense of tranquillity enveloped the premises. I closed my eyes, absorbing the serenity as the sun prepared to rise.

I was roused from my contemplation by a high-pitched voice. Before me stood a large crowd of enthusiastic youngsters, some adorned with peacock feathers. An older man in saffron robes began to sing and dance. The celebratory atmosphere was infectious. As one group departed, another entered, continuing the festive spirit. The priest explained that the celebration is called Govardhan Pooja, which celebrates a story about Lord Krishna lifting a hill to protect villagers from heavy rains. During Diwali, people in the area wear peacock feathers and go to temples to dance. Sadhus and devotees also sing songs to show their devotion. Such unexpected moments of celebration seemed woven into my journey, reminding me that happiness resides even in the most unexpected encounters. With every turn, I could sense the joy of the people I encountered.

Descending the hill, my excitement grew as I approached Narmada. The feeling was distinct, much like meeting someone I had yearned to see. I was about to meet the girl depicted in my paintings, who had played a game of hide and seek with me.

We set out on the tranquil waters on a boat. The boatman pointed out the sights, and I was captivated by Narmada's presence. Flanked by white marble on both sides, she exuded an ethereal beauty, reflecting the hues of the setting sun. The moment was surreal as I engaged in a conversation with her, falling deeper in love with her form. Her curves and features mirrored those I had painted—a dazzling reflection of her beauty.

As we approached the riverbank, I began sharing my experience of painting her, my emotions welling up. In response, JJ suggested we take another ride. They swiftly gathered kumkum, clothes, coconuts, and sweets for offerings, allowing me to present them to Narmada. JJ's gesture touched my heart deeply, and I felt grateful beyond words.

Turning to look at her one last time, it felt as if she was bidding me farewell. I knew I would return to see her again. I could sense her calling. Regret lingered for not staying by the banks longer, as I did not know that was possible. A peaceful silence enveloped me, these thoughts settling in. We returned to the hotel. The experience left me feeling like an eighteen-year-old girl, aware of her beauty and femininity. I felt a sense of liberation, an energy that flowed freely, capable of transforming and nurturing. The texture of her presence, the same I had felt while painting Narmada, lingered as a sweet memory.

Day 7: Badoh

We departed from Bhedaghat early in the morning. Unlike the temples we had visited, the ones we visited the day before were lesser known and took us into unfamiliar territory. There needed to be more information available about these temples or their locations.

As we journeyed, I pondered that our travels were not just confined to the present time. It felt like we were traversing through different eras and layers of time. It is quite intriguing when your mind becomes an observer of itself. You can see and understand things better. Being spiritually attuned gives you the power to explore and move in various directions without needing logic. It is like collecting old fragments and crafting a new space where you can experience without bias. This phenomenon had occurred several times on this journey. I could completely erase the previous day's experiences and immerse myself in the new day. That day was one of those instances. My mind was open without preconceptions.

The Gadammal Temple in Badoh in Vidisha District, Madhya Pradesh, was said to be built by a herder. We had to ask local villagers for directions because Google Maps led us to a different temple. Finally, we found the correct path, a bit away from the main road. The temple's impressive height was visible as we approached and parked outside the temple gate.

While I was walking towards the temple, I noticed numerous small yellow butterflies fluttering around me. It struck me that I had seen butterflies of different colours and sizes throughout this journey, as if they were companions on our voyage.

The pathway to the temple was flanked by the scattered stone remains of the temple itself—squares, circles, padmas (lotuses), and various geometrical motifs. They reminded me of my earlier paintings, which were connected to the symmetry of nature. Even though the temple was not in the best condition, its designs felt deeply connected to nature.

The Badoh Yogini Temple, also referred to as the Gadarmal Devi Temple, in Badoh, is approximately 48 km away from Dudhai, in Vidisha District of Madhya Pradesh. Constructed in the 9th century CE by Gadariya, the temple's local moniker derives from its builder. This temple's architectural style blends elements of the Pathihara and Parmara styles, showcasing a captivating fusion. The Gadarmal Temple of the Mothers stands out as another yogini temple in the vicinity, hosting forty-two niches and possessing a unique rectangular structure. Remarkably, eighteen fragmented goddess images, once fitting into the temple platform's grooves, have been preserved from the waist down. Comprising a rectangular shrine and an imposing, towering shikhara, this temple stands adjacent to some Jain temples, enhancing its cultural and historical significance.

As we moved closer to the garbhagriha, we were startled by the sound of bees suddenly swarming out like a battalion. For a moment, fear gripped us, but I felt they were guardian angels and messengers of wisdom. I silently prayed to Brahmarahi, the yogini of bees, asking for her protection and composure. We spent the afternoon in that temple, and none of us were bitten. A powerful feminine presence pervaded the space despite the absence of physical idols. I felt accompanied by divine energy as I wandered around the temple, though I did not voice this to anyone.

The wall motifs conveyed the cultural essence of the temple. The energy was lonely. I felt the presence of goddesses that felt loneliness. It was as if all the children had left their mother and gone away, leaving her lonely. The insights I received were vast, almost overwhelming, and needed further exploration. Feeling the weight, I must have displayed it in my demeanour as JJ attempted to lighten the mood with jokes. He pointed to the words on his T-shirt and humorously remarked, "At the end, UNITED." I must have given him a puzzled look, struggling to grasp the meaning. I realised that meaning much later.

As we walked out, I turned back to the feminine energy within the temple and expressed my gratitude. I sat on the lion statue and took a photo with pride. From there, we headed to a nearby Jain temple. The team kept cracking jokes, and JJ playfully asked if I was alright. I responded that sometimes I have these moments. Occasionally, I prefer being alone, even in a crowd.

Day 8: Dudhai

It was just an hour's journey to Dudhai in Lalitpur, Uttar Pradesh, where we stayed before, bordering Madhya

Pradesh. Upon reaching Dudhai, a lively village, JJ and his team began shooting scenes of village life while we planned to head towards the temple. The road led us into the town. We noticed some small broken temples and statues by the roadside along the way. When we turned back to ensure the other car was following, we found that they were not. I tried to call them, but there was no mobile network. It looked like a forest area where there seemed to be no way forward. We decided to halt the vehicle.

Suddenly, we heard distant sounds. A group of girls approached with pots on their heads. Intrigued, we stepped out of the car to see them, and they seemed excited by our presence. I felt that they were a group of yoginis. I enquired if there was a yogini temple nearby. They replied that they were not aware of a yogini temple but had just come from a nearby Shiva temple where they had offered water to Lord Shiva. I thought that the temple they referred to might be the yogini temple, and they said it was not far from that spot.

Hardly a few hundred meters ahead, we noticed a sign saying "64 Yogini Temples—Archaeological Site". We disembarked and were glad to meet a man who identified himself as working for the Archaeological Survey of India (ASI). We informed him about the missing car. He asked us to wait while he rode his two-wheeler to search for the lost team. The surroundings were forested and quiet, with only the sounds of the forest.

After some time, we spotted two boys approaching. Curiously, they asked if we had come to the ruined temple. They offered to take us to a better temple. The condition of the place was quite distressing. I shared with them the temple's significance and suggested that they bring people to visit it.

Situated in Dudhai and locally referred to as Akhada or Akhara, near Lalitpur in Uttar Pradesh, the temple holds distinct features. Its circular layout encompasses an open central space, adorned with niches to accommodate forty-two yoginis. Constructed during the 10th century by the Chandala kings, this temple spans a diameter of approximately 50 feet, showcasing its historical and architectural significance.

I was left blank, utterly devoid of feelings. The space felt like a broken home without anyone inside; even the energies seemed to have departed. There was no role for conscious thought in that silence—the silence that is not meant to be experienced. I was in a state of beautiful emptiness. In the scorching heat, my mind shifted into thoughts, and I became aware of Abirami preparing a delicious breakfast with bread, jam, and butter. I sat on the steps in the shade, observing butterflies fluttering around.

My mind was unusually tranquil, free from comparisons, complaints, or even mental images. JJ joined me, and I began to enjoy our conversation. His words were intriguing and stimulating. I appreciated his thought-provoking questions. It felt like mere questioning on the first day, but now it had evolved into conversations. He asked, "Don't you think this place is about life?" He was breaking through my defences. His role was not just limited to cinematography; it was more significant.

He asked me about the director of the documentary. I informed him that currently there was no director. He suggested that I needed one. I looked at him and asked if he could do it. His abrupt response: "Oh no, I don't have the time." JJ confirmed, "I don't think I can invest more time into it." Inwardly, I felt JJ would be the one to do it, and I expressed my confidence with a smile. Why don't you ask Anil? I told him I asked Anil once but will ask him once again.

I strolled down, savouring the moment and enjoying the breeze and the butterflies. My mind transitioned from silence to quietness to a heightened state of aliveness. The two boys guided us to a nearby Shiva temple, an old and dilapidated structure.

We resumed our journey in the car, stopping for lunch. During this time, I contacted my friend Anil and I discussed with regards to directing the documentary. His response was as firm as before, reconfirming that I should only do it. He told me we would find a talented editor once we finished the shoot, and when he mentioned JJ's name, I said to him that JJ was not interested due to lack of time. Anil's reply was, "That's okay. You can handle it yourself."

Abirami took the driver's seat, and we indulged in singing, dancing, and laughing, relishing our girl time. Our driver was catching up on his sleep in the backseat. Upon reaching the hotel, we gathered for an evening meal, growing increasingly comfortable in each other's company. Later, JJ and I engaged in a lengthy conversation about me and my experiences. This time, I could take his questions lightly and comprehend their depth. Unlike the first day, when I had felt defensive, now I was prepared to offer more.

Day 9: Chattarpur and Khajuraho

Our next destination was Khajuraho. On the way, we planned to visit the Chattarpur museum. As I settled into the car, I was puzzled by something that lacked a proper explanation. There was an inner force within my aura, something different from before. Until now, it had been just me and my goddess, and I had not let anyone influence my thoughts. Was I allowing JJ to become a part of my journey? I did not want this to remain an unanswered question—it felt quite heavy.

Sitting in the car, I asked Abirami to play the Kanda Guru Kavacham and then the Chandi Kavacham. These mantras were like protective seals for my aura. Tears streamed down my face, and Abirami looked concerned. I understood what it was. I was giving JJ space, allowing his thoughts to enter my journey. It was becoming more prominent with each passing day. I prayed deeply to my goddess to guide me to the right path and be by my side.

At times, you become a regular human being. No matter how spiritually enlightened you are, introspection of your actions are always beneficial. As usual, I surrendered to her guidance. Without doing so, we burden our brains and find ourselves torn between conscious and subconscious thoughts. I knew there was something I needed to comprehend. Instead of constantly processing the divine data and entering a defensive mode, I needed to ask my brain to relax. Comparing with past data was not necessary. My faith was the answer; I knew I was within her embrace.

Upon arriving at the Chattarpur museum, I got out of the car. Everyone looked at me and asked if I was alright. My inner contemplation seemed to reflect on my face, creating a not-so-great scene. The incident reminded me of my friend Pramela's words during a discussion about me—that I love everyone but maintain a certain distance, not allowing anyone to get too close. She suggested that I should open up more. I was not surprised by her insight, but it did make me feel a bit uncomfortable. I confirmed this perspective with my close friends, and they all shared similar opinions.

As I mentioned earlier, I had never discussed my journey with anyone, nor had I allowed any thoughts to influence me. However, with JJ, that seemed to be changing. The comforting aspect was that his influence did not stem from his practices.

Being a devout Christian, his connection with me felt like direct divine intervention, like how I connect with my goddess. Chattarpur had many yoginis. I briefly observed them, not being particularly drawn to the iconography. Moreover, the place was filled with bees. Leaving the museum, I sat on a garden bench, surrounded by butterflies, my fellow travellers, dancing around me. Throughout this time, my mind was still grappling with thoughts. Yes, I believe that divinity exists within, but it is also present externally. My ignorance and arrogance made me think I have welcomed all energies without bias or doubt. No one can influence me except someone who is a part of the goddess's master plan. I trusted Bala, my inner self, to guide me through this. It was another surrender of the "I".

We reached Khajuraho, had lunch, and prepared to explore the much-awaited Khajuraho temples. The Khajuraho yogini temple would be our destination the next day, as we needed to shoot there. The temple is an exceptional example of Aryan architecture. Walking through it with a knowledgeable guide, I understood that the temple's fame for erotic sculptures is just one of its facets. The temple represents various elements of life, with sensuality being just a part of the story—it is all about what you choose to see.

The temple has a beautiful story behind it, which I read in a book purchased locally.

As we strolled amidst the aesthetically carved structures, they seemed to come alive, depicting human emotions and the physical and spiritual dimensions of life. One remarkable feature was the Varaha Temple with 672 intricately carved figures of gods and goddesses. I felt that the creators of the temple and these sculptures had truly lived life to the fullest, a life that was now visible on the walls of Khajuraho. As the sun began to set, the team showed interest in a light and sound show. We sat there for a while, and I noticed the moon casting its glow on the temples, creating a romantic scene.

We all retired to our rooms. JJ and I shared dinner and a lengthy conversation, which ultimately veered into the topic of life. He talked about his family and his four children and his passion for his career. The way he cherished his career and his family resonated within me: my family is my anchor, while my work and my art are my passions. It was a heart-to-heart exchange between two human beings, discussing our paths, visions, and approaches. That evening brought me comfort, silencing the chaos in my mind. I was able to settle my uncertainties and fears, drifting off to sleep in a state of peace.

Day 10: Yogini Temple, Khajuraho

I began to enjoy the process of Pradeep, the assistant camera person, coming over and asking me about the saree I was wearing to approve it. I felt elated at the indulgence and pampering I recieved. I realised that I had been a spoilt girl, cared for by my parents, friends, and family. Being pampered is a blessing, and it nurtured the divinity within me. This thought brought me great comfort.

The temple of the sixty-four yoginis was just a fifteen-minute journey from the hotel.

The Chausath Yogini Temple, situated in the town of Khajuraho in Madhya Pradesh, stands as a ruined structure with historical significance. Dating back to 885 CE, it holds the distinction of being the earliest surviving temple within the Chandela capital, Khajuraho, and is often referred to as the oldest enduring temple in the area. Characterised by a rectangular layout measuring 31.4 m x 18.3 m, the temple follows the hypaethral design, exposing its interior to the open air. Positioned within the western group of temples on a raised platform standing 5.4 m high, the temple is constructed from coarse granite blocks and features an open central courtyard. Originally encompassing sixty-five shrine cells—ten on the front wall, eleven on the back wall, and twenty-two on each side—only thirty-five of these cells have survived over time. Among the ruins, three sizable statues of mother goddesses or Matrikas were discovered, now housed in the Khajuraho museum. These statues, identified as Brahmani, Maheshwari, and Hingalaja or Mahishamardini, offer a glimpse into the temple's historical and religious significance.

The empty temple did not disrupt my peace. I interpreted the emptiness as a journey from the tangible to the formless, from the concrete to the abstract. The real essence lies not in monuments, temples, or idols but in connecting with the dynamic energy of the land, a reservoir of accumulated spirituality. How much you draw from this well of spirituality is up to you. I felt like immersing myself in that flowing energy. From where I stood, I could see the "concrete" western group of temples, symbolising life, while the spot I occupied represented the abstract—the yogini temple in ruins, devoid of idols. The experience was the pinnacle of spirituality and material existence.

> While my blank canvas
> Whispers riddles and unspoken words,
> My heart and toes tap to the silence.
> The brush dances alongside my trembling hands,
> Expressing the colours of my inner soul,
> Unseen colours, unheard music.
> Instead, I breathe life into my canvas,
> Creating hues beyond imagination,
> Like an eternal classical love story.
> I remain inseparable
> From the blankness that completes me.

With the goddess's grace and blessings, I could perceive the various layers of divinity. There, I felt alive and fully comprehended life, experiencing its nuances and forming the foundation of my spiritual journey. This journey allowed me to harmonise and elevate different aspects of life to unite with her. This place is ideally suited for such growth. Each element complemented the other, distinct yet unified in the experience of oneness. You do not need to escape from your life. A different flavour of happiness emerged. I am getting to know more of its reflection within me.

It was a long drive from Khajuraho to Gwalior. Reflective moments happened in the car. I had been moving from one place to another, and it was an incredible blessing. We arrived late at night at the Hotel Deo Bagh and went to bed. The next day would be the final shoot.

Day 11: Morena, Gwalior

Gwalior was a familiar place. I had been to Morena before. I had stayed at the same hotel the last time I had visited. Waking up there, I heard the chirping of birds and saw the lush green fort amidst the chaos of the city. This 17th-century property has ancient family temples nestled among trees and a beautiful green garden. There was a Kadambam tree. Its flowers are of Goddess Kadamhavana Vasini, who resides in the Kadambam forest. I plucked a flower for my Bala.

The last day of the shoot was approaching. Morena was nearby. The drive through Chambal was exciting. Chambal, known for its dacoits, is a part of many legends and stories.

Situated in the village of Mitaoli, also spelled Mitawali, near Padaoli in the Morena district, 40 km from Gwalior, stands the Chausath Yogini temple, also known as the Ekattarso Mahadeva Temple. This remarkable temple is perched atop an isolated hill, approximately a hundred feet high. Its name stems from the multitude of Shiva lingas housed within its chambers. Dedicated to the worship of sixty-four yoginis, this yogini temple holds historical and spiritual significance. Constructed in 1323 by the Kachchhapaghata king Devapala, the temple holds a unique legacy as an educational venue for astrology and mathematics based on the sun's transit. Its external circular shape spans a radius of 170 feet, housing sixty-four small chambers within its interior. Notably, the main central shrine features slab coverings with perforations, designed to channel rainwater into a large underground storage facility. The temple's robust architectural design has even withstood earthquake without sustaining damage—a testament to its enduring artisanship.

This yogini temple structure resembled a seed turning into an embryo at the centre. The structure is like when a milkweed pod opens and its seeds float through the air on its delicate white silk wings. The passing breeze carries them. Most people who encounter a seed make it fly higher with their breath. I feel blessed that the seed that fell in my garden germinated and grew into another plant and blossomed. Now the time has come for the pod to burst open. It is time to disseminate the wisdom I have received. This thought was in my mind.

After a few shots of the temple, they were about to shoot my part, my reflections and thoughts. JJ was discussing about what I was going to talk about, and I was recording it. During the journey, there were times when I recorded our conversations. Although I felt vibrant and happy, my mind was going blank. Beyond my vision, in my mind, I could only see circles like the temple's structure, and they were moving. It felt like they were engulfing me and filling me with information, about to move in another direction and leave me. Many processes had happened, and I thought that the pod was ready to break open, disseminating the wisdom I received to a broader space where it could land in receptive minds, growing healthier and more beautiful. This journey must continue. Today, it is me, and tomorrow, it will be someone else.

We often try to hold on to the energy we receive without realising that we are processing centres that process it in a way the next generation can absorb. We cannot hold on; we need to share. Through this process, we become enlightened and balance our spiritual and material spaces.

Feeling light, I stepped outside and sat on the steps. Two large butterflies were flying around—my messengers. We had to return as there was a shoot in the hotel premises, a fireside shoot. Our driver started causing issues on the way, and I got angry. He had been troublesome throughout the journey, but I had considered it his character. But this time, I lost my temper. Abirami tried to calm me down.

After reaching the hotel, Abirami and I went to JJ's room to finalise the evening shoot. JJ said I could not wear a saree or a big bindi. He asked me to wear a dress. I looked at him as if I did not understand, and he firmly continued, "Wear anything other than a saree. Don't wear a big bindi, and tie your hair up." He was asking me to be without my protective elements.

I told him that a saree is a beautiful garment. He replied, as if he had read my mind, "Yes, it is, but for you, it is cover, and you seal it with your bindi."

Abirami laughed, and I understood why. She used to tell me that I would look good in a dress. She told JJ, "Don't say anything more; she's in her Kali mode." She then told him about the incident with the driver.

JJ said, "Beena, we want the energies of Uma and Gowri. Please relax, get ready, and come."

I strolled behind Abirami to my room to get dressed. On the lawn, the team was preparing the bonfire for the evening shoot. JJ's words reminded me of a few lines of poetry I had written long ago:

> Six yards of feminine beauty and grace
> Carefully carelessly draped six yards of energy
> Changed its spirals with complexity to a shell of mine
> Proclaiming its years of inner pain
> Strangling and choking, stealing my breath.

I got ready and came out of my room. I looked at my mirror reflection and headed to the lawn. JJ tried to reassure me, saying that sometimes we need to break conventions and step out of our comfort zones, as they are often the most significant barriers in our lives.

The fire was lit, and JJ sat before me with the fire between us. He asked me questions about my journey, and I answered deeply and sharply, attempting to stir the energies we had encountered. Although I felt mechanical, my mind was drawn to the masculine energy before me. I sensed something was opening up but could not figure out what it was.

The shoot lasted only forty-five minutes but was successful. We wrapped up, and I approached JJ and asked him, "I'm making this offer for the last time."

He asked, "What offer?"

I replied, "Direction!"

He enthusiastically said, "Of course, it's a yes. I'm ready to direct it."

I was happy, and I asked if he was sure and could commit the time. He reassured me saying he could, and he would. He was entering my project willingly, and I felt content because I had known what his response would be when I asked if he would direct.

That night, we had a wrap-up party with the team, a perfect end to our twelve-day shoot. When the group said they had a wonderful vacation, I felt relieved. Everyone enjoyed it thoroughly and was happy. The following day, JJ and his team left for Cochin. As he left, he said, "Prepare the script's first draft with the data, your thoughts, and your reflections. Then we'll meet." I was not stressed about it as, by that time, I was already in the process of writing this book.

> Standing there again,
> Before the boundless sea's devotion,
> I felt like a child, innocent and free,
> holding a bag of treasures in my hand
> A bag filled with shells,
> Gathered through my journey,
> I'll explore their depths like secrets in the night,
> Unveil their mysteries, like stars so bright,
> For in each shell, a chapter is concealed,
> A memory, a moment, a story revealed,
> And in the whispers of the ocean's song,
> I'll find where these shells truly belong.

81

Scripting

I came back to Chennai with a different energy. I felt happy with my feminine feeling. I wanted the memory of this journey to be embedded within me for this lifetime. I went to a tattoo artist and got a butterfly tattoo on my left wrist. I always felt that butterflies were showing their presence during the trip. I also had my goddess's name, Sreebala, tattooed on my hand. It was a wonderful experience. When I showed it to my sons, they did not believe I had done it. My elder son, Arjun, asked why I chose a butterfly since it did not match my character. I wondered what else I should have chosen, and he suggested something powerful like a trishul (trident) or a tigress. I understood that I embodied a powerful energy.

Masculine Energy—My Bhairava, My Guiding Force

I started scribbling the script while listening to the recording of my discussion with JJ during my travel. While listening to it, I felt that he sounded like a divine intervention. I was in the office and realised that tears were rolling down my face. I was emotional. A colleague walked in to pick up a book she had given to me earlier. On seeing me in tears, she became worried and suddenly said the book's name, *Tripura Rahasya*. I told her I had not read it and asked what it is about. She replied, "The *Tripura Rahasya* expounds the teachings of the supreme spiritual truth. The book is about knowing your consciousness and understanding the ultimate reality. It is also about achieving liberation after realising this truth and acquiring genuine wisdom, which Lord Shiva imparted to Lord Vishnu. When Vishnu incarnated on earth as Dattatreya, he passed this wisdom on to Parasurama." Every word of this was incomprehensible to me.

While I was listening to her, she said, "If you want to read it, I will leave the book here."

I immediately replied, "No, I have found the answer. Once I finish writing, I will read it." I felt through her words that my journey with my paintings is towards understanding my own consciousness.

I thought back to the early days of painting and had several questions about the steps I took. Why had I painted Ardhanareeswarar first and then Bhairava? What were my thoughts? I thought about the strange pull of masculine force. I painted Ardhanareeswarar to honour the masculine energy within me. I painted Bhairava with the belief that he would assist and guide me in depicting his consorts. I comprehended that a masculine energy was guiding me throughout the process. While listening to the audio of the recording, I sensed that this force was leading me towards a destination to reveal something profound. JJ served as a metaphor to make me feel Bhairava's presence.

Bhairava, who guards the eight directions of the universe, possesses the energy to transcend the seeker to the highest realms of consciousness and the supreme reality. I understand now why JJ was trying to break down my experiences, thoughts, and processes. I am delving into the deeper layers of my journey, unlearning what I have learned.

JJ is a Christian, a religious person. I felt that whatever was coming from his thoughts was divine intervention. If someone who practised tantra had been in his place, their perception might have differed as per their experience. Hence, JJ was a channel for delivering these concepts to me. The divine energy knows I need more explanations and direct interventions to help me understand. This information and my acceptance of it were crucial to completing this journey. He was a milestone in this journey, a physical catalyst to hold my hand to take me to the roots.

After two weeks, I travelled to Kerala to meet JJ and discuss the evolving thread of the script. I explained that this documentary is a dialogue between me and time, with time symbolising Bhairava. I shared the reasoning behind this concept with him, and it resonated with him. Together, we delved into the foundational structure.

Anchoring Point of the Journey

Our subsequent meeting took place two weeks later. We were scheduled to attend the annual Women Economic Forum (WEF) event in Delhi for a week and decided that the script would be finalised by the end of that week. I aimed to have my base script ready before reaching Delhi.

In Delhi, we reviewed the entire script. I had completed about 80 per cent of the script, including a rough draft of my travel experiences, thoughts at each temple, stories, and substories. As I began to read, he bombarded me with question after question. His questions triggered a flood of memories and brought forth vital aspects of the journey. He skilfully fit the pieces together like a jigsaw puzzle. Many fragments coalesced, lending meaning to my experiences. He said,

"Everything is good, Beena, but I lack an anchoring point or a core, the essence and significance of the whole picture."

I was puzzled and fell into a thoughtful silence. JJ's numerous questions prompted me to dig deep within. What was the purpose of this journey? What had triggered it? I explained to him that after I began painting and immersing myself in the experiences, my connection with the goddess's love and energy became so potent that I had lost sight of the original goal. I shared that I was following her master plan, eagerly awaiting her revelation of the purpose that ignited this journey.

He responded, "Yes, Beena, I understand, but now you need to respond to that energy and ask questions. Otherwise, you might miss the destination. They must be waiting for your questions too. So, what do you think was the trigger for you to embark on this journey?"

I thought out loud. My mentor suggested writing about Srividya—did that ignite something within me? A yearning for my femininity and a desire to grasp and unleash feminine power emerged. Was that the purpose?

I meticulously dissected my thoughts into fragments. After my mentor's passing away, an irresistible compulsion or energy propelled me forward. I felt as though I was meant to be doing something more. To write about Srividya, I needed to learn Srividya Upasana, which meant delving into tantra, finding a guru, and embracing a level of discipline that was not my forte. As I ventured deeper, my goal extended to painting the presiding deity of Srividya, Maha Tripura Sundari, which had also been a long-cherished dream. However, the idea of writing about Srividya seemed off the table.

However, painting Tripura Sundari may have been the way forward. There was one significant hurdle; I struggled to connect with my own feminine power. How could I depict her, the universal feminine, authentically? For me, painting was my meditation, my prayer, and my devotion. I believed that the easiest way to understand her truly was through my art. With unwavering conviction, I decided to embark on this path. To gain clarity, I undertook a nine-day fast during Navaratri. After that, every step flowed effortlessly, without any doubt.

I told JJ that Dr David's wish was for me to write about Srividya, which became interconnected with my search for femininity. For both points, the answer lay in painting the presiding goddess of Srividya, Maha Tripura Sundari. I affirmed that this was my trigger point.

Revelation of Srividya by Bhairava, the Lord of Time

JJ did not wait. He was ready with the question "What is Srividya?"

I answered, "Srividya is a tantric ritual or process, a puja for the highest Shakti, Tripura Sundari, who embodies the universe's creative force."

He continued, "Why is it practised?"

I replied, "It depends on the devotee—for salvation or to fulfil desires, with the guidance of a guru."

My answers and expressions made it clear to him that I did not know much about it. He suggested, "Beena, why don't you talk to a few people who practise Srividya? It will provide clarity, and that will really help us script it. Only then can we convey it to the audience."

I called Mr Viswanathan of Sumeru Madam, who is a scholar in this subject, to explained the situation, asking for a simple explanation.

"Srividya is considered the most secret and powerful knowledge in the spiritual world. Srividya Sadhana is a practice of great significance. It centres on understanding and honouring Ma Lalitha Tripura Sundari, commonly seen as the mother of the universe who encompasses all aspects of the world. Srividya Sadhana is fundamentally about self-realisation, recognising that everything is within oneself. It represents a journey to establish a connection with the highest goddess.

"During the practice, practitioners visualise the Srichakra within themselves, perceiving the presence of goddesses within. They gain insight into certain spiritual principles and energies, elevating their spiritual energy to the highest level and experiencing a sense of unity symbolising the union of Shiva and Shakthi.

"In essence, Srividya Sadhana is a specialised training provided by a guru who profoundly understands tantra, mantra, and yantra. This training is designed to assist individuals in establishing a profound connection with the Supreme Mother, Ma Lalitha Tripura Sundari, through these spiritual practices."

JJ fell silent for some time and asked, "Don't you think your journey is nothing but Srividya? Don't you see the purpose is the same? The method of approach may be different."

I was awestruck, and tears welled up. I was speechless and frozen for a moment. I wanted to react but could not even open my mouth.

He continued, "You used your creative force to understand her." Deep within, I heard an internal voice say that the destination is one but the method varies.

I remembered my mentor reciting Srividya. He would recite the mantra aloud and instruct me to listen closely. Several times after that, I asked him if I should write it down, to which he responded, "No, it's getting imprinted in your internal system."

Dr David gave me a book and told me that I would write about Srividya. I told him I knew nothing about it. He sarcastically said that time will reveal everything. Time, for me, represented Bhairava. Without analysing all of this, I told JJ that this documentary is a conversation between me and time. I was now wondering if this was what Dr David meant. All these thoughts were running through my mind, and I was thinking out loud.

JJ did not stop there. He pressed further, saying, "You need to go beyond this. You said that painting Maha Tripura Sundari had been a long-standing dream. Where did you first hear about her to have that desire?

I shared the story of Krishnan Potti, who had sensed a feminine energy within me. That conversation had attracted me to the goddess. I wanted to draw the Sri yantra and the goddess Maha Tripura Sundari. I told Krishnan Poti that I should learn from someone. When I expressed my need for a guru, he inscribed something on my tongue with a sharp object and gave me a silver face of Adiyogi, saying, "He is the guru of this universe. Whenever you want to learn something, ask him."

Everything felt intricately connected, and I could sense it.

Silence enveloped us. I was also convinced. Yes, it is Srividya, and Bhairava, the lord of time, has revealed it to me. It was a very powerful revelation for me, and both of us felt it. We needed time to absorb it and formulate our thoughts around it.

The next two days were very powerful and a time for celebration. I had my first interview about the yoginis with Dr Bibek Debroy for Sansad TV, which felt like a gift from my Bala. I was overwhelmed by the interaction with Dr Debroy.

On the last day of December, JJ and I celebrated with women from all around the world who had come to attend the WEF event. Then we both travelled to our hometowns.

After reaching Chennai, I had to travel to Kerala the very next day. My son's wedding was scheduled for 15 January, and the celebrations were planned for an entire month. It was an occasion of great festivity, a celebration of profound revelations. I was fully prepared to welcome my daughter-in-law, Harini, my goddess Lakshmi in her physical form. She is a vibrant embodiment of femininity, bubbly, intelligent, and beautiful.

Delving Deeper

During the first week of February, JJ came to Chennai to finalise the script.

"Do you have any uncertainties about where we left off?" JJ enquired.

I responded, "No, I don't, but I still cannot grasp the thought that the entire journey was Srividya. I believe it will take some time for me to fully comprehend it."

JJ remarked, "Srividya is our core point for this journey. We'll continue with the script."

We proceeded to build upon the foundation of the initial script I had crafted. The points were very clear to me now, I explained my thoughts to JJ in a flow.

Surrender of My Ego

In the Hirapur temple, I realised the presence of my ego and the importance of surrendering to go beyond or deeper.

Connecting to My Deeper Layer

In Ranipur, my connection with the Divine as thoughts delved into forms and their expressions. These concepts prompted me to explore deeper within myself, peeling back the layers. It was essential to understand the divine expressions.

Connecting to My Inner Child

The next destination was Bhedaghat. My experiences there emphasised creative energy and not my physical self, which established an internal connection with my inner child.

Connecting to the Elixir of Life—Shiva and Shakti, the True Balance

At Badoh, the geometric shapes in the stones in the temple ruins—circles and squares—resembled yantras and stirred something within me. The symbols hinted at structured thoughts and equilibrium between internal and external forces, reflecting the interplay of microcosm and macrocosm.

The beehives I encountered in the temple symbolised balance and symmetry. The hexagonal cells formed by equilateral triangles represented the union of masculine (Shiva) and feminine (Shakti) energies, generating the elixir of life. This union marked the convergence of seeker and the search.

The abstract, formless realm of transcendental consciousness (a realm beyond the confines of physicality), which is represented by Shiva or the masculine energy, and the concrete realm of manifested forms (the physical, tangible world that we perceive through our senses), which is Shakti or the female principle, represent two facets of the same coin. Our life is an interplay of these concepts. The abstract form encourages introspection and spiritual growth, and the manifested forms keep us engaged with the physical world. The ability to balance these aspects can lead to a more holistic and fulfilling life, the stage of Paramananda. This is where the seeker becomes one with the search, one leading to another.

I continued to read the script to JJ.

I really did not know why I painted Ardhanareeswarar first. After visiting these temples, when I was able to connect Shiva and Shakti to the essence of life, the true balance, I understood that the reason I painted Ardhanareeswarar is to have a balance before embarking on such a divine project.

JJ's questions came rapidly: "Then, in that case, after Bhairava, you should have painted Mahamaya, the Maha Lalitha Tripura Sundari, the embodiment of supreme feminine divine energy."

Yoginis—The Seed of Manifestation

"Why then did you paint the yoginis? Who are they, and what is their connection to this journey?"

I looked at him in despair. More questions?

I posed these queries to the goddesses while praying to decipher the goddess's master plan—why she had guided me to paint the yoginis. However, that discussion went on for a few hours, and it was a very powerful interaction.

I told JJ that I encountered distinct energies and expressions with each painting. Every experience was different. The yoginis are the different energies of the goddess with different purposes.

As we continued our conversation in the car, JJ seemed entranced. As if he knew the answer to his question, JJ said, "Mahamaya embodies abundant possibilities and layers of energies. When her expressions—called yoginis—merge with the male energy within, they become potent emotions with the manifestation of power. They signify the facets of Mahamaya. Each yogini holds a unique blend of powers, and while there are sixty-four, their numbers can be infinite."

I looked at him and continued, "Ashta Matrikas, Bhairavis, Dakinis, Yakshinis, Sakinis—640 crores of yoginis."

Suddenly, I recalled my discussions with a doctor about why people fear the ferocious forms of the goddess, and I shared the details with JJ. "Human beings, regardless of gender, embody various combinations of energies. Motherly energy is not confined to giving birth; it manifests in both men and women across ages. They are diverse expressions of her—Uma, the lover, and Maheshwari, the wife. Similarly, ferocious forms are also for a purpose. So why should you fear them? Even mothers punish their children, scold them, and get angry with them, all for a good purpose. The goddess is just your reflection."

What we see is only the external appearance. One must go beyond appearances to understand their energies, love, and purpose. Our understanding must expand beyond our vision.

Secret of Manifestation

JJ continued, "When the flowing creative feminine expression that you call yoginis converges with the male consort, masculine energy with structure, manifestation flourishes across domains."

I said, "Yes, JJ. I realise with experience that masculine and feminine energies are not confined to gender. We embody both. Their union is the universe's secret."

I continued, "Now I am beginning to understand why I painted the yoginis."

I interpreted JJ's idea as a hierarchical structure: Mahamaya represents the system. Beneath her, multiple divisions exist, each led by their respective heads, that are further divided into subdivisions. These entities are known as yoginis. Understanding one yogini alone does not equate to comprehending Mahamaya. To grasp Mahamaya fully, I needed to explore all her manifestations.

I came to understand the root cause of fear. Approaching the outer layer is relatively easy, but reaching the core demands significant effort. The misuse of this accessible outer layer, akin to a security guard assuming responsibilities beyond their role, disrupts the entire structure and exposes the individual to potential destruction. This misuse has resulted in a layer of fear surrounding the yoginis.

This entire structure is the creative life force existing within every being. This innate capacity for creativity and vitality comes to life when it unites with divine consciousness, the masculine energy. This union signifies the activation and manifestation of creative potential. Whether it is a spiritual or material context, its outcome is consistently positive, yielding goodness on both personal and universal higher purposes.

In the real world, a yogini is not merely a yoga practitioner. She is one in harmony with her masculine counterpart. The masculine counterpart here is not the physical partner but is within yourself. This union is always misinterpreted as physical union, which is why yoginis are connected to sexual acts. The union is internal. A yogini is a seed of manifestation. I understood clearly why I was directed to paint the yoginis before painting Mahamaya.

Over the next two days, we focused on shooting the goddesses I had painted for the documentary project. We both realised that scripting could not be done in just one day. After each point, we had to go deeper to absorb the energy it held individually. It was very heavy, and we needed time to settle and ponder over it. JJ went back to Kerala after the shoot.

Following these two days, I had to rush to Kerala due to my aunt's demise. While there, I decided to stay in Kochi for an additional week. JJ's hometown was Kochi, and he could spend some time for discussions.

Unleashing Feminine Energy

One evening, when JJ came to meet me, I read the portion that we had discussed during our last meeting in Chennai. Playfully, he asked, "Was your travel an unleashing of your feminine energy or a realisation of the importance of union with the male energy?"

His question upset me as if he had touched a sensitive nerve—my feminine energy. On the same humorous note, I told him not to try to change my path. I knew I needed to understand more about it. Even though I understand that both energies are not powerful without each other, why am I perceiving them as different? I should have told him both the energies are one and the same. I need to cleanse myself more to be able to say that.

His second question was about the difference between Shiva and Bhairava.

In response, I remarked, "They must possess two layers of the same energy."

JJ promptly replied by drawing a parallel between breath and belief, asking, "Is it similar to Swaswam (breath) viswasam (belief)?" When people breathe in, they believe they will breathe out. I said it resembles the three-syllable Bala Beej mantra, which is recited as "One two three. Three two one". The three syllables are recited normally and then in reverse order. It resembles breathing in and out.

This idea led to a profound discussion between us that delved into these layers, providing us with newfound clarity. Remarkably, this conversation seamlessly continued from our earlier discourse on yoginis.

Coexistence—The Secret Power

Bhairava and Mahakal (Lord Shiva) both embody the essence of time. In non-linear time, Bhairava represents the masculine energy in the creation process. He unites with the expression of Shakti, the yoginis, to manifest in the physical world. Bhairava and the yoginis are dualities that can exist independently. In contrast, Shiva is beyond duality and beyond time, in union with his feminine energy, Mahamaya, the supreme goddess.

Our breath seems to connect these energies in time and beyond time, possibly the secret behind pranayama. The rhythmic movement of breath bridges these two points, much like day and night. Bhairava and Lord Shiva reside in manifestations and transcend time—a profound philosophical concept that emerged from our conversations.

For me, this concept finds its embodiment in my breath, which I refer to as "Bala". The "Bala" Beej mantra establishes a connection between these spaces, bridging the gap between the present and the eternal.

I have come to recognise the importance of uniting the feminine and masculine energies within me, unlocking their true potential as genuine expressions of myself. The key to achieving harmony and peace lies in the coexistence of these energies within us and around us.

Feminine energy is characterised by qualities such as care, emotions, flexibility, creativity, and inspiration, which are strengths rather than weaknesses. However, relying solely on feminine energy can result in excessive nurturing, forgiving too easily, and allowing others to take advantage of your kindness. This idea is applicable to all genders.

Conversely, masculine energy involves traits like structure, direction, and decision making. People who lean too heavily into logic, planning, and methodical thinking without acting may miss tapping into their feminine energy and become overly authoritarian but unproductive.

Success ultimately depends upon understanding the presence of both the energies within ourselves and finding a balance between these two forces. Knowing when and where to harness them to manifest your dreams makes you powerful. The union of the material (Prakriti) and the spiritual (Purusha) aspects of existence are responsible for developing true intellect or wisdom.

Union with My Male Energy

The power I sensed within me was not masculine but rather a potent feminine energy seeking unity with the masculine aspect within me. Hence, I struggled to express it fully.

While creating the Ardhanareeswarar painting, incorporating the masculine aspect proved challenging as it lay dormant within me. The balance emerged unknowingly when I painted Bhairava, enabling me to unlock the sixty-four feminine powers and to paint them.

I discovered that I carried all these feminine energies within me. It was a beautiful realisation of my own completeness. To unleash my full potential, I needed to embrace the masculine aspect and integrate it within myself.

I told JJ that I understand the importance of uniting with the male energy within me. I am grateful for his guidance in uncovering these revelations through my experiences.

>Red, green, yellow, and pink,
>A riot of colours around me,
>The vivid hues of life,
>Shades, tints, and hues of blue
>A pure pigment of the colour wheel
>Drifted onto my canvas
>Dark blue, the "true blue"
>The colour of my male in me

Blue, the colour of my spirit,
Inducing calmness and peace
Like the bottomless ocean
Tint of blues so serene and sedative
Holding my conscious and subconscious
So dynamic and dramatic
Blue, the colour of my breath,
The celebration of my life
Signifying the divinity of you in me
Merging with you completely.

The next day, another beautiful experience unfolded. We visited the music director of our documentary, and I was happy to know that my poem was going to be the lyrics of a song for the documentary. Adding to the surprise, the music director began talking about the *Vigana Bhairava Tantra*, a Shiva tantra from Kashmiri Shaivism that is a discourse between Bhairava and the goddesses, describing it as a fascinating read. He said he felt a connection with our concept.

Reconfirmation by St Michael, the Archangel

Thereafter, we had to meet a friend. We had to wait for my friend's call to confirm the location. JJ said, "It's Sunday, so I'll head to the church." He pointed to a church by the roadside and said, "You can wait there." I said I would also join him as I am fond of churches. During my childhood, I studied at St Joseph's School and visited the chapel daily. Even when I went to temples back then, I would draw crosses. I smiled on remembering a secret desire from that time. I wished to marry a Christian for two reasons: first, I wanted to wear a white wedding gown, and second, I thought that Christian families were very modern as my Christian neighbour's house always had joyful gatherings. I was not even allowed to go out alone and felt a lack of freedom and fun.

I shared this story with JJ, laughing like a child. It felt as though the carefree spirit of my youth was returning. I felt very happy as I could talk without any inhibitions.

JJ commented, "You have a story for everything."

The church was grand, and I entered and sat down. I closed my eyes and offered a prayer of gratitude. I experienced a beautiful vision: a growing blue light in front of me, pushing away black clouds and enveloping me in its embrace. This made me incredibly happy, and I sensed a conversation happening with this energy.

That evening, I stayed at JJ's house, surrounded by the love he and his wife shared with their four children. I enjoyed spending time with them, yet an internal dialogue persisted beneath the surface. JJ must have felt that there is something on my mind. He enquired about my comfort, and I assured him I was indeed comfortable. However, I did not share the experience in church as I wanted to delve deeper into it.

The next day, on the flight back to Chennai, I dozed off and had a vision reminiscent of my church experience. This time, there were no black clouds. Instead, wings held me close. I saw a lotus with an orange-yellow flame at its centre, gradually expanding into a larger flame and turning to complete blue. It then opened again, revealing an enchanting orangish hue.

Upon arriving at the airport at Chennai, I went straight to my office and sat meditatively, pondering this energy's nature. An answer came to me: "I am Michael, the archangel. Blue is my colour." The word *archangel* was very new to me. I was baffled by this revelation, and as I gazed ahead, I saw the flame again. It transformed into blue.

I messaged JJ immediately, asking for the church's name.

He replied, "St Michael's. Are you okay? Do you have anything to tell me?" I explained the vision to him. He had many questions as usual but later called to share that St Michael is associated with blue. I understood that this was a reaffirmation of masculine energy. The blue flame opened to reveal the presence of the feminine energy through the orange and red hues. My gratitude for this confirmation was immense. Perhaps the revelation was because of the true essence of my quest. I took a break from work, went home, and immersed myself in that energy of vision. I sent back that energy with a lot of gratitude.

Vijana Bhairava Tantra

The next day, while sitting down to document our discussion, my thoughts shifted to our conversation with the music director. I searched my computer and unexpectedly found an ebook, *Vigana Bhairava Tantra*, sent by my cousin Sreekumar, although this was the first time I had opened it. The book is a conversation between Shiva and Parvati where Shiva answers Parvati's essential questions, explaining what the Divine is and its supreme intelligence.

Flipping through the pages, I became motionless. I felt that Bhairava was leading me towards the light. I wanted to avoid going through each page. I wanted to stick to my plan. Only after completing my writing would I read the book. These texts are like a guru, guiding you along a path. I wanted to enjoy the freedom during this journey.

I just glanced through the text, and my mind got hooked on a few translations, which I correlate to my journey. The comparison of a mother using rewards and threats to influence children. The explanation about the gentle and fierce forms of the goddess was fascinating. I had felt all through that all the fearsome forms of gods are manifested for a purpose. We need not fear them. The goddesses Lakshmi and Chamunda represent different energies. Lakshmi is associated with wealth and abundance, while Chamunda is a fierce and powerful form linked to destruction and transformation. Lakshmi's qualities inspire growth, while Chamuṇḍa's fierce nature inspires courage and change.

In the text, Bhairava explains that feeling complete is called "antaḥsvānubhavānandā". True happiness can be found only by delving deep within oneself, uncovering the essence that often goes undiscovered. True happiness can only be possible if you engage in introspection. Many people miss out on this profound sense of fulfilment because they neglect to explore their inner thoughts and emotions. This fulfilment is unique and can only be achieved by experiencing a personal journey of self-discovery.

My mentor used to say that if you can look beyond your visions and thoughts, you can connect to the network of energies around you and distil its essence. That can only be done with your experience, unwavering belief, sincere intentions, and complete surrender.

Soundarya Lahari

There was deep silence in my mind as I glanced at the goddess I had painted, and a sudden thought emerged. Like a child, I asked my goddess, "Bhairava is saying this, but what do you want to convey?" I got up and went to take a random book from the almirah. I closed my eyes and took one. It turned out to be the *Soundarya Lahari* by Adi Shankaracharya (Swami Satyasangananda Saraswati 2009). I opened the book to page 210, which said:

Shiva shares his knowledge through conversations with Parvati, guided by Shakti's influence. Parvati, who is knowledgeable, asks questions, and Shiva answers, revealing the universe's secrets. These discussions are called agamas, and there are sixty-four agamas, essential texts about tantra.

The sixty-four tantras cover various topics, from everyday matters to profound concepts. On one side, they are the guide to achieving success in worldly affairs, while on another level, they provide techniques for attaining spiritual liberation.

Human thinking has changed over time. First, people wondered where gods lived—like in the sky or on land and then moved to the sun, moon and other planets to pray to avoid problems. Then, they evolved to have them in unique places and argued about their looks and whether they were male or female. This made different sects and beliefs.

Over time, some started understanding divinity is within. This understanding is the most important one a person can have, as it changes everything and life transforms completely.

So, this knowledge from Tantra that Shiva shared after getting permission from Shakti is extensive. Shiva explains this tantra to Devi, who needs no explanation as it has emanated from her so that any deserving listeners nearby may overhear and convey it to others. This tantra holds the highest position because it allows one to directly understand or sense the energy and consciousness within one's body. Which is samaya tantra, which is his favourite

The sixty-four tantras are connected to the sixty-four Shakti Peeths and sixty-four yoginis, but they represent only a part of Shakti's energy. Sixty-four tantras talk about expanding the mind and liberating power, which unites with consciousness and fulfils different human desires.

Beyond that, it also goes further into becoming one with the divine. This is the vision of Tripura Sundari in profound spiritual union with Shiva, radiating beauty and bliss, and appears as the reigning and most supreme tattva, the ultimate "coexistence".

Unveiling the Book: The Complete Circle

My heart skipped a beat. Suddenly, I thought of the book Dr David had given me. When I wanted to start the paintings, I searched for the book but could not find it. While I was painting, we shifted our house to a new place. So, when I sat down to clean the almirah, I found the book. I did not open it then. In the next few days, I met Dr David's close friend Elayettathi, and we spent a lot of time together, sharing our experiences. After two days, Elayettathi and her daughter, Lakshmi, came to my house, and I mentioned this book. She asked me to show her the book, so I took it out. It was inside a plastic cover, and I gave it to her. She opened it and realised that the pages could not even be flipped. The pages crumbled to powder on being touched. To our surprise, the book was emitting an aroma. She closed it, put it back in the cover, and gave it back to me. I had not even looked at it.

However, the time had come to see the book. I took it out and saw that it was *Soundarya Lahari*—a sign for me to understand that the path I took to know Maha Tripura Sundari was right. I could not shake that feeling, and I became numb. How can I comment on the precision of her plans?

Is It Samayacharam?

I discussed this experience with JJ and shared the text with him. He suggested that I talk to someone about Samaya Tantra. I called Sumeru, a Srividya practitioner, to discuss it. He explained about the four schools of tantras. I then asked him, "I have painted the goddess with divine intervention. Is this Samayacharam?"

Samayacharam is one of the schools of Srividya Tantra where one worships the goddess internally. He said it could not be as even Samayacharam requires knowledge of tantra. It is also a defined method, just that it is a mental process.

I was not worried about that answer. The energy of Samaya (time) and the lord of Samaya, Bhairava, alone has led me throughout. With his and my guru's blessings, I reached here. It was time to wind up this chapter of my journey so I could see beyond my experiences.

I chose the path of creation. My bhakti was my method, and my surrender was my method. Art can happen only if there is a union of these forces. The divine formula of "coexistence" is the secret of manifestation of the spiritual physical world and the creative world.

Direct Experience of The Absolute—Self-Realisation

After a few days, as part of our documentary, we met some people who practise Srividya and had discussions with them. Every discussion endorsed my thoughts, and I always saw a reflection of respect and love in their eyes—it must be because I reflected the energies I have encountered.

Our last shoot was with Dr Bibek Debroy, and I asked him about the difference between Bhairava and Shiva. His answer was straightforward: perception. When I asked about tantra, he said, "Beena, tantra is a set of practices defined by a disciplined method to reach goddesses. If you follow it correctly with the guidance of a good guru, results are assured. But the most challenging path to know her is the path you have taken to paint them—'surrender', the way of bhakti. People think it is an easy path, but it is the most difficult one. Surrendering 'I' (aham), 'mine' (mama), possessions, and ahamkara (arrogance) is not very easy. If you do that, I do not have to tell you that you will see her—because you have seen her." He smiled at me.

JJ and I looked at each other and said, "It is done." The path I followed is Srividya, my Tripura Sundari, and her gift was her Bala to me, the child in me.

JJ called me the next day and said to search for *Aparokshanubhuti*, a book by Adi Shankara. The word *Aparokshanubhuti* is a compound consisting of the words *aparoksh* (perceptible) and *anubhuti* (direct cognition or direct experience of the absolute), meaning self-realisation.

82

Reflections

After I had penned down the final page, I felt as though torrential rain had washed over me, and I could sense the last drops trickling down my face. I allowed them to descend without any resistance. To me, this feeling unquestionably marked the path of my spiritual journey. I held all my experiences, encounters, and reflections in high regard, recognising that they all contributed to a profound and enriched understanding. I could discern that these experiences and encounters were messages. They were glittering threads intricately woven into the fabric of my life, forming a splendid tapestry brimming with meaning. I unearthed a teacher in every person and circumstance, humbly setting aside my ego to forge meaningful connections and transcending distinctions of colour and creed.

We always try to connect spirituality with religious practices, stopping when we are unable to go deeper. Being a spiritual practitioner guided by a guru is only one of the methods to attain the ultimate knowledge. Understanding God and spirituality is much more profound than mere rituals. Spirituality connects you with the essence of all living beings, infusing meaning into every action and enlivening each moment. With this understanding, perspectives shift.

Each layer of this journey was an act of introspection, allowing me to perceive every facet in a wholly different light. The interplay of masculine and feminine energies in every creation, both within myself and around me, carried a profound significance.

I felt as if I had unlocked the secret of the power of manifestation through my depictions of yoginis, which had been concealed within the formula of coexistence.

I became aware of my complete femininity and understood the presence of masculine energy and its enchanting influence, making me powerfully feminine. Male energy is powerless without understanding and accepting the power of the feminine creative force within them. Using that feminine creative energy knowingly or unknowingly will make living beings productive and successful in any field.

The journey had commenced with a yearning to discover my femininity and had culminated in a profound spiritual awakening of understanding the power of unity.

At the apex of this spiritual odyssey, I stand at the threshold of self-realisation, a testament to the profound beauty of coexistence, embracing the unity of masculine and feminine energies, and the eternal quest for the Divine within. Therein lies the secret of manifestation, whether one's path is spiritual or worldly.

Ultimately, my journey led me to profoundly understand Srividya, the embodiment of feminine divine energy and a journey within oneself.

Reflecting on all these experiences and revelations, I comprehended that my voyage had come full circle, a self-realisation with complete surrender.

It was clear that the path I had taken to reach the goddess was bhakti, the true devotion to her. For me, my creative energy is my devotion. I have used this tool to reach the goddesses and understand self-realisation. Only through art could I surrender entirely, listening to the whispers of the unseen energy around me, connecting me to my feminine essence. Enlightenment and self-realisation may seem like distant dreams, but one needs to understand the basics to get there. This understanding of energy will allow me to view my life with new, insightful eyes. This knowledge is the secret to keeping your inner child alive. For me, my inner child is my Sreebala.

I realise nothing ends here. My journey continues in search of experiences and fresh insight.

> A breeze passed by, caressing my hair,
> With the same tender touch.
> I wondered, is it she, my Bala?
> I caught myself smiling in that moment's grace.
> Still, my intensity of search is pure.
> The longing and desire, as fresh as morning dew,
> To merge with her again and again,
> Till my existence dissipates into thin air,
> Where my essence merges, bearing no name.
> My search for her shall persist, unswayed,
> Through my life's winding paths,
> In the ever-turning cosmic play,
> I seek you, find you, in each new day, in a new way.

Acknowledgements

Col Unnikrishnan and Kids

My life changed completely after my marriage. It was not an easy journey. We are complete opposites in our thoughts, actions, interests, discipline, and even food preferences. Anything you mention, we differ on, but despite these disparities, we remain together. I was not the only one who had to adjust; he must have found it equally challenging to adapt to me. We are both strong-willed individuals, but we have carved out space for each other to breathe. He has never imposed his ideology on me, and I have never tried to do the same to him. I can confidently say he is my backbone.

Whether success comes or not, he believes in my thoughts, respects my personality, and acknowledges my talents. From the beginning of our project to today, he has been an unwavering source of support. We may have never explicitly discussed my experiences, but his eyes and ears have always been open. He has always been aware of what is happening around me. There has always been an unspoken connection between us.

I know that without him, exploring my journey would have been impossible. He is my wellspring of strength. He ensures that nothing disturbs me when I paint or engage in any creative activities. He served as my first critic after I finished painting, and his insights are astute.

He is an ardent fan of Bala. Sometimes, when he lights a lamp, I have overheard him talking to her, which fills me with happiness. Without him, I would not have reached where I am today.

My sons Arjun and Akash are my sources of inspiration. I discuss everything under the sun with them and value their advice greatly. They serve as my bridge to the next generation's perspectives. One of them has been consistently by my side while I paint. When I need clarification about the postures, particularly when I paint hands, they often pose as models for me. Bala has become an integral part of their lives as well. Expressing my gratitude to all three of them is a challenging task.

Girl power and a woman's touch hold a special place in my heart. Harini, my daughter-in-law, has been a powerful source of strength. Whenever I hesitated to speak in public or lacked confidence in my writing, she consistently empowered me and boosted my self-confidence. Her support has truly made a significant difference in my life, and I am immensely grateful to her for it.

Annamalai Subbiah

I have never encountered anyone as spiritually committed as Annamalai Subbiah. He is an essential part of this yogini project and a strong pillar of support. He has been involved in every step of the process, from the initial painting to the present. Whenever I need anything at any point in time, he is just a phone call away. His unwavering belief in me and his commitment to bringing this project to the world for dissemination are genuinely remarkable. We both believe that many people will come to know about yoginis and their powers, inspiring them to visit temples to see them. He is an integral part of this journey, and my gratitude to him knows no bounds.

Dr Bibek Debroy

I thank a dear friend for introducing me to Dr Bibek Debroy. It was indeed a miracle for me. Although I have had only a few meetings with him, his impact on me is immense. He is an exceptional listener and patiently lends an ear to all my stories. Conforming with a scholar of his stature gave me the strength to complete this book. Every person I have encountered on this journey has been a godsend. Bhairava must have orchestrated this connection. I am humbled and consider myself too small to discuss him in detail. I offer him my most profound respect and gratitude with a sashtanga pranamam for his invaluable guidance and unwavering support. Dr Bibek Debroy is an Indian economist, serving as the chair of the Economic Advisory Council to the Prime Minister of India.

Jain Joseph

JJ has played a crucial role in deconstructing my thoughts and experiences, providing invaluable guidance to help me gain a more comprehensive perspective on my journey. He helped me view my entire experience as unified, which I had struggled to do alone. JJ's advice and support in this regard felt like a godsend.

Despite his firm adherence to his beliefs, JJ has the remarkable ability to look beyond his personal convictions and respect the belief systems of others. This quality is a testament to his exceptional humanity. JJ dedicated eight months of his time to help me unravel the intricate puzzle that was this endeavour, and in doing so, he is a guide and a profound philosopher. My sincere gratitude to his wife and children for their support to him. He must have taken a lot of time for this from his family time.

JJ is, by nature, an artist, and this inherent artistic sensibility has enriched his character. I extend my heartfelt gratitude to him for every second he devoted and his unwavering support.

As a person, he believes in blending dualities to generate value. He innovates methods that combine creative chaos, confusion, and madness, transforming them into harmonious and meaningful compositions with a sensory appeal to beauty. JJ is a filmmaker and the founder and chairperson of Neo Film School in Kochi, Kerala.

His ability to sculpt individuals and help them recognise their talents and capabilities is remarkable. Through my association and discussions with him, I have personally experienced this transformation. He adeptly dismantles the barriers that hinder personal growth and encourages you to explore the world around you. In today's generation, having a teacher like him is invaluable.

Rashmi Govind

I have known Rashmi Govind for a few years now. Our paths first crossed when she served as the editor for a short film in which I was involved. Later, as part of my NGO's research team, we embarked on a project centred around mythological stories and temples, with the aim of creating a documentary.

Rashmi joined the research team in April of 2022 and her dedication was apparent right from the beginning. While I prefer writing on paper instead of typing, she graciously offered her assistance by transcribing and even conducting the initial corrections. Whenever I needed to go into additional stories, Rashmi was always there to research and enrich the content. Our reading sessions, too, proved to be immensely valuable.

Although Rashmi's formal engagement with the project officially lasted only two months, our collaboration continued over the course of two years. She consistently demonstrated excellence in her work, and I had initially hoped she would be with me until the project's completion. However, due to time constraints, she was unable to assist in its conclusion. This project followed its own unique path, guided, perhaps, by divine decisions. The determination of who should do what and when was never solely mine; it was influenced by divine interventions.

I want to express my heartfelt gratitude for Rashmi's unwavering support, and I genuinely treasure her invaluable contribution to this endeavour. Completing this mission without her would have been an immensely challenging feat.

Abirami Vivek

Abirami was indispensable in my yogini project, and her involvement was extraordinary. She effortlessly assumed various roles within the project—sometimes appearing as a dear friend, at other times taking on the part of a sister and even that of a nurturing mother figure. Her unwavering support throughout this creative journey was undeniable and profoundly meaningful. When delving into the realm of divine energies, I have realised that those by your side must possess exceptional patience. My creative process often led to fluctuating moods, and Abirami exhibited a remarkable ability to navigate these shifts with grace and understanding. She was the one person other than my husband who was a steadfast source of patience and encouragement.

Although Abirami and I share a close friendship, we rarely discussed work-related matters while I was engrossed in the act of painting. However, she assumed a pivotal role when it came to executing the project. She was an integral part of my documentary team from the initial planning stages to the project's completion. During this time, I was often on the move, and Abirami took on the responsibility of looking after my needs and ensuring that everything ran smoothly—a level of dedication that is truly hard to fathom.

Expressing my gratitude toward her is a task that words alone cannot adequately convey. Over the past two years, as I prepared for my son's wedding, Abirami provided unwavering support and was an indispensable pillar of strength, which helped me to concentrate on my project. In every sense, she has become my wonderful soul sister, and her contributions to my creative journey are immeasurable.

Sakina Ansari

The first time I laid eyes on Sakina, there was an inexplicable attraction, almost like experiencing love at first sight. She radiates a bubbly and effervescent personality that can light up your world and infuse it with vibrancy.

Sakina became an integral part of my painting journey. She is spiritually inclined and inherently optimistic, making her a person with whom I could share my stories, knowing that she would truly understand and appreciate them. I was going through a challenging phase in my business, filled with its fair share of ups and downs. However, Sakina stood firmly by my side, extending her unwavering support and helping hand.

Her presence during that period felt reminiscent of our college days. She often stayed overnight at my house, engaging with the energies surrounding us. To me, she was like a yogini, providing the essential support I needed for this transformative journey. Even now, Sakina remains just a call away, ready to offer her support and encouragement.

She is a source of positive energy, and spending time with her left me feeling recharged and inspired to tackle my painting endeavours with renewed vigour. Her kindness and dedication were further highlighted when she celebrated my birthday after I completed my painting. Such genuine gestures are rare, and it was evident that this celebration was her unique way of expressing her friendship and support. Sakina is not just a friend; she is a friend for a lifetime and a cherished presence in my life journey.

Sreekumar

Sreekumar believes in my artistic journey and experiences. Sreekumar has been a part of my painting journey from day one. Having known me since I was a small child, as he is my cousin, he never needed an introduction to people I have interacted with as he knew all of them personally. So he could easily connect with my thoughts. He is a deeply spiritual person who embraces all religious processes and continues to do so.

The moment I finish a painting, I send it to him, and he shares his thoughts about what he felt upon seeing it. Remarkably, his impressions always align with my own experiences, bringing me immense happiness and peace. He must have witnessed the various facets of my artistry and the different energies I have channelled into my work. We used to engage in lengthy discussions about my paintings, and his patience and capacity for listening are truly commendable. He has been a steadfast pillar of strength for me, and I express my sincere gratitude to him.

Harbeen Arora Rai

Dr Harbeen Arora Rai is an angel who has connected millions of women worldwide. In life, we come across numerous individuals, and even a moment spent with someone can profoundly impact your life. Dr Arora Rai, the founder and president of G100, ALL, WEF, WICCI, and the SHEconomy, has made an immense difference in my life. Her passion for making a positive impact on the lives of millions of women is truly extraordinary, and I find her mission to be infectious.

As a strong and empowered woman herself, she played a significant role in entrusting me with the responsibilities of national president of WICCI's Art Leadership Wing and later as the G100 global chair of Art Leadership and Films. There was a time when I felt like I did not have many friends, but she has connected me with people worldwide. It was an infusion of feminine energy that propelled this project forward. She inspires me to become the best version of myself.

I extend my heartfelt gratitude to this remarkable woman who believes in the power of coexistence and the potential of women.

Friends and Family

I express deep gratitude to my friends and family, whose unwavering support has been pivotal in my journey. The invaluable encouragement from my parents, brothers and their families has significantly bolstered my artistic pursuits. I am truly fortunate to be surrounded by such exceptional individuals who have enriched my personal and professional paths. Their insights have been instrumental in realising my dreams, particularly in my work with yoginis. The overwhelming support received at every turn has been a source of strength. To all those unnamed but equally essential contributors, I offer my heartfelt thanks for being an indispensable part of my life's adventure.

Bibliography

Roy, Anamika. *Sixty-Four Yoginis: Cult, Icon and Goddesses* (Delhi: Primus Books, 2022).

Deheja, Vidya. *Yogini Cult and Temples: A Tantric Tradition* (New Delhi: National Museum, 1986).

Das, Adyasha. *The Chausathi Yoginis of Hirapur: From Tantra to Tourism* (Delhi: Black Eagle Books, 2019)

———. *The Yoginis of Ranipur Jharial: Tantric Goddesses of Yore* (Delhi: Black Eagle Books, 2021).

About the Author

Beena Unnikrishnan is an artist with multifaceted personality. Her career spans over three decades, encompassing various fields such as education, entrepreneurship, healing practices, filmmaking, and artistry. Her journey began in 1992 as an educator and has evolved into a remarkable exploration of diverse domains. At the core of her identity lies an unwavering connection to art as a medium of spiritual expression and transformation, drawing inspiration from mystical traditions.

www.ingramcontent.com/pod-product-compliance
Lightning Source LLC
Chambersburg PA
CBHW031104020326
40488CB00011B/140